NORTH CAROLINA
STATE BOARD OF COMMUNITY
LIBRARIES
SAMPSON TECHNICAL COLLEGE

P9-CMP-519

DISCARDED

HV
881
R86

3-26-81

17361

RUNAWAYS — ILLEGAL ALIENS IN THEIR OWN LAND

Implications for Service

DOROTHY MILLER

DONALD MILLER

FRED HOFFMAN

ROBERT DUGGAN

PRAEGER SPECIAL STUDIES • PRAEGER SCIENTIFIC
A J.F. BERGIN PUBLISHERS BOOK

Library of Congress Cataloging in Publication Data

Main entry under title:

Runaways, illegal aliens in their own land.

A J.F. Bergin Publishers book.
Bibliography: p.
Includes Index.
1. Runaway youth—United States. 2. Social work with youth—United States.
I. Miller, Dorothy L.
HV881.R86   362.7'4   79-11682
ISBN 0-03-051051-1

Published in 1980 by Praeger Publishers
A division of Holt, Rinehart and Winston/CBS, Inc.
383 Madison Avenue, New York, New York 10017 U.S.A.

© 1980 by J.F. Bergin Publishers, Inc.

All rights reserved
J.F. Bergin Publishers, Inc.
65 South Oxford Street
Brooklyn, New York 11217

0 056 987654321

Printed in the United States of America

CONTENTS

ACKNOWLEDGMENTS

This research was made possible by a grant from the Social Rehabilitation Services section of the Department of Health, Education and Welfare. We wish to thank Phil Grossman, the project officer, for his kind assistance and many helpful suggestions. We also wish to thank the directors and staff of Huckleberry House, the Way Home Foundation, the Charila Foundation, Hillsides Episcopal Foundation, Traveler's Aid Society of San Francisco, The Alameda County Welfare Department, and the Los Angeles County Department of Public Social Services for their assistance with this project. Thanks also are due to those whose work brought this project to completion, especially Martin Orlick, Barbara Fisher, Ruthie Marks, Amy Eisenberg, Martha Griswold, Suzanne Olson, Mark Lipschutz, Olivia Loewy, Laurie Engelberg and to Lia Stahrlite for proofreading and compiling the index. Consulting scholars were Harry Kitano, Manuel Miranda, David Gold, and Scott Kester. To all the foregoing persons and organizations we acknowledge our gratitude and appreciation, while insisting that the responsibility of this text is our own.

Scientific Analysis Corporation   Dorothy Miller
2410 Lombard Street   Donald Miller
San Francisco, California 94123   Fred Hoffman
                                          Bob Duggan

Executive Summary

A two-year study of youthful runaways and runaway services in two metropolitan centers on the West Coast was conducted to (1) develop a useful runaway typology and (2) determine the needs of runaways currently and how these are or are not being met.

The research design purposefully sought out hitherto largely "unseen" runaways systematically along with the usual groups of agency clientele officially labeled "runaways." A total of 214 runaways and 38 parents of runaways were interviewed intensively. Similarly, eight agencies servicing runaways (among others) were identified and studied in-depth with regards to their views, attitudes, and experiences with their runaway clients. A detailed description of runaway client characteristics and agency policies and attitudes was also sought by means of a mailed questionnaire locally and nationwide. Interviews with staff and observations of agencies were conducted, leading to an analysis of program policies, goals, problems, and plans. These data, along with a search of the growing runaway literature, served as the basis for our findings. A brief historical sketch traced changes in social attitudes toward childhood (and the runaway phenomenon) from antiquity to the present century. In recent times, it was noted, runaways were perceived as an important national problem in the Depression of the 1930s, but with World War II the problem disappeared as the war effort extensively employed the labor of women and juveniles. After the war, the baby boom created severe strains on the institutions rearing children, such as the schools and other agencies.

The 1960s brought another phenomenon with large-scale exodus of youths from home, the birth of the so-called "hippy" or youth culture, and the increase in juvenile crime, drug use, and delinquency. For the first time, not only the poor and the dispossessed were involved, but the "middle-class" youth as well, leading to a redefinition of runaways as not just "delinquents" or "hoods," and to a quest for alternatives to incarceration and jail.

Based on the view that the basic socialization process was either breaking down or being completed at an earlier age in contrast to the trend toward a longer and longer span of adolescence, the study of runaways in all their diversity was seen as needed, with typologies sought which would allow for different approaches and different solutions to the different problems being presented.

A comparison of the study's sample of runaways with other youth populations revealed that some evidence of differences in degree, but not differences in kind exists. A survey of a high school sample of youth found that about 13 percent had run away (and returned) and another 20 percent had considered running away at some time. Apparently, running away is a problem (actual or potential) common to many, if not most, youth today and cannot be viewed as an isolated phenomenon. Other evidence also testified to the universality of this phenomenon, with nearly all socioeconomic strata represented among runaways, for example, and a majority reporting knowing friends or classmates who had run away, with some also mentioning relatives who had run away. Many youngsters also reported doubts about the value of school and having problems in school; some reported thinking about dropping out of school altogether.

In all these examples, the main runaway sample tended to be more extreme in its endorsement than did the nonrunaway segments, but it was noteworthy that sizable minorities of the latter groups commonly endorsed these same views and experiences. This was taken as an indication that runaways, including the more chronic cases who have not returned home, may well present the same problems or features, differing *only in degree,* as nonrunaway samples of youth their own age.

RUNAWAY TYPES

For a better understanding of the runaway phenomenon, an attempt was made to classify the runaway sample into types. Many other attempts have been made to this end, developing typologies based on a wide variety of criteria and theories. The resulting labels have tended to impute one motive or another to the actor, some stigmatizing, some condemnatory, some dramatizing, and others romanticizing. Most of these labels reflect the interests and preoccupations of the investigators and the goals of their own particular networks and agencies.

Some examples of the various classifications are given, ranging from the clinical models of Levy (1972), to the criminal or delinquent models of Jenkins (1971), to the hedonistic conceptualization of Homer (1973), and the eclectic methodology employed by Brennan (1974). None of these models is either founded on or consistent with the social science approaches to human behavior and its patterning. The social-psychological approach to the study of human behavior in social systems and the importance of the individual actor's perceptions of the world around him are ignored or overlooked in these classification schemes used previously.

A VOCABULARY OF MOTIVES

Based on a social science perspective, human behavior is seen as emerging or following from the individual's internalized definition of objects, self, situations, and views of the world around him. These definitions are a result of socialization, learning experiences in social systems, family, school, and so on. This study utilized the runaways' self-reports and their own perceptions and thus reflects very much the "natural" world of the runaways as seen from their own perspective, rather than that of some clinician, professional, or researcher.

Content analysis of the verbalized reasons for leaving home and the circumstances surrounding the runaway episode tapped the "vocabulary of motives" of the runaway sample and yielded two general categories of response on the basis of the "root causes" for the act. One category, making up some 44 percent of the sample, consisted of all those subjects reporting the parents as the primary cause of leaving. This group was called the "Parent-Locus" category. The second group (56 percent of the sample) consisted of those who reported self or other reasons, or at least not primarily parental reasons for leaving. This group is called the "Child-Locus" category. Both general categories contained three subtypes. The three subtypes in the Parent-Locus category were called "victims," "exiles," and "rebels" and were defined as follows:

Victims are those runaways who feel they are fleeing for their lives from physical abuse and assault by parents or stepparents. These youth feel their parents are their enemies and that to return home is to endanger their lives. While at home, the victims are possessed by an acute ambivalence: they fear their parents, see them as capricious and unjust, and yet at the same time they are dependent upon their parents, referring to them as a source of support and security. Once the underpinnings of that support are torn asunder by some climactic episode, they confront the world as hapless and helpless vagabonds.

If a runaway acknowledges his dependence upon his family, and then explains his leaving home in terms of parental rejection, he is an *exile*. Such runaways report that they were driven out and rejected. These runaways are characterized as exiles, that is, they are banished and outcast among their own kind. (Other studies have labeled such subjects as "kickouts," "throwaway children," or "pushouts.")

Rebels describe their motives for running away in terms of serious and longstanding "hassles" or involvement in authority struggles with their parents. They hope their running away will help them "win" this struggle. They want to live at home, but want to live by their own rules.

The three types of *Child-Locus* runaways were termed "fugitives," "refugees," and "immigrants."

The *fugitive* is running from the consequences of his or her own behavior. Fugitives leave home because they feel that they have to in order to escape from some form of retribution, arrest, disgrace, or punishment. Fugitives are afraid to face their parents, the school, or community social control agents. They ran away to avoid further trouble, but may maintain contact with their home, communicating periodically with someone there. They may also be partly dependent on support or assistance from parents or siblings while they are in flight.

The *refugees* are without a family, they run away from foster homes and institutions. These children, like the fugitives, are running from a social control situation. But, unlike the fugitives, they are not running from the consequences of their own behavior. Their dependency upon parents has been truncated and they feel they belong to no one; they do not view themselves as culprits or as being in flight because of an antisocial act.

The *immigrants* are independent runaways who have taken matters into their own hands and have resolved unpleasant home or community situations by choosing the alternative, to be "free." These youth have truncated their parental dependency relationship in order to be "on their own." Their departure from home takes the form of autonomy rather than flight. They run away in order to find "adventure," "freedom," and independence rather than merely to escape parental or social "hassles" or "authority." They consciously view themselves as persons who are able to take care of themselves. The independent runaways have terminated their socialization under the family tutelage in order to determine their own life-style. In a sense they are "emancipated" although without court adjudication.

Wide variations between the six runaway types in terms of personal characteristics, family background, school problems and others, runaway experiences, and adventures emerged from analysis of the research data. Judging from these variations and differences, it would seem impossible to speak of *a* runaway policy in the singular, but rather a policy based on the multifaceted features of the runaway phenomenon seems necessary.

SOCIAL SERVICES

In the second part of the study, that part dealing with social services for runaways, involving both formal and informal sources, the activities and programs of eight local agencies *vis à vis* runaways are examined at length along with information about client characteristics and the attitudes of a national sample of agencies. Runaways' own accounts and views of agencies, and their contact or lack of contact with different types of agencies were surveyed.

Beginning with the runaways' views of social agencies, it was noteworthy that more than half (55 percent) saw *no* agency as either helpful or appealing, with a high of 32 percent reporting such facilities as free clinics, crash pads, and so forth, as helpful while at the other extreme some 8 percent mentioned public agencies and the like as being helpful. A total of only 14 percent felt that any formal agency would be either helpful or appealing.

Concerning the extent of the runaways' knowledge of services and programs that are available to them, a high of 48 percent had heard of free clinics while only 15 percent had any knowledge of the free food stamp program. The least well known as serving runaways were the aforementioned food stamp program, public welfare agencies, runaway shelters, and Traveler's Aid—all known of by less than 20 percent of our sample.

A very low correlation was noted between knowledge of services and the use of them, indicating that the nonuse of facilities involves more than simply a need for more advertising of programs. Public agencies particularly fared poorly with respect to maximum utilization of services. In contrast, while less than 20 percent of the runaways knew about runaway shelters, all who knew about them used them. Similar trends were noted with respect to the other "counterculture" facilities listed. This greater utilization of "free" facilities in the informal networks probably results at least in part from the difficulties posed by being an "illegal alien" on the one hand and being eligible for services on the other. Some 59 percent "distrusted" public agencies, fearing detention and return to homes they were fleeing. Instead, most runaways facing specific problems tend to rely on friends or the more informal sources of help, such as "counterculture" agencies.

An organizational analysis of eight social agencies, two public agencies, two private agencies, two diversion agencies, and two "counterculture" agencies revealed the following:

1.   Social agencies of all types serve only a very few of the runaway population, and when they do so, it is because of unique or special problems other than that of running away, for example, pregnancy, drug use, venereal disease, accidents, encounters with the law.

2.   Most runaway youth served by social agencies are "multi-problem" children and are often wards of the juvenile court as well.

3.   Social agencies find their services are generally inadequate or inappropriate for a large percentage of the runaway youth they do serve.

4.   Most social workers do not view the runaway youth as a "special category"; rather they view him or her as a disturbed or a-bused child not unlike other youth in their caseloads, albeit one they are not especially equipped to serve.

5.   Services given runaway youth by social agencies are often brief contact services, are not followed up, and may result in either return of the youth to his or her family, or placement with a social control agency, such as a diversion program or juvenile hall.

6.   The legal status of runaway youth is ambiguous, and nearly all social agencies deal with the police or courts in working out treatment plans for runaways. "Treatment" can only follow legal disclosure and sanction——the runaway must be "labeled" and his case adjudicated before he can be served.

Described for each agency was the type of services offered, intake procedures, sources of clients, sources of funding, staffing patterns, and various barriers existing with respect to servicing runaways——either internal or external.

The public agencies included in this study consisted of two public welfare agencies, which are responsible for developing and administering the official county programs to meet the welfare needs of the populace. Specialized services for children, including runaways, are organized as the Children's Services Division. No special sets of services are earmarked for runaways, hence no specific statistical data on runaways are available. Intake tends to be a formal and time consuming process with most referrals coming from community agencies such as the police, courts, or probation offices. Counseling, medical services, foster home placements are the main form of assistance rendered in children's services along with income maintenance. Staff qualifications are guided by civil service rules and college graduation is required at the entry level, with graduate work in social work valued for advancement. Most staff felt lack of funding and lack of staff were the main barriers to providing services for runaways, along with the aforementioned illegal status of the runaway.

For the two established private agencies studied, one featured a residential treatment program and the other, transit services. Staff at both have professional degrees, usually in Social Work. Relatively brief counseling services for "transients" and newcomers, along with referrals and funds, are the mission for one such agency—the Traveler's Aid of San Francisco. The other, Hillsides, has long-term residential services with a therapeutic community approach and psychiatric consultation available. Traveler's Aid gets many clients from walk-ins while Hillsides' clients are primarily referred from other agencies in the county and supported by public funds. Both agencies see the legal restrictions as the greatest barrier to effective services for runaways.

The diversion agencies were both relatively new projects receiving most of their funding from criminal justice programs. One, a residential treatment center, featured a live-in residential cottage program for girls, the other was an outpatient counseling center with an emphasis on family counseling. Most of the staff had professional backgrounds and degrees. Both groups saw the legal problems as the main barrier to servicing runaways, with some mention of the need for better relations with the older, more established agencies in the community.

The two counterculture agencies, one church-sponsored and the other originating from self-help efforts in the "hippy" heyday of San Francisco's Haight-Ashbury community, offer largely informal services on an around-the-clock basis, usually involving young professional staff. Services range from the survival type, such as food and lodging, to legal and medical assistance.

Unlike the other agencies described, the counter-culture programs deal primarily with runaways, although a sizable minority of their clients are youth with other problems. The church-sponsored program is funded by the church and contributions from individual church members and other residents in the community. The other program receives some funds from community sources (for example, churches and the United Way), but most of its funds are supplied by a variety of federal, state and county programs. However, even the funding for the latter program is not stable, being subject to the fluctuations of private philanthropy and the budgetary variations of the several governmental agencies. Staffs of both agencies see inadequate and/or fluctuating funding and the legal status of runaways as the principal barriers to servicing runaways.

Unlike the other agencies listed earlier, the primary source of clients for the counterculture agencies surveyed was walk-in traffic, although a few were referred from other agencies.

In general, most of the agency staff felt that running away was a serious problem, but did not constitute a separate category for services. Instead they saw running away as symptomatic of serious family problems. Most felt additional servicing was needed, however.

NATIONAL AND REGIONAL SURVEYS OF SOCIAL AGENCIES

Three surveys of social agencies—two national studies, and one local study—were conducted to create a better understanding of the runaway problem and its solutions as these are evidenced around the United States. The first survey used as its sample the agencies represented at a series of three regional conferences dealing with the runaway problem in 1974. Later, the same questions were used with a local sample of social agencies and another national group.

In general, the findings from all three surveys indicated a great deal of consensus on the nature of the runaway problem, the type of runaways being seen, and the type of services being offered.

First, the majority of all agencies contacted viewed the runaway problem as serious and long-lasting, not likely to go away, in fact, perhaps even increase in severity in time.

Second, most of those surveyed indicated that survival problems were the greatest area of concern, followed by possible exploitation and legal problems created by the illegal status of the runaway.

The typical runaway seen, in terms of personal characteristics and background factors, was white, female, aged 13-15 years, from a moderate family income setting, usually from a broken home and on the road for only a short time. This consensus on runaway characteristics may account for the great similarity in the perceptions of the problems encountered.

Runaways with family problems were the most prevalent type seen by these agencies and constitituted the most serious group seen, with adventuresome, independent types of runaway youth viewed as the *least* serious type encountered.

A wide variety of services, although not sufficient by any means, were reported, ranging from various forms of counseling (individual, group, family) to referrals and including "survival" services such as food and shelter.

A follow-up on the representatives who attended the national conferences revealed that those attending had different levels of influence in their respective communities and upon returning home had engaged in varying degrees of activity as a result of attending these conferences. In general, the greater the degree of local influence reported, the greater the level of activity on return. This finding tended to confirm the hypothesis that "agencies and professionals serve as 'pressure groups'" in influencing and changing policies and programs vis a vis social problems such as that of the runaway. This was also seen as evidence of the important role that national conferences can play in influencing local programming.

THE UNDERGROUND LIFE

Having seen earlier that there is relatively little contact by runaways with the established social agencies or any agencies for that matter, some 70 percent reported contacting none, a question of how the runaway survives at all arises. Thanks to the illegal status of the runaway, which does not permit gainful employment for the most part, it would seem the runaway must seek other avenues of "getting by." These means may include unsavory and even illegal activities and lead to deviant life styles on the part of the runaway.

Several means of survival were found including working, dealing drugs, stealing, panhandling or begging, prostitution, or being supported by others.

Representative cases are drawn from each of the six runaway types listed in this study and their runaway experiences and patterns of coping with survival problems are delineated in the text (Chapter 7).

UTILIZATION OF SOCIAL SERVICES

We observed that involvement of our runaway sample with various types of service outlets was minimal, with only some 27 percent actually using any one of the available programs. A rather low order correlation between knowledge of a given program and its use was also noted in general, with many runaways apparently avoiding programs for fear of being caught and returned home.

Closer examination of the interview data revealed that different types of runaways utilized different sources of help or services. When services and programs were dichotomized into public and counterculture types, differences between the runaway types emerged clearly or were highlighted.

IMPLICATIONS FOR RUNAWAY SERVICES: A DISCUSSION OF FINDINGS

Any policies or programs must take into account the varied nature of the runaway population and begin by admitting that no single solution or answer is possible. All the data collected in this study suggest that while certain common problems do exist among runaways, a wide variety of specific problems also obtain which require specific solutions. Having said this, several possibilities or avenues do seem open and worthy of further exploration, each with a great deal of potential impact program-wise.

First and foremost, we have the runaways basically in an illegal alien status. Until something is done about this fundamental condition, programs and services will be operating under severe handicaps. If *decriminalization* could be achieved, there seems to be every possibility that greater contact with and use of existing programs would follow. Indeed for those runaways already in trouble with the law before leaving home, *diversion* programs could be implemented and in all probability could significantly reduce or eliminate the *Fugitive* type of runaway. This decriminalization effort, by encouraging *legal* solutions or programs, would by definition reduce the involvement of runaways in their criminal pursuits on the streets. Much of the runaway problem thereby could be contained or reduced by such efforts.

Second, based on interviews and data of this study, the existing programs frequently are not designed with the runaway in mind and hence tend to be either irrelevant or ineffective. This is specially true in the *public* sector where programs frequently do not exist to meet immediate survival needs of the runaway population. Also, some of the existing programs, e.g., foster home programs, seem very ineffective judging from the high rate of recidivism and flight from them, involving the *Refugee* type of runaway particularly. Redesigning and improving such existing programs seems to be necessary. Better communication channels and advertising of these programs seem to be needed also. Crisis intervention programs and other similar approaches also seem indicated as avenues of servicing in the runaway sector. The existence of long-standing and multiple problems—in the home, in the larger community, with the law, with the school—seems to suggest that school counselors, social workers, welfare workers, and law enforcement people should be able to identify potential problems and react in an organized, coordinated fashion as outreach workers and take preventive action.

Finally, it would seem clear that a variety of alternative services is needed similar to those developed in other countries where hostels and wayside services exist to reduce the hazards of travel and survival for youngsters away from home. Such a variety of legitimate, alternative services could be provided if runaway status were decriminalized. In this way, the many and contradicting conditions facing the runaway and those who would serve him could be more honestly and rationally handled.

CHAPTER 1

Scope of The Study

Runaway youth are illegal aliens in their own land. They are persons without papers, without credentials, rights, or support. Because they are underage, they are under laws that tend to restrict and limit their access to citizenship and independence.

Laws against disorderly conduct, hitchhiking, drug and alcohol use, as well as runaway warrants account for most detentions of runaways (Ambrosino 1971). Most such detentions are handled by juvenile courts, but as D'Angelo (1974) has suggested, juvenile courts are "hopelessly ill-equipped" to consider the health, education and personal needs of runaways in the 10 to 15 minutes allotted to most juvenile court hearings.

In 26 states, the police have the right to take a child into custody if he is "believed to be a runaway" (Beaser 1975). Many state laws are contradictory, vague, or punitive with respect to runaways. As Beaser states: "While not specifically so expressed, [these laws] sometimes seem to carry with them an implied presumption against the runaway child and seemingly place upon such a child the burden of proving that his running away was justified, without specifically spelling out what would constitute legally justifiable grounds for a child leaving home" (p. 89).

On the other hand, society is touched by the plight of the runaway and reaches out to help. Two major pieces of federal legislation have attempted to place the runaway youth in a nonpunitive legal category. The 1977 fiscal year will see a total of $7.9 million dollars available for social services under the HEW Office of Youth Development projects (Youth Alternatives, April 1976). The Runaway Youth Act (P.L. 93-415, 1974) declared that runaway youths constitute "a substantial law enforcement problem," and also noted that many of them are significantly endangered, living on the streets, without resources (Section 302, Title III, 1974).

This law goes on to state: "The problem of *locating, detaining and returning* [emphasis ours] runaway children should

not be the responsibility of already overburdened police departments and juvenile justice authorities and in view of the interstate
nature of the problem, it is the *responsibility of the Federal Government* [emphasis ours] to develop accurate reporting of the
problem nationally and to develop an effective system of temporary care outside the law enforcement stucture." The issue of "care
outside the law enforcement structure" is addressed by the other
piece of relevant federal legislation, Title XX of the Social Security Act, which permits service to runaways without eligibility requirements.

Yet the runaway is properly under the legal jurisdiction of
state laws and local law enforcement. Through these three over-
lapping areas of jurisdiction, caught between detention or services,
runaways are living in a prison without walls.

The purpose of this study was to develop a typology of runaways based upon their own motives for running away, and to examine the services available or not available to them. Why do runaways leave home? How do they survive? What services are available? What else is needed? These questions guide our research.

METHODS OF STUDY

This study focuses upon runaways and three correlates: parents
of runaways, agencies that serve runaways, and the underground
world that many runaways live in while on the road. In Appendix I,
details of our sampling design and data collection methods can be
found. Briefly, we chose our runaways to represent two theoretical groups of runaway youth, *the seen* and *the unseen.* We did not
attempt to select a random, representative sample; we chose our
subjects to represent youth being served by different types of
agencies and youth "free," that is, unseen. As Shellow (1967)
noted: "We knew that those (runaways) who were reported missing to the police were merely the tip of the runaway iceberg and
that beneath the surface lay an undetermined number invisible to
public agencies." Thus, we chose to pursue the "unreported" as
well as the "reported": the "unseen" and the "seen."

The sample of "seen" cases comprises 124 subjects referred
from the eight social agencies that cooperated with our project.
These eight agencies represent four types that service runaway
youth: (1) public social service agency; (2) private social agency;
(3) juvenile court diversion agency; and (4) counterculture agency. We selected these four types of agencies from two West Coast

runaway "terminals": The Los Angeles area and the San Francisco Bay Area. Our unseen sample was recruited on the street, using
street contacts, word-of-mouth messages, payment of voluntary
subjects, and so on. We were able to locate 91 "free" (or "unseen"
by social agency) runaways who talked with us about their lives
and their needs. The 215 runaway interviews, plus interviews with
38 selected parents of runaways, forms the data base for our study
of runaway youth. The interviews with the parents of runaways,
chosen to illustrate each of the runaway types, give us a dynamic
view of the parent-child interaction leading to the runaway act.

We also studied the services available to runaways and the a-
gencies that delivered them. In this phase of our study we examined in depth the eight agencies that supplied our "seen" sample.
Additionally, for a more comprehensive picture of how agencies
view runaways and their families, we used a structured questionnaire to elicit the perceptions of a wide range of agency workers,
nationally and locally.

Based on these data, we developed our analysis of the world
of the runaway and the services needed and received.

THEORETICAL PERSPECTIVE

Who is a runaway? Why does society come to define runaway
youth as a social problem?

Historically, "running away" has been viewed in many
different ways. For example, in the ancient world, running away
from home was probably minimal because the custom of enslav-
ing powerless strangers and the practice of disposing of unwanted
children by infanticide. Roman law drew no age distinctions in
subjecting children to their father's control. The father could put
sons, daughters or other dependents to death or sell them into
slavery without explanation.

Children were no less subject to parental control during the
feudal period, although boys and girls sometimes could find asy-
lum in convents or monasteries. Running away violated feudal
obligations, but the medieval cities provided sanctuary for those
who could find a place within their walls under the local bishop's
protection or as apprentices of some guild master. Relatively ma-
ture youth might join the many wandering bands of mercenary
soldiers as drummers, grooms, or camp followers, depending on
their sex and physical abilities.

In the era of rising nation states and the breakdown of the
feudal order, diverse pressures forced serfs and peasants off the
land. Poor laws and vagrancy statutes were enacted to control un-

attached persons and indentured servants who violated their contractual obligations. Few distinctions separated youths from adults although guardianships were established whenever an heir was too young to administer properties. Land and wealth were so closely linked that only the children of the poor really had the sort of mobility we today associate with running away.

The industrial revolution altered the family constellation and destroyed the guild system. Skilled workers were replaced by machines in centralized industrial enterprises organized around tasks a child could perform as well as an adult. Young people faced prospects and conditions that had not been experienced by their parents. When child rearing books began to appear in English around 1825, loss of parental control over their children was the common theme.

Although many American colonists fled religious controls and a patriarchal economic system, it would seem peculiar to characterize them as runaways since they had royal permission to leave and many adult heads of households were among them. Parental rights were regulated by English common law, and statutes were promulgated to help family heads maintain discipline in the new world. A Connecticut law of 1642 banned "incorrigibleness" by forbidding in children "any stubborn or rebellious carriage against their parents or governors." A Massachusetts statute of 1646 prescribed the death penalty for children over 16 who cursed or struck their parents except in self-defense. Other laws required single minors to attach themselves to a household.

Indentured servants, usually orphans and paupers recruited from almshouses, were among the earliest settlers in the colonies. They came to America under contract to pay for their voyage with service; to run away from this service was to violate the contract, to become an outlaw.

After the Civil War the tide of migration swiftly overwhelmed the native Americans on the frontier. Controlling Indians by bureaucratic administration or by force became a major priority of the Department of the Interior and the U.S. Cavalry. When all the Indians had been captured, punished, and sent to their reservations, popular novels and films generated the idea that Indians were rebels and fugitives running away from homes that had been given them. A common administrative procedure, which continues to the present, has been to take the children from their homes and place them in special schools run by the Bureau of Indian Affairs. This removal of Indian children from their homes meant that if these children should leave the Indian school without permission, even if only to return home, they would be dealt with as runaway offenders.

Late in the nineteenth century tremendous waves of immigration swelled population in the eastern cities. Use of child labor continued, with many young people working 16-hour days and 6-day weeks in unsanitary sweatshops. It was not unusual for employers to make these children wear chains to prevent them from running away. Abandoned children, orphans, and runaways were seen as a social problem, potential members of the dangerous classes, in an era whose street life was unfettered by compulsory education, child labor laws, or other restrictions on the freedom of youth.

The practice of treating adolescents as dependents was formalized into law by the reformatory movement as a practical application of the idea that youth is a distinct stage in life. Minors could be sent to reform schools for vagrancy, incorrigibility, or other ill-defined offenses to serve indeterminate sentences and be released upon reaching majority or when the authorities considered them rehabilitated. It was partly because of the failure of the reform schools to meet their goals that the juvenile court movement was instituted.

The concept of a special court to hear cases involving minors, to deal humanely with children whose conduct endangered themselves or others and avoid labeling such children as criminals, evolved around the turn of the century.

Efforts to increase the scope of compulsory school attendance and to enact child labor laws coincided with the juvenile court movement. The child labor laws were designed to protect the health, welfare, and safety of minors, to buttress the compulsory school attendance laws, and to protect children from unscrupulous employers. This whole legal structure of well-intentioned reform also provided a rationale for placing "runaways" into a special category and labeling them as antisocial transgressors. If they were still within the compulsory school age, by running away they automatically became truants. If they were under the legal working age, they tended to become vagrants. Simultaneously, the establishment of a separate law enforcement system for juveniles facilitated the metamorphosis of runaways into status offenders.

The economic conditions of the 1930s produced a wave of youthful nomadism. With one-fourth of the nation's labor force out of work, economic destitution in the home impelled many adolescents to leave. Hundreds of thousands of young people roamed the countryside, drifting from one town to another, "riding the rails." The federal government created the Federal Transient Service to aid in social service efforts for the massive numbers of people on the move. Outland (1938) studied 3,352 boys who registered in the Southern California regional camp of the

Transient Service and concluded that financial strain on the family was the "usual reason" for running away.

Leaving home took on a completely different meaning with the outbreak of World War II. Many youths were lured into wartime jobs, and others ran off to join the armed forces. When enforcement of the child labor laws was relaxed, there was a dramatic increase in the number of employed youth.

The New Deal period witnessed the entry of the government into the welfare sector on a massive scale. Public social agencies increased the scope of their activities to include counseling and psychiatric social services. By the end of 1944 about 400 counties in the United States had special children's workers whose services were supported by federal funds under the Social Security Act.

Running away did not seem like an important social problem during the early postwar era. With the return of prosperity, middle-class values became more firmly established. Glorification of youth was exploited by the media and the advertising industry. College education became the theoretical prerequisite to economic success just as the extended family and the multigenerational community were breaking down. The divorce rate rose perceptibly in the 1950s, and migration of nuclear families to the urban centers increased. As agrarian America faded it was becoming more difficult for adolescents to understand or participate in many of the historical traditions from which their parents' thoughts emanated.

The unique demographic situation of the 1960-1970 decade, with massive increases in the proportion of adolescents in the population, produced immense strains on the institutions that dealt with youth, and the number of runaway youth increased dramatically. With little access to the more desirable apprenticeships, runaway youth could at best hope for marginal, low-paying work in the secondary labor market. At worst, the problems of finding legitimate employment without valid working papers would lead many runaways into contact with hustlers and unscrupulous entrepreneurs who exploited young transients.

The legal distinctions separating juveniles from adults were partly undermined in 1967 when the Supreme Court's "Gault decision" overturned many provisions and practices of the juvenile courts. The high court's blow at the concept of the status offense came during an upsurge of runaway behavior, when thousands of kids were running away to join the hippies, that is, during the "love-ins" of the sixties. This phenomenon, associated with a youth counterculture, has faded away.

In the 1970s intergenerational conflict appears to be taking different forms as the proportion of single-parent and stepfather-headed families increases. Aside from the major cities, which have always drawn mobile youth from other areas, there are no special meccas for runaways who must compete for survival with all others of the underclass in the cities.

The findings of most researchers are sample specific and center on white children. The story of runaways among blacks, Chicanos, Asians, and native Americans has not been told, yet we are aware of cultural differences among runaway youth.*

From the disappearance of the frontier through the growth of technological society, running away has been a problem for adults who perceive it as a problem, for parents trying to control their children, and for authorities trying to rationalize the situation. Parents' usual response to a child's running away is worry, criticism, and denial of guilt. Evidence of the child's mental instability is eagerly reviewed, and incidents of delinquency are cited. Although some investigators have tried to see both the parent and the runaway perspective, the usual research products have been reports for various authorities, explanations for parents, and "treatment" for the kids. Observers have often commented on "family pathology," but they have not always attended to the home situation as the child perceives it when assessing the determinants of runaway behavior. Minimal attention has been given to the experience of youth once they have left home or to what happens while they are on the road.

Various studies purporting to report findings on runaways have not focused on current runaways at all, but present the reminiscences of former runaways, the intuitions and impressions of helping professionals, or other data from secondary sources. With numerous diverse methodological approaches and lacking representative samples from which to generalize, researchers have had tremendous difficulties in constructing an integrated and complete picture of the runaway phenomenon.

The first issue is that of defining the runaway. The operational definition of a runaway is indeed a difficult problem. Other studies of runaways have utilized either the strict legal definition or have left the definition relatively vague. In this study, we approach the problem by utilizing a three-pronged definition. First, the legal definition of a California runaway, that is, a child (under 18) who is away from his home overnight, *without his parents' consent,* is necessary but not sufficient. Many young people are on the streets, seemingly *with* their parents' consent, or at least, without any visible signs of parental concern. Yet these are considered

---

*See Chapter 3 for an analysis of the data on our sample along ethnic lines. As a part of this study Dr. Harry Kitano has written a paper dealing with ethnic minority runaways.

"runaways" by law enforcement officials or perhaps by the youth and his immediate peer group. Thus, our operational definition considers the secondary deviance labeling impact; that is, if the agencies label a child as a "runaway," he is treated as a runaway. Or if a child *considers himself to be a "runaway," he behaves as a "runaway."* Thus, we accepted into our sample youth 17 or less who are (a) away from home without their parents' consent, or (b) are defined as runaways by law enforcement or service agencies, or (c) identified by themselves or by their relevant significant others as "runaways." Subjects in our study meet one or more of these three criteria.

By applying a wider approach based on theories of socialization it is possible to conceptualize the runaway phenomenon as one of deviations from the "norm" of white middle-class child-rearing patterns. Instead of a youth's lengthy dependence on parents, we see some youth rushing to independence, to the establishment of autonomy by 14 or 15 years of age. These young people *look like* young adults; a girl of 14 may well resemble a girl of 18; a boy of 15 may appear as a 29-year-old man. Early physical maturity is lending visible credence to many young people's claims to autonomy, to independence, to "freedom." Serious authority struggles may erupt within these families. One possible outcome of these struggles is that the youth will leave home. This leaving phenomenon may be a relatively long and repetitive process, with the youth "taking off" for a few days, returning only to leave again when the parent-child struggles become virulent. In some cases, this "leaving the scene" is with parental consent, sometimes covert; other times overt (complete with payments to stay away). In some cases, the parent-child relationship has been broken, and the child has been placed in foster care or institutionalized. These are "state-raised" children, who flee from such arrangements.

The parental home or the surrogate arrangement (that is, foster home, institution) is a primary socialization agency. Thus, a child's flight from either environment may be viewed as a socialization failure.

Another possibility, however, is that when a child leaves home early this may be not a socialization failure per se, but rather an incidence of socialization completion, particularly for children from some ethnic subcultures. For example, among the poor or various cultural groups (blacks, Indians) leaving home in mid or late adolescence may be an expected "natural" act; they are "grown."

Thus, we posit two types of parent-child terminations, the *discontinuous* (result of socialization strain) and *continuous* (result of expected behaviors).

Our approach in this study has been to consider the runaway phenomenon from the perspectives of adolescent socialization patterns, those which are both continuous and discontinuous. Every society has formal and/or informal autonomy. Even in societies where young men and women become part of an extended family structure, their new role as adults is clearly defined. In American society the phenomenon of adolescent separation from the family is complicated by the adolescent phase of development, which is absent or greatly truncated in many other cultures. The rationale for an extended period of adolescence is that this society is highly complex, and it appears a longer period of apprenticeship is required in order for individuals to cope with the complex adult roles. There are less comforting but perhaps equally valid explanations for prolonged adolescence. One is that the economic system can neither support an influx of younger wage earners, nor furnish the kinds of controls which parents provided in the past. Another explanation coming from theorists of the "youth culture," such as Bettleheim and Kenniston, is that parents are unwilling to relinquish control and attempts at guidance of their children, since the interdependence relationship would be totally severed after separation. Still others believe that excessive permissiveness and/or neglect on the part of the parent has led to premature autonomy and a lack of proper socialization of the young, producing the "bad child."

The process of separation may be viewed along a spectrum ranging from continuous at one end to discontinuous at the other. There may be several types of termination. The "normal" type is graduation from both the primary and secondary social institutions (family and school) into the labor market, self-sufficiency, and adulthood. In cases where separation occurs at this stage, both the youth and his parents have prepared for this act by the granting of adult privileges by degree until separation finally occurs.

There are several points of strain throughout this process, and many deviations from the "normal" pattern can occur. One of these deviant patterns of failure in the normal socialization process is that of "running away," that is, of leaving the adolescent socializing institutions, such as family and school, and choosing the wider social arena as the source for new roles and behaviors.

If we view runaways along the continuous-discontinuous spectrum, it becomes clear that service and intervention strategies for a youth at one point of the spectrum may be totally inappropriate for a runaway at another point. Our procedure is to identify runaway youth along this continuous-discontinuous spectrum, and relate them to places where we find them after running away, either in official or unofficial terminals, that is, either "seen" and "captured" or "unseen" and "free."

When a youth becomes a runaway, there are only very limited roles available in the larger society. As the structure of society has been urbanized and highly stratified and the possibility for employment has been closed off and as adolescents become "surplus property," the fate of the runaway becomes problematic.

Within the structure of these changes in American society, the diverse socialization patterns of youth, the velocity of change and strain in all youth socializing institutions, we see runaway youth as possibly forming an emerging youth-adult category, that is, persons who are now illegal aliens in a society not yet ready for their presence. These are precocious adults, torn between homes without love and the streets without support.

CHAPTER 2

How Different Are Runaway Youth from Other Youth?

How unique are runaways in comparison with other adolescents? Are they different in kind, or only in degree?

In order to examine this issue, we asked a random, representative sample of high school youth a series of questions about their running away behavior. The high school was situated in one of the cities* in which we interviewed the runaway sample. We found that *13 percent of these high school students reported that they had run away from home one or more times,* although they had returned and were in school at the time of the interview. In addition, another *30 percent told us they had "thought about"* running away, although they had not actually done so. Thus, it would appear that among urban high school youth, running away from home is not a totally unique or uncommon experience.

The estimated runaway prevalence rate has varied because the problems of obtaining an accurate rate are indeed complex. However, the 13 percent rate we found in our Berkeley high school sample falls within the range of variations reported by other studies. Kupfer (1967) found that in a Canadian high school sample, 17 percent of the subjects reported running away. A survey of youth in Denver (1973) by Behavioral Research and Evaluation Corporation estimated that approximately the same percentage had run away from home at least once. Mobley and Swanson (1973) and Elliott and Vass (1974) reported the incidence of running away closer to 10 percent among all adolescents. The discrepancy between incidence and prevalence is not likely to be great because the runaway classification is confined to a restricted age bracket, and there is the marked tendency among runaways to become re-

*This sample was drawn from Berkeley High School, randomly selected students from the ninth, tenth, eleventh, and twelfth grades, a total of 436 students. This sample was selected for a larger study, under a National Institute of Education contract, to evaluate alternative schools in Berkeley. There is no overlap of subjects between this high school sample and the 215 "seen" and "unseen" runaways in our study. The Berkeley High School subjects serve as a control group.

peaters. If the above estimates are near the mark, it means that somewhere between one-tenth and one-fifth of the country's adolescents run away, and given an adolescent population in the 20 million range, it also means that the runaway experience has been shared by two to four million adolescents. This is a mass phenomenon, not an isolated vagary.

One problem in accurately estimating runaway prevalence is the reluctance of parents to report that their children had fled. Shellow, et al. (1967) found that only one out of every six self-reported runaways had been reported missing. Thus, studies that rely exclusively on data derived from parents are likely to understate the extent of the problem. Many parents feel that a child who runs away from home casts doubt upon their own capabilities as parents and are thus reluctant to discuss such events with "outsiders."

In our interviews with parents of runaways, we found this to be true. In fact, it was difficult to obtain access to them. Most parents did not want to discuss the situation. Those parents who sought help from social or psychiatric agencies were also reluctant to discuss the incident with "researchers," feeling that their child needed "help" or "treatment" and that they were caught up in a difficult situation, too embarrassing to reveal to "strangers."

Further, we found approximately one-fourth of the runaways had no functioning parents to report their leaving. These are "state-raised" youth who ran away from the very services designed to "help them."

The family background of runaway youth tends to reflect the changing American family, that is, more step-parents and more mother-headed households. Children reared in such families are reported to have greater socialization problems, although the research on this issue is not clear, but is rather compounded by amount of income, degree of extended family support, amount of conflict in the home, and so on.

One measure of comparison between our runaway sample and the other adolescent sample is the educational background of the mothers (since so many of our runaways are from fatherless homes, it appears a comparison of mothers is the best control for background differences).

As Jencks and many other researchers have found, the socio-economic status of the family is a most important predeterminant of a student's educational adjustment and achievement. Thus, we would hypothesize that most runaways would come from homes where the mother's educational attainment is relatively low, and where the student's educational achievement might be expected also to be relatively low in comparison to those with other types of backgrounds.

TABLE 2.1: Mother's Educational Background as Reported by Nonrunaways, Potential runaways, Ex-runaways, and Current Runaways*

Mother's Educational Status	Non-Runaways (N=189)	Potential Runaways** (N=88)	Ex-Runaways (N=47)	Current Runaways (N=123)
High School or less	31%	33%	23%	69%
B.A. or less	41%	38%	40%	29%
More than B.A.	28%	29%	36%	2%
Total	100%	100%	100%	100%

*Includes only those cases where data on mother's educational status were given.
**Those who said they had thought of running away but didn't.

As can be seen (Table 2.1), the runaways in our sample are much more likely than the control group runaways to come from families where the mother had only a high school education or less. In the control group ex-runaways came from families where mothers had greater than average educational levels. It appears that highly educated parents of runaways tend to return their runaway children to the family and to school. Thus, our sample may include a high proportion of youth from lower classes, whose parental ties are extremely weakened by multiple problems, and thus represent the most needful and socially deviant group of runaways.

Further differences between ex-runaways from the high school and our current runaways can be seen in the average number of runaway incidents for each group, for ex-runaways, the average is 3.1, while our current runaways average 5.2 times. Thus, the ex-runaways in the control group appear to be of a different strata in terms of parental background and in terms of long-term commitment to a runaway career. These control group ex-runaways may be youth caught at an earlier stage in the runaway career, while our sample runaways are a more chronic, more deviant group and therefore less likely to return to schools or families, that is, to resume "normal" adolescent roles.

Within the school system from which the adolescent control group was chosen, there exist two types of school structures. Students who attend one continuation and one alternative school appear to resemble those whom James Coleman (*Adolescent Society,* 1960) labeled as the "disaffiliated."* Therefore, it would seem likely that "disaffiliated" students who attend these schools would also be those most likely to become runaways.

**TABLE 2.2: Percent of Runaways among Students from Continuation/
Alternative High Schools and Regular High Schools**

	% Runaway
Continuation/alternative high school (N=42)	45%
Regular high school (N=343)	9%
Total percent of runaways	13%

As can be seen, youth who are already disaffiliated in some
sense from regular high schools, that is, they attend a continuation
or alternative school, have a statistically significant greater incidence of runaway behavior, as compared with students who attend
a regular high school.

As youth move along a process of assuming a deviant role or
move into a "runaway career," they leave behind membership in
regular, nondeviant groups.

We asked both the control group and the current runaways a-
bout their peer groups' experiences with running away. That is,
did they associate with significant others who also ran away? The
findings are reported in the following table.

**TABLE 2.3: Peer Group Runaway Status as Reported by Nonrunaways,
potential Runaways, Ex-runaways, and Current Runaways**

Peers Who Ran Away	Non-runaway (N=235)	Potential Runaway (N-126)	Ex-Runaway (N=53)	Current Runaway (N=215)
Friends	45%	73%	84%	87%
Classmates	41%	60%	58%	71%
Relatives	22%	40%	43%	48%

As can be seen, (Table 2.3) as a youth enters a runaway career, he picks up runaway reference groups, friends, classmates,
and relatives who have also run away.

As a youth proceeds from a high school student "career" into
a deviant runaway "career," he loosens his commitment to the im-

*In Coleman's definition, "disaffiliated" youth are those who are "disaffiliated"
from the standard high schools and are placed, voluntarily or involuntarily, in other
schools or institutions. Students are consigned, as a rule, to continuation schools when
they have dropped out of a mainstream high school or have been excluded from it because of educational and/or behavioral problems. Alternative schools are options for
students, who, for one reason or another, are alienated from the mainstream school or
have special interests or problems that are not met adequately in that school. The
distinctions between continuation and alternative schools are not always quite that rigid.

portance of the student role and tends to attach lesser degrees of importance to school, as can be seen below.

TABLE 2.4: **Importance of School as Perceived by Nonrunaways, Potential Runaways, Ex-runaways, and Current Runaways**

	School Important
Nonrunaways	93%
Potential runaways	89%
Ex-Runaways	78%
Current Runaways	77%

While current runaways attach less importance to school than do ex-runaways, the difference is in degree. Most runaways recognize the importance of school, even though they have left the scene.

Runaways' attitudes regarding the importance of school also seem rooted in their school learning experiences. We asked all control group and runaway subjects to rate themselves on their general reading ability. These are self-ratings, and do not reflect "measured reading scores."

TABLE 2.5: **Self-ratings of Reading Ability by Nonrunaways, Potential Runaways, Ex-runaways, and Current Runaways**

	Above Average	Average	Below Average
Nonrunaways	57%	36%	7%
Potential runaways	53%	38%	9%
Ex-runaways	57%	36%	7%
Current runaways	42%	40%	18%

As can be seen, current runaways are more than twice as likely as the control group ex-runaways to rate themselves "below average" in reading ability. Perhaps those runaways who feel they are poor in school are even less likely to return to school, where they will only be open to further feelings of failure and inadequacy. However, 42 percent of the current runaways and 57 percent of the ex-runaways rate themselves as "above average" in reading, so that performance in school, as self-assessed, is not necessarily a determinant of the general disaffiliation, which also includes disaffiliation from school, that is implicit in running away.

Using a "troublesome scale," we asked each subject whether his teachers, parents, and friends saw him as "trouble in school" as well as how he saw himself. These self-ratings are shown below.

TABLE 2.6: Perceptions of Others and Self that Subject is "Trouble in School" as Reported by Nonrunaways, Potential Runaways, Ex-runaways, and Current Runaways

	Non-runaway	Potential Runaway	Ex-Runaway	Current Runaway
Teachers	9%	12%	14%	47%
Parents	8%	22%	33%	70%
Friends	7%	20%	14%	20%
Self	8%	13%	11%	36%

If the self-view of "trouble in school" could be taken as a measure of self-esteem, it can be seen that our current runaways are very self-demeaning, over one-third of them indicating they felt they had been "troublesome in school." The table indicates a clear correlation between running away and the subject's feeling that his parents consider him troublesome in school. The trend seems clear that runaways will feel most estranged from their parents. The more likely they are to consider themselves as "trouble," the more open they are to selecting a deviant career, that is, to be a highly potential runaway.

This is further buttressed by the percentage of the high school students who stated they had thought of dropping out of school:

Nonrunaways	8%
Potential runaways	27%
Ex-Runaways	49%

Thus, the runaway career is a tempting one to a student who is thinking of dropping out of school.

School disciplinary problems are a good prediction of potential running away, as indicated by the subjects' responses to questions about school suspensions or expulsions.

TABLE 2.7: School Suspensions and Expulsions as Reported by Nonrunaways, Potential Runaways, Ex-runaways, and Current Runaways

Nonrunaways	10%
Potential Runaways	27%
Ex-runaways	32%
Current Runaways	69%

Here, again, the trend is clear (Table 2.7). If a student is suspended from school, he becomes a potential for running away—just as parents "suspend" the youth, so the school also "suspends" him, and running away from such "suspensions" seems only a further process of disengagement with those primary and secondary institutions of socialization.

By comparing our sample of current runaways with youth of the same age who now attend school, we find strong evidence that similar processes of disengagement from home and school are at work toward establishing a runaway career.

It appears that our sample of current runaways is more extreme on most measures as compared with the control group. However, we can see that as a student is disaffiliated from the school system, and as he views his parental relationship negatively, so he becomes more runaway-prone. It appears our sample of current runaways, while not selected to be representative, does reflect the extreme of observable disengagement trends in nonrunaways, potential runaways, and returned runaways.

This permits us to generalize to all potential runaways from much that we have learned from our current runaways, and much that we have documented appears to point to early-warning signs of runaway-prone youth who may still be in school.

Runaways are different from other adolescents in degree, not in kind. They represent those youth who are in difficulty in many areas of life and have few family or institutional supports.

TYPES OF RUNAWAYS

The purpose of classification is to lead to better understanding of phenomena. By developing a set of classifications describing different types of runaway youth, we propose that such classifications will lead us to better understanding of what is needed. Many other studies have also developed classifications of runaways, based on a variety of criteria and theories. Many have led to the assignment of labels to runaway youth—some stigmatizing, some condemnatory, some dramatizing, and some romanticizing. All *impute* motives in one way or another.

The elaboration of typologies to classify the various labels, summarize experiences, and impute motives or dispositions has been common in studies of runaways. Such labeling is part of administrative channeling, a device to create common reference points for selection and recording of treatment careers. As Shellow, et al. (1967) have noted, the interpretation given the runaway act depends in large part on which of the social networks the youth becomes entangled in: the legal, correctional, the mental health, or the welfare service network. Most typologies of runaways have originated in the intuition of investigators who were serving in social control agencies where their tasks required categorizing runaways as juvenile delinquents.

Many studies have reported that runaways suffered from some type of psychological disorder (Armstrong 1932; Reimer 1940; Berachyahu 1955; Leventhal 1963), and others have defined them as having criminally delinquent tendencies (Robins and O'Neal 1961; Kanner 1950; Foster 1962; Hildebrand 1963; Shinohara and Jenkins 1967; Jenkins 1971). Another researcher has argued that youth who leave home without parental authorization do so in search of "the pleasures of the runaway's world" (Joos, et al. 1970).

Lowrey (1941) distinguished "runaways" who are seeking a better life from "nomads" whose errant behavior is chronic. Bergeron (1954) drew a similar distinction between runaways and vagrants as two types of "misadapted youths." Berger (1958) differentiated "spontaneous" from "reactive" runaways, finding variant personality and family conflicts in the two groups. Spontaneous runaways have an "inherent urge" for "change of environment, flight, and motor activity," whereas reactive runaways are influenced by parental rejection, unsatisfactory school situations, and their need to be considered adults.

Shellow et al. (1967) distinguished two types of runaways, the "disturbed minority" and the "nondisturbed majority." Rosenwald (1967) found four types of suburban adolescent female runaways, the hyper-mature, the hypo-mature, the impulse-ridden, and the unclassifiable. Levy (1972) catalogued five types of girls running from a residential treatment center—the defiant, the psychotic, the escapist, those who desire to be on their own, and those who desire to be with their parents. Greene (1972) distinguished three types of runaway girls: the rootless, who are hedonistically careless of the consequences of their actions; the anxious, who come from problem families and experience feelings of depression and powerlessness; and the terrified, who flee from a threatened incestuous relationship with the father.

Homer (1973) distinguished two types of runaway girls, those who are "running from" a tense family situation and those who are "running to" the real or imaginary "pleasures of the runaway world." Homer noted that runaways have something to tell helping professionals about their own values, assumptions, and rescue fantasies.*

Steirlin (1973) identified four types of runaways along a continuum of differing degrees of success: abortive, lonely schizoid, crisis, and casual. Abortive runaways fail to complete their "missions," which might indicate strong, intact psychological ties to the family as well as rejection of a stressful situation at home. The "lonely schizoid" youth are rejected and have no peers to run to. The crisis runaway is more a fugitive escaping from a threatening situation than a reject. The casual runaway is more or less independent.

English (1973) developed a taxonomy based on time spent on the run. His approach uses the picturesque terminology a counselor in a runaway agency might hear. Thus, according to English, the largest number of runaways are "floaters" who run away to release home tensions but only stay away for a couple of days. Then there are "recurrent runaways" who stay away longer to resolve an unhappy family situation and "splitters" who find their welcome upon returning home appealing and seem to find an increasing number of situations to run from. Then there are the "hard road freaks" who are very streetwise and have severed ties with their families to make their home in the streets. The runaway's situation is seen as a function of the actions of the youth, with little consideration of the effects of other forces.

Most of the above typologies are ill-defined, offer no objective quantitative validation, and fail to encompass all runaways. Based upon the clinical experiences of a few researchers with a few runaways, they fail to do justice to the phenomenon. Furthermore,

---

*Girls who were seen as running from family conflicts were significantly helped by the therapeutic intervention but therapy was "virtually useless" for the girls who were "running to." They were interested in doing their own thing and showed no interest in examining the reasons for their running. According to Homer, "...their energy was primarily directed toward seeking the lack of controls and the freedom to do their own thing which they found in the runaway's subculture..." And this forced a shift in treatment approach away from communications problems in the home to the girl's "ability to take responsibility for her actions and to help her set controls on her behavior. There was a strong emphasis on raising the anxiety of these youngsters and working with the guilt which surfaced. The shift involved changing from an insight-oriented approach to more confrontation, more emphasis on the setting of limits and more emphasis on looking at the direct consequences of the acting-out behavior... Within this framework, it was clear that those girls who continued to run frequently, and on a regular basis, were not able to control their behavior; even with the assistance of a helping person. It became apparent that the gratification they experienced while on the run made it worth their while to risk the consequences they incurred when picked up by the police."

with the exception of Homer's classification of "running from" and "running to," these taxonomies have little or no predictive power.

Brennan, et al. (1974, 1975) elaborated a provisional classification of runaways based on previous research and then tested it empirically. Brennan argued that the classification of "the sick," "the bad," and "the free" may oversimplify matters. Two subtypes of "bad" or delinquent runaways were distinguished—criminal delinquents and conflict delinquents. Two subtypes of "free" runaways were also distinguished—rebels and adventurers. This process produced a five-fold typology. Then computerized clustering methods were applied to empirical data taken in a household survey of runaway and nonrunaway youth and a sample of agency related youth to examine the degree of separation of the types and the ease of accurately classifying any new runaway youth. This empirical analysis prevails and that the five-fold typology is unrealistic. Brennan, et al. divided the runaway youth population into seven classes:

1. Nondelinquent youth in the lower age brackets running from high stress family situations;

2. Middle-class "loners," nondelinquent youth who appear to exemplify a "running to" model of runaway. Most of them are girls;

3. Highly "autonomous" older runaways from a loose-knit family situation. Social class is low;

4. Delinquent lower social class runaways who are embedded in a wide variety of delinquent behaviors;

5. Delinquent girls with highly stressful home and school situations and strong peer pressure toward delinquency;

6. Higher social class delinquents with extremely high commitment to peers and high peer delinquency. They lack interest in school and have highly rejecting families;

7. Delinquent boys in the lower age brackets from highly rejecting families. Strong normative pressure from peers toward delinquent behavior.

These types were differentiated according to levels of delinquency. Three of the types have low involvement in delinquency, and it was found that this relationship is conditioned by the presence or absence of severe family stresses. Delinquent runaways are subject to stress at home and in school. They may be expected to have lower self-esteem and higher levels of social alienation than nondelinquent runaways. Peer pressures seem to be the common factor among the four categories of high delinquency runaways.

Brennan, et al. also developed a typology of episodes. Five types of episodes were described:

1. Spontaneous unplanned episodes: minimal planning, short duration, voluntary return, and noninvolvement with the police characterize this type;

2. Deliberate successful episodes: deliberate, careful preparation and long duration are found here. The police become involved and the youth do not usually return voluntarily;

3. Temporary "good time" escapades: hedonistic "good times" are common to this type. The youths travel to "fun" places and tend to return voluntarily within a week;

4. Difficult, long-term escapist episodes: many girls trying to "escape" from difficult home situations are found here. They intend to leave permanently and are usually gone for a long time. They do not generally enjoy the runaway experience, yet they do not return voluntarily;

5. Temporary escapist episodes from unpleasant home situations: this type also seeks escape from difficult home situations, except that they clearly intend to stay away only for a few days. They usually go to a friend's house and return home within a few days.

The episodic classification supplements Brennan's structured typology of personality profiles. The sevenfold etiology may or may not be applicable to the majority of runaways. Brennan's analysis is basically concerned with delinquency and is derived from a social control orientation. Such an approach is inevitably one-sided and needs to be supplemented by a fuller, more painstaking analysis of the perspectives of the runaways themselves, as well as mitigated by the situations in which runaways and agencies or others interact.

Brennan, et al. conducted a household survey to interview former runaway and nonrunaway youth at home. Such a survey can include only runaway youth who have returned and must inevitably miss all those who are currently on the run. The researchers also surveyed former agency clients who had run away in the past but their response rates for this sample were extremely low. The number of runaways in the residential sample is also quite small and may only represent the population of a semirural mountain state. Nevertheless, Brennan's typological approach reconciles most of the contradictions in other research findings and is easily replicable.

We interviewed 124 "seen" and 91 "unseen" runaways (94 boys and 121 girls). Whereas Brennan used random sampling techniques to survey households, which he supplemented by a mail survey to former client populations, we used cluster and snowball sampling procedures on agency and nonagency populations. Although the two studies agree in most of their findings, there are also some discrepencies that may reflect regional variations but more probably derive from different sampling procedures.

Classifications of runaways have often been constructed out of deviant labels and have rarely attended to what runaway youth have to say about themselves and their situation. Typologies derived from stereotypes and the extant laws against running away tend to protect and maintain social institutions rather than explain or service the needs of runaway youth.

All runaways must be viewed as illegal aliens, persons without status in their own land. They may find themselves adrift for family or personal reasons, depending on how they view themselves and their situations, yet they must also face their illegal status as runaways. Some may want to return to their homeland, others may not; irrespective of such preferences, runaways are forced into an underground status because of their illegal position in our society.

These runaways' different definitions of their situations lead to different implications for services. But this social-structural ambivalence between control and assistance, between detention and support, between captivity and freedom, underscores every aspect of their relationship to the formal agencies of society.

Various means and data can be used to develop typologies, with some employing background social, demographic data, some using behavioral data or various diagnostic or clinical labels. All of these approaches can have their uses, and their strengths and weaknesses, and all have been used in studies of the runaway phenomenon. In the present study, the typology was developed on the basis of the runaways' own reports of conditions and events shaping their flight and other related behaviors. The sum total of our sample's selfreports will be classified and called a "vocabulary of motives," and the following sections will attempt to explain and describe this approach and its rationale more fully.

Viewed from a particular perspective, that of self-theory or the "symbolic interactivist" orientation, human behavior is seen as stemming from the way the individual structures the world around him in terms of meanings and symbols. Behavior is not random or capricious but rather a systematic response to the definitions of objects, self, and situation held by the actor. The best predictor of behavior is knowledge of how the actor sees the world around him. Using these views, definitions, or this "vocabulary of motives," is then seen as important not only in terms of understanding runaway behavior and its varieties but also as important in terms of predicting future behavior, and such things as response to service modalities available or being planned. Obviously, the degree of legality or illegality of the situation as seen by the runaway can be an important determinant of his or her behavior vis a vis services and agencies in general. For both theoretical and utilitarian reasons this study, unlike many others, will base its typological classifications on the "vocabulary of motives" experienced by the runaway.

VOCABULARY OF MOTIVES

Instead of looking at the prevailing social responses to running away, we examined the youth's own perceptions of his or her situation during the period that the situation was a source of concern.

We feel that the most useful typology of runaways would not be based on the clinical or counseling experience of helping professionals, nor on the reminiscences of former runaways, but on the reasons given by youth currently on the run, that is, the vocabulary of motives used by youth who at that time were running away. Such a typology would be based on the fundamental processes, which these young people define, by sorting out their own accounts of their reasons for leaving. Such a typology might better reflect the "natural world" of the runaway, seen from his own perspective.

Two basic types of runaways were derived from a content-analysis of runaways' responses to a series of open-ended questions intended to assess the reasons they ran away. The data derived from these responses permitted us to reclassify them in degrees ranging from dependence to independence in relationship to their families. In our typology these categories ranged from the most dependent victim types to the most independent immigrant types. All such vocabularies of motives given by individual runaways were set against the larger social problem, that is, that runaways are illegal aliens, irrespective of the reasons given for their action.

Parent-Locus Motives

Parent-Locus runaways are those who explain leaving home in terms of something the parent or parent-surrogate *did.* Under Parent-Locus motives we found three groups of runaways: the *victims,* the *exiles,* and the *rebels.*

Victims are those runaways who feel they are fleeing for their lives from physical abuse and assault by parents or stepparents.

These youth feel their parents are their enemies and that to return home is to endanger their lives. They feel helpless and undefended, and yet dependent upon their parents. While at home the victim runaways refer to their parents as a source of support and security, but once the underpinnings of that support are torn asunder they confront the world as helpless vagabonds.

If a runaway acknowledges his dependence upon his family, and then explains his leaving home in terms of parental rejection he is an *exile.* Such runaways report that they left home because they were no longer wanted. They feel they were driven out and rejected. These runaways are characterized as exiles, that is, they are banished and outcasts among their own kind. (Other studies have labeled such subjects as "kickouts," "throwaway children," or "pushouts".)

The third group of runaways, *rebels,* describe their motives for running away in terms of serious and long-standing "hassles" or involvement in authority struggles with their parents. They hope their running away will help them "win" this struggle. They want to live at home, but want to live by their own rules.

Child-Locus Motives
Runaway youth of this basic type use a self-referrent in their vo-cabulary of motives, that is, they see themselves as the source of the action, they are in flight because *they* seize the initiative. The three subtypes are *fugitives, refugees,* and *immigrants.*

The *fugitive* child is running from the consequences of his or her own behavior. Fugitives leave home because they feel they have to in order to escape from some form of retribution, arrest, disgrace or punishment. Fugitive children are afraid to face their parents, the school, or community social control agents. They ran away to avoid further trouble but may maintain contact with their home, communicating periodically with someone there. They may also be partly dependent on support or assistance from parents or siblings while they are in flight.

The *refugees* are runaways without a family, who run away from foster homes and institutions. These children, like the fugi-tives, are running from a social control situation, but, unlike the fugitives, they are not running from the consequences of their own behavior. Their dependency upon parents has been truncated, and they feel they belong to no one; they do not view themselves as culprits or as being in flight because of an antisocial act.

The *immigrants* are independent runaways who have taken matters into their own hands and have resolved unpleasant home or community situations by choosing the alternative, to be "free."

These youth have truncated their parental dependency relationship in order to be "on their own." Their removal from their home takes the form of autonomy rather than flight. They run away in order to find "adventure," "freedom," and independence rather than merely to escape parental or social "hassles" or "authority." They consciously view themselves as persons who are able to take care of themselves. The independent runaways have terminated their socialization under family tutelage in order to determine their own life-style. In a sense they are "emancipated" although without court adjudication.

RUNAWAY TYPOLOGY

This phenomenologically derived taxonomy is based on the language of youth on the road and is interpreted within the social context of the life conditions of runaways. The same typology might have been derived by logical means had we begun with the notion of dependency on the family instead of making a content analysis of runaways' responses to our open-ended questions. Using this approach it has been possible to consider running away from the viewpoint of the children rather than relying exclusively on the viewpoint of social agencies or researchers.

The distribution of the two basic types with the six subtypes ranges along a continuum of parental dependence to independence. The exiles, victims, and rebels are still tied in some way to their parents and are running away in reaction to their home situations. These groups constitute 44 percent of our total runaway sample.

The other three subtypes of the child-locus motivation type constitute 56 percent of our sample of runaway youth. These youth are straining toward precocious adulthood—they are less and less dependent upon parents, and more and more independent and self-directed. These subtypes range from the fugitive, to the refugee, to the immigrant. The following table presents the distribution of our 215 runaways by types (Table 2.8).

We now turn to the presentation of our research findings on runaways in each of the six subtypes, based on the runaways' own motives. We first describe each of the six subtypes by variables that reflect these runaways' socioeconomic background.

The father's occupational status is one indication of the social class background of runaways.

As can be seen (Table 2.9), rebels are most likely to come from middle-class families, refugees and immigrants from working-class families, and fugitives and exiles from welfare or fatherless families, as based upon the reported occupational status of their fathers (many of whom are no longer in their homes).

If the vocabulary of motives types are to be meaningful, the special types of problems faced by both runaway boys and girls must be taken into account.*

TABLE 2.8: Distribution of Runaways by Type of Motives for Running Away (N=215)

	N	Percentage
Parent-Locus	93	44%
Victim	42	20%
Exile	19	9%
Rebel	32	15%
Child-Locus	122	56%
Fugitive	20	9%
Refugee	43	20%
Immigrant	59	27%

TABLE 2.9: Father's Occupation by Type of Runaway

	White Collar	Blue Collar	Unemp./D.K.*	Total
Victim	29%	51%	20%	100%
Exile	32%	42%	26%	100%
Rebel	50%	25%	25%	100%
Fugitive	30%	30%	40%	100%
Refugee	7%	83%	10%	100%
Immigrant	29%	64%	7%	100%

*It may be inferred that, in most instances, the "D.K." (don't know) answer signifies the father's absence from the home.

The sex distribution is 94 (44 percent) boys and 121 (56 percent) girls, and we now examine the runaway types by sex.

As can be seen (Table 2.10), more girls are found among rebels and refugees, while more boys are among fugitives and immigrants.

Over two-thirds of the runaway girls came from "broken homes" or had no real homes at all. Only 30 percent of the girls

*Due to the relatively small sample size for each of the six subtypes, we felt it would be best to describe generally the factors most influenced by other important variables, that is, sex, ethnicity, number of prior runaways, and present service status. We proceed to do this, relating each one to the basic vocabulary of motive type.

were residing in a home with both parents at the time they ran away—actually, only 50 percent of the girls ran away from a home with *any* parent present. Family conflict and separation had already caused structural breaks in many of these girls' families, and they ran away from relatives' homes, foster, or adoptive homes, or from institutions (refugees). Eighty-four percent of these runaway girls said they did not try to contact anyone "at home" because they felt *no one* cared. Within whatever type of family they had resided, we found that they reported considerable amounts of conflict with parents and siblings, as can be seen in the following table.

TABLE 2.10: Runaway Types by Sex (N=215)

	Boy (N=94)	Girl (N=121)	Total
Victim	43%	57%	100%
Rebel	34%	66%	100%
Exile	47%	53%	100%
Fugitive	55%	45%	100%
Refugee	35%	65%	100%
Immigrant	52%	48%	100%

As can be seen (table 2.11), the greatest difficulty appeared between father and daughter, between son and mother, although the differences are not statistically significant. Some subjects had difficulties with *all* family members—and we found that 80 percent reported difficulty with at least one member of their respective families. Nearly three-fourths of all runaways reported their parents did not understand them and that they were treated "unfairly."

We asked all subjects if they felt their parents had abused them, and if so, in what way. About two-fifths of all runaways, both boys and girls, felt they had suffered some form of parental abuse, as shown in Table 2.12.

TABLE 2.11: Runaways' Reports of Poor Relationship with Family Members, by Sex* (N-215)

Did not get along well with:	Boys	Girls
Father/Stepfather	41%	44%
Mother/Stepmother	43%	41%
Brother/Stepbrother	19%	25%
Sister/Stepsister	14%	26%

*Table applies only to those with one or more parents in the home and covers multiple responses, therefore, figures do not add up to 100%.

As can be seen (table 2.12), 12 percent of the girls reported sexual abuse by fathers or stepfathers. Two girls, in fact, reported being sexually molested by both father and stepfather. "My stepfather raped me, and my real father sent me a plane ticket to California and then he raped me." For this girl and all the girls involved in incest, sexual molestation by a father or a stepfather was more than a rare occurrence. Some of these girls had to cope with incest on a fairly regular basis. One girl stated that her father beat her, stuck his finger in her vagina, took off her clothes, and that this happened three or four times before to her as well as to her sisters.

TABLE 2.12: Runaways' Report of Type of Parental Abuse, by Sex*

	Boys	Girls
No abuse reported	62%	60%
Sexual abuse	0	12%
Physical abuse	38%	32%
Verbal abuse	10%	4%
Neglect	1%	10%
Alcoholic parent	10%	13%
Other type of abuse	6%	9%

*Table adds up to more than 100%—multiple responses given.

In fact, these girls who reported incest incidents stated that sexual abuse, or the threat of it, was their major reason for running away the first time. One girl, when asked why she ran away for the first time, said that her "stepfather was beating her and also having sex." Interestingly enough, almost all of these girls were returned home after their first runaway episode.* In these cases the pattern of sexual abuse and incest soon reemerged. One girl remarked that she left the first time because her "stepfather kept forcing her to do things (sex)" and that she left the last time because of "stepfather trouble (rape)." Thus, it can be seen that a pattern of incest and running away emerges in these sexually abused girls' lives.

*In the state of Connecticut in 1973 and 1974, among reported cases of child abuse, incest constituted only 3 percent of the total amount of child abuse. Rape and sexual molestation by others was more common, consisting of 9 percent of all reported child abuse. Our incest report rate of 12 percent among girls is *very* high, as, according to the best prevalence estimates, incest is a problem in less than 3 percent of all families. We felt that the stepfather/daughter relationship, so common among our runaway girls from "broken homes," is the primary sources of this high incidence. See Suzanne M. Sgroi, "Sexual Molestation of Children," *Children Today*, DHEW Publication No. (OHD) 74-14.

Boys were more likely to report physical or verbal abuse by a parent, but were also somewhat more likely to report trouble outside the home as well. Thirty-one percent of the boys stated their parents reported them as missing, while only 19 percent of the girls said their parents reported them as being runaways. In fact, 74 percent of the boys, as well as 84 percent of the girls, stated that they felt no one cared for them—and thus, no one cared if they ran away.

Girls were likely to be running away with or to a lover, or to be running away because of problems of sexual promiscuity or pregnancy. Boys were more likely to be seeking adventure, jobs, or fleeing from some type of delinquency problem.

Thus, irrespective of the type of motives for running away, social service needs for each type would vary by sex, or be directly different in some ways. In general, runaway girls appear to be more sophisticated than runaway boys, more "hardened" to the streets, and somewhat less attached to their original family. They are as likely to engage in illegal behavior as are boys to support themselves while on the road.

We asked each runaway how he or she supported him/herself while on the road, and the responses are shown in the following table.

TABLE 2.13: Source of Survival Support on the Road by Sex*

	Boys	Girls
Work	18%	13%
Panhandle	59%	45%
Steal	28%	33%
Deal drugs	62%	56%
Prostitution	19%	23%

*Table contains multiple responses—does not add up to 100%

As can be seen (table 2.13), both boys and girls occasionally engage in one or more forms of illegal behavior to support themselves on the run.

One difference of note between boys and girls while on the run is that girls are more likely to maintain contact and to spend time with relatives (47 percent), while boys are more likely to stay with friends (43 percent). Thus, despite the girls' greater tendency to break with their parents, they are still family-connected with siblings, grandparents, cousins, and so on. This factor offers clues for social service agencies as they work with these runaways.

ETHNIC RUNAWAYS

We now turn to an analysis of the runaway data, using ethnic categories as the primary classification tool. First, we look at sex distribution by ethnic category.

TABLE 2.14: Runaways' Ethnic Identity, by Sex*

	Boys	Girls	Total
White	47%	53%	100%
Black	55%	45%	100%
Chicano	24%	76%	100%
American Indian	22%	78%	100%
Asian	20%	80%	100%

*Three subjects fell into an "Others" category.

The table (2.14) invites some intriguing speculation about different sex roles in the several ethnic cultures, but our ethnic samples were neither large enough nor sufficiently representative to pursue such speculation. However, the findings do suggest a significant area for further investigation that might encourage greater sensitivity to ethnic diversity in sex roles when dealing with runaways.

Next we compare the vocabulary of motives types by ethnicity in order to further specify the various motivational types (table 2.15).

TABLE 2.15: Types of Runaways by Ethnicity

	White	Black	Chicano	Native American	Asian
	(N=127)	(N=38)	(N=33)	(N=9)	(N=5)
Victim	17%	21%	27%	11%	20%
Exile	9%	8%	6%	11%	20%
Rebel	17%	11%	12%	22%	0
Fugitive	11%	8%	3%	11%	20%
Refugee	9%	39%	45%	11%	20%
Immigrant	36%	13%	6%	33%	20%

Proportionally, more whites and native Americans tended to be immigrants, whereas more blacks and Chicanos tended to be refugees; Asians were evenly divided among all the types, except the rebel type.

Kitano and Miranda (1975) have documented differential arrest rates for youth among the various minority groups and present a theoretical framework which attempts to explain such differences.

Runaway arrest rates were highest for whites, native Americans and Japanese, and lowest for blacks and Chinese in 1972-73. (The arrest rates were not available for Mexican-Americans.) The limitations of FBI statistics in determining the prevalence and incidence of "true runaway" rates is well known. For example, black runaway youth tend to be arrested for more serious crimes than running away.

All ethnic groups produce runaways, and the cultural differences produce different meanings for the situations. As Klenebery (1966) states:

> There are great variations in the frequency of delinquent behavior in children of different ages, as well as changes in such frequency from time to time, which at least to some extent reflect the influences of peer cultures and cannot wholly be explained by the stage reached in biological development. Delinquency in any community will be influenced also by the pattern of police behavior, the judges of juvenile courts, and all the other official personnel with whom the young offenders, actual or potential, come into contact: both initial reactions and recidivism may vary considerably according to whether "they are regarded as friends or foes."

The feelings of trust toward others and confidence in the self will be deeply rooted in the culture and heritage of runaway youth, and any intervention strategies designed to aid groups from different minority groups will of necessity be influenced by culturally derived definitions.

For example, as noted previously, we asked the runaways what survival strategies they employed while on the run. The following table gives the percentage of each ethnic group by type of strategy employed for survival during the runaway episode.

TABLE 2.16: Runaways' Survival Strategies, by Ethnicity*

	Own Resources	Work	Panhandle	Steal	Deal Drugs	Prosti-tution
White	42%	23%	76%	43%	57%	10%
Black	13%	5%	40%	66%	87%	21%
Chicano	54%	0	36%	38%	90%	42%
Asian	60%	100%	80%	60%	80%	80%
Native American	33%	0	33%	17%	57%	33%

*Percentages do not add up to 100 percent, since each column represents only the positive responses to each question.

As can be seen, minority runaways are more likely to be dependent upon illegal strategies for survival, while white runaways appear to have other means of survival. Minority runaways are not as likely to have employment or to have their own resources, or to be able to panhandle. (Panhandlers must have a sense of presence and be able to approach potential contributors without sanction. Minority group members find it difficult to panhandle whites who appear prosperous for fear of complaint and arrest. In addition, few prosperous minority passerbys seem likely to be approachable by a minority runaway.) Rather, minority runaways are forced into more illegitimate means of survival, such as dealing in drugs, stealing, or prostitution. These illegitimate activities are not yet "true" criminal careers, but rather are temporary strategies utilized in times of extreme need. Most runaways sought support from friends or within legitimate structures whenever possible. Often their return to a relatively intolerable home situation was motivated by the hardships of everyday life "on the run."

Those hardships seem very real, and the erosion of a sense of trust in others occurs very quickly. We now analyze, by ethnic group, our sample reports of runaways ripping off other runaways and other persons and their reports of having been ripped off.

TABLE 2.17: Runaways' Perception and Experience of "Rip-Off,"
by Ethnicity

	Think Runaways Rip Off Others	Think Runaways Rip Off Runaways	Have Been Ripped Off
White	90%	54%	49%
Black	81%	36%	22%
Chicano	68%	45%	25%
Asian	80%	80%	56%
Native American	78%	67%	56%

As can be seen, whites, Asians and native Americans were most likely to report having been ripped off, while only approximately one-fourth of the black and Chicano runaways reported they had been ripped off. (Black and Chicano runaways were also the group that reported they were best able to protect themselves.) Whites were most likely to feel that runaways rip off others, while Asians and native Americans believed runaways rip off other runaways.

Grant Johnson (1974) has proposed a strategy for aiding youth to develop as productive members of their community. He suggests three ways of implementing this developmental strategy: (a) increase youth access to socially desirable roles; (b) reduce negative labeling of youth; and (c) increase the sense of personal control which youth feel over the direction of their lives.

Let us examine our sample of ethnic runaways to see how they might be measured along the three dimensions indicated by Johnson.

Adolescents who are suspended or expelled from school prior to running away from home are a group partially denied access to socially desirable roles (that is, a "successful school career"). Among our subjects, we found school suspensions and/or expulsions as follows:

TABLE 2.18: Runaways' Reports of Suspension/Expulsion from School by Ethnicity

White	69%
Black	71%
Chicano	70%
Asians	60%
Native Americans	79%

Thus, between two-thirds and three-fourths of all runaway youth are partially blocked from achieving a "socially desirable" role, the darker skinned minorities more so than Asian or white runaways (although the differences here are not statistically significant).

Adolescents who experience trouble with the law, who are on probation or parole, experience negative labeling which can be viewed as another blockage to productive adolescent development. The following presents the proportion of runaway subjects who were so "labeled."

TABLE 2.19: Runaways' Reports of Trouble with Law, by Ethnicity

	Trouble With Law	On Probation	On Parole
White	66%	18%	3%
Black	68%	24%	5%
Chicano	52%	13%	0
Asian	40%	0	0
Native American	56%	11%	0

As can be seen (Table 2.19), Asians, Chicanos and native Americans had less negative labeling than did black and white runaways, although the majority of the runaways in all ethnic groups, except the Asian, experienced some type of "negative labeling."

They tend to see themselves and to feel that others view them in negative terms. As previously mentioned, we asked each runaway if he felt others viewed him as "trouble in school" (parents, teachers, or friends) or if he viewed himself as "trouble in school." These responses along ethnic lines to the "troublesome scale" are shown below (Table 2.20).

TABLE 2.20: Perceptions of Others and Self that Subject is "Trouble in School," as Reported by Runaway Ethnic Groups

	Teachers	Parents	Friends	Self
White	50%	70%	20%	35%
Black	42%	68%	18%	37%
Chicano	34%	69%	22%	34%
Asian	80%	100%	25%	40%
Native American	56%	79%	11%	33%

Asian runaways were the most likely to feel they were "troublesome" to all, showing the lowest degree of self-esteem, the greatest sense of negative labeling. Blacks were next in degree of self-labeling of "trouble," while Chicanos, native Americans, and whites had the least amount of damage from self-derogation.

However, most runaway youth feel both parents and school view them as "trouble," thus cutting them off from important sources of self-esteem.

Runaways appear to have a very poor sense of personal control, as measured by scores on Srole's anomie scale. This anomie score purports to gauge the amount of a sense of "worthlessness" or "normlessness" felt by a subject. The following present those ethnic runaways who indicate a poor sense of personal control, that is, who score high on the anomie scale:

TABLE 2.21: High Scores on Srole's Anomie Scale, by Ethnicity

White	40%
Black	56%
Chicano	62%
Asian	20%
Native American	50%

As can be seen (Table 2.21) Asian runaways indicate the highest degrees of personal control as compared to blacks, Chicanos, and native Americans, who evidenced poorer views of their ability to conform and to control their personal worlds.

All three sets of criteria toward a strategy for productive adolescent development appear to indicate runaways in general, and various ethnic runaways in particular, experience grave difficulties in making a successful adjustment.

All these ethnic variables must be taken into account in designing programs for each type of runaway youth.

CRISIS VS. CHRONIC RUNAWAYS

Not all runaways are veterans committed to life on the road. Some are "newcomers" or "tourists"—trying out their freedom by making initial breaks from their homes. If a runaway returns with only one or two runaway experiences of a few days duration, it seems likely that certain family or institutional problems could be worked out, and that person's runaway career might end at that point. It seems likely that many runaway episodes end in just that fashion. The runaway event is a "danger sign," one that many parents view with alarm. In such cases, parents and the runaway attempt to come to some resolution of their difficulty and try to prevent further ruptures. In these circumstances social services may indeed be helpful. For example, in our interviews with parents of runaways, we found that while they could neither accept nor understand their child's actions, they did try to effect some change in the relationship in order to prevent further embarrassment or trouble in the home. But there seems to come a point, after a child has run away from home three or four times, that parents "give up," and turn away from the parent-child relationship, leaving the runaway to his own devices.

In working with runaways and their parents, agencies must be especially aware of these crisis runaway situations as they differ from the chronic runaway situation. We have classified as "chronic" runaways those who ran away five or more times, and as "crisis" runaways those who have left four or fewer times.

TABLE 2.22: Crisis and Chronic Runaways, by Type of Runaway

	Crisis	Chronic
Victim	66%	34%
Exile	50%	50%
Rebel	63%	37%
Fugitive	64%	36%
Refugee	47%	53%
Immigrant	75%	25%

As can be seen (Table 2.22), the immigrant is most likely to be leaving home for the first few times, while refugees who are running from foster care or institutions are most likely to be chronic runaways.

The exiles and refugees both seem to present the greatest degree of chronicity and represent the two runaway types least likely to be reunited with their families, natural or surrogate.

Most runaways are relative "newcomers" to the runaway scene, although if a runaway becomes chronic, he may run away dozens of times, until there is nothing left for him to run away from, in the sense that the relationship with "home" is too tenuous to constitute a meaningful tie.

For example, 40 percent of the crisis runaways, as compared with 60 percent of the chronic cases, report parental neglect and abuse, which supports the trend toward permanent parent-child separation.

Thus, the number of times a child has run away, as well as his own motivation for doing so, has implications for social services.

Not only the number of times a runaway leaves, but his length of stay away from home is also an important determinant of the outcome of each episode.

In the following table (2.23), crisis and chronic runaways are compared by the length of time they stayed away during their first runaway.

TABLE 2.23: Duration of First Runaway, by Crisis/Chronic Type

	Crisis	Chronic
Less than 5 nights	47%	61%
Less than 1 month	27%	31%
More than 1 month	26%	8%
Total	100%	100%

Thus, it appears that the chronic runaways—the repeaters—tend to stay away from home for shorter periods of time during their first runaway experience. However, as the frequency of running away increases so does the length of time on the road, until the chronic runaway is well established in his itinerant role.

THE "SERVED" CAPTURED AND "UNSERVED" FREE

Because a primary purpose of our study is to examine and evaluate the services provided to runaways, we found it useful to seek out two groups of runaways: (1) those who were receiving some form of social service; and (2) those who were not, and hence were not under the supervision or control of any social or legal agency. We then compared the "served" or "captive" runaways with the "unserved" or "free."

We compare each of these categories by our six motivational subtypes, as seen below (Table 2.24).

TABLE 2.24: Captured and Free Runaways, by Runaway Type

	Captured	Free
Victim	62%	38%
Exile	47%	53%
Rebel	75%	25%
Fugitive	60%	40%
Refugee	86%	14%
Immigrant	30%	70%

As can be seen, those runaways who have already been institutionalized, that is, the refugees, are also most likely to utilize the social service agencies in some form while on the road. Rebels are also likely to turn to agencies for help with their intense authority struggle with parents, and victims seem to come to the attention of social agencies for protection and care.

Immigrants are the most likely group to be living outside of agency contact or control, that is, to be "free," while over one-half of the exiles were also "making it on their own."

Yet, most of these runaways had only superficial contacts with social agencies, and, in fact, many were not aware of the potential services available to them.

Even among those runaways we selected in our sample based on one or another agency referral, few were actually receiving any form of services, aside from referral to other resources at the time of our interview with them.

Thus, we feel the "served" and "unserved," the "captured" or "the free," classification may indeed be misleading, since few of our runaways actually utilized social services, aside from police or diversion agency referrals. Those who use counterculture agencies were the most likely to be receiving at least temporary services.

We now turn to a further analysis of each type of runaway, using the runaways' vocabulary of motives as the basis for analyzing our findings. If we can understand the different backgrounds and needs of each type of runaway, using his own definition of the situation, social services could be better tailored to meet the unique needs of each type.

We first examine the sociodemographic backgrounds of each of the six subtypes, beginning with family composition, as shown in the following table.

TABLE 2.25: Family Composition, by Type of Runaway

	Natural Parents	Step Parent	Single Parent	Foster Parent	Other	Total
Victim	31%	24%	24%	12%	9%	100%
Exile	26%	21%	53%	0	0	100%
Rebel	44%	22%	25%	3%	6%	100%
Fugitive	5%	25%	50%	10%	10%	100%
Refugee	2%	9%	0	63%	26%	100%
Immigrant	46%	22%	24%	8%	0	100%

As can be seen (Table 2.25), immigrants and rebels are most likely to be residing with their natural parents, victims and fugitives with a mother and a stepfather, exiles and fugitives with a single parent, refugees (by definition, of course) in foster homes or institutions, or with friends or relatives outside the nuclear family.

These findings underscore the frailty of family structures that produce runaways and highlight the need to understand the strains facing many American families today, given the mounting divorce rate and the increasing number of female-headed households.

Thus, merely returning runaways to their "parents" may indeed be a policy without much substance, since the "natural family" is relatively rare among runaway youth.

Given this family structure, the determination of the social-class background depends heavily upon the mother's employment and income rather than on the natural father's.

We now examine the mother's occupation as reported by each type of runaway.

As can be seen, (Table 2.26) over one-half of all mothers of runaways are employed (or are seeking employment) outside the home. Fugitives and rebels are most likely to have mothers in white-collar occupations, whereas exiles' and victims' mothers are most likely domestics or blue-collar factory workers. Among many of the single-parent families, the mother receives public welfare, with refugee runaways most likely to be products of a welfare home (that is, moved from a welfare home into a foster home or institution prior to their running away).

TABLE 2. 26: Mother's Occupational Status, by Type of Runaway

	White Collar	Blue Collar	Not in Labor Market/Don't Know	Total
Victim	35%	21%	44%	100%
Exile	21%	32%	47%	100%
Rebel	41%	13%	46%	100%
Fugitive	45%	15%	40%	100%
Refugee	14%	9%	77%	100%
Immigrant	37%	19%	44%	100%

The runaways report coming from impoverished homes as follows:

Victims	21%
Exiles	10%
Rebels	13%
Fugitives	7%
Refugees	30%
Immigrants	18%

In home situations where one or more parents were present, we asked each runaway how he got along with his family members. In the table below, we can see the findings of those runaways who report that they got along poorly with one or more of their family members prior to their running away.

TABLE 2.27: Reports of Intrafamily Difficulties, by Type of Runaway*

		Got Along Poorly With		
	Father	Mother	Brother	Sister
Victim	59%	42%	24%	24%
Exile	44%	72%	22%	20%
Rebel	30%	44%	26%	30%
Fugitive	30%	40%	8%	15%
Refugee	31%	42%	21%	13%
Immigrant	48%	33%	23%	20%

*Table reports multiple answers and does not add up to 100 percent. (These findings refer only to cases where these family members were present.)

As can be seen (Table 2.27), victims got along poorest with both parents, while nearly three-fourths of the exiles report they did not get along with their mothers. Nearly one-half of the immigrants reported they had poor relationships with their fathers or stepfathers. Nearly one-fourth of all runaways also reported poor relationships with their siblings as well. Thus, we can see that most runaways experience some degree of poor intrafamily relationships, with victims and exiles evidencing the greatest degree of family trouble, since child abuse and rejection played such an important role in forming their motives for running away. These situations present difficult problems for the conventional "detention and return" policies generally applied to runaway youth by most social and legal agencies that deal with them.

We asked each runaway if he felt abused, and the percentage of affirmative responses is recorded in the table (2.28) below.

TABLE 2.28: Reports of Parental Abuse, by Type of Runaway*

	Felt Abused
Victim	69%
Exile	47%
Rebel	13%
Fugitive	25%
Immigrant	29%

*Table contains responses to multiple questions, therefore does not add up to 100%.

As could have been expected, victims reported the greatest incidence of abuse. Interestingly, the rebels, those most in conflict with parental authority, were the least likely to have felt abused.

Many studies have found a correlation between parental abuse of children and parental abuse of alcohol or drugs. Percentages of our runaway sample reporting alcohol/drug abuse by their parents are recorded below (Table 2.29).

TABLE 2.29: Reports of Parental Alcohol and Drug Abuse, by Type of Runaway*

	Alcohol	Drugs
Victim	55%	14%
Exile	47%	21%
Rebel	44%	6%
Fugitive	50%	20%
Refugee	40%	30%
Immigrant	27%	12%

*Only for runaways with one or more parent in the house.

The reasons youth run away from home are complex and multifaceted. No one, single element could be seen as "the cause." Therefore, the typology, drawn from open-ended discussions of the runaways' own motives, was further compared with runaways' responses to a series of structured questions covering a range of "reasons" for running away. We asked each runaway if one or more of these reasons (personal, family, school, law, adventure, job, or friend) played a role in his or her decision to run away. We found that the runaway has many reasons for leaving home, although some are more salient than others.

Actually, most runaways gave a number of reasons for running away, both because of problems *and* because of a desire to "seek adventure" or to join friends. Running away is a complex act, and service workers need to be mindful of this complexity and ambivalence in the runaways' relationship with his parents and peers.

These are indeed multiproblem youth, who experience both personal and family problems, and seek solutions in running from trouble and toward adventure, jobs, and friends. Over half of the immigrants had trouble in school as well as in the family, and 81 percent felt "adventure" was an important runaway reason. Victims had serious problems with both parents and the law, as did exiles. Thus, irrespective of each subject's vocabulary of primary motives, he/she reported additional problem areas entering into his/her decision to run. Most of these youth are in difficulty in many areas of their lives, with both primary and secondary social institutions. Most of these are not simple situations that will yield to a simple solution, such as a return home ticket or a brief counseling session.

Aside from runaways' relationships with their parents, the other more important socialization experience is within the school system.

We questioned runaways about their school problems, and we found that nearly three-fourths of the victims, exiles and refugees reported they had been suspended or expelled from school, while nearly two-thirds of the table (2.30) below, dropped out after suspension and/or a stint in continuation school.

TABLE 2.30: School Problems, by Runaway Type

	Suspended/ Expelled	Continuation School	Dropped Out
Victim	74%	26%	33%
Exile	74%	21%	53%
Rebel	69%	38%	34%
Fugitive	65%	5%	45%
Refugee	79%	19%	37%
Immigrant	59%	22%	61%

As can be seen in the above table, these runaways were, in general, making a poor school adjustment, with immigrants having the least difficulty and refugees, victims, and exiles the greatest difficulty in school.

Many runaways reported negative family relationships, and they found similar climates at school. In fact, runaways seemed to equate their parents' negative attitude toward them with their perception of teachers' negative attitudes as well. We asked each runaway if he/she felt his/her parents, teachers, or friends considered him/her to be "trouble in school." We then asked him/her if he/she considered *himself/herself* to be "trouble in school."

TABLE 2.31: Perceptions of Others and Self that Subject is "Trouble in School" as Reported by Runaway Types*

	Parents	Teachers	Friends	Self
Victim	76%	48%	22%	36%
Exile	83%	53%	16%	37%
Rebel	72%	53%	23%	34%
Fugitive	70%	40%	5%	50%
Refugee	67%	50%	31%	45%
Immigrant	64%	41%	14%	25%

*As the reader will note, this table (2.31) and several others (Tables 2.30, 2.32, 2.34 and 2.36) cover areas that were covered previously, but from a different analytical vantage point, in our treatment of our runaway sample by ethnic group.

This was used as a self-evaluation measure. We found nearly three-fourths of all runaways felt their parents saw them as trouble in school, while one-half thought their teachers saw them as trouble in school.

The exiles were most likely to see that their parents thought them trouble in school. The rebels and exiles were most likely to think their teachers saw them as trouble, while refugees were most likely to have friends who thought they were trouble in school. About half of the fugitives and refugees felt they were "trouble," while one-third of the victims, rebels, and exiles rated themselves as "trouble in school." The immigrants tended to be somewhat more positive in their self-evaluation, although one-fourth replied that they felt they were trouble, while two-thirds judged their parents felt they were "trouble in school."

Not only did these subjects feel they were in trouble in school, but many also reported trouble with the law, both prior to their running away and while "on the road." We asked about trouble with the law, if the trouble was "serious," if they were on probation or parole. The results are in the following table.

TABLE 2.32: Reports of Trouble with the Law, by Runaway Type

	Trouble	Serious Trouble	Trouble As Runaway	Probation	Parole
Victim	71%	13%	34%	32%	2%
Exile	68%	9%	41%	0	5%
Rebel	47%	25%	40%	13%	0
Fugitive	70%	46%	50%	25%	5%
Refugee	63%	21%	37%	19%	5%
Immigrant	63%	24%	48%	12%	2%

As can be seen (Table 2.32), nearly two-thirds of all runaways had been in trouble with the law *prior* to their running away, while nearly half of the fugitives reported *serious* legal problems, which motivated them to flee. Over one-fourth of the fugitives and victims were on probation at the time of their runaway, while half of the fugitives and the immigrants got into legal troubles while "on the road." Many writers are concerned with delinquent behavior of runaways, and as can be seen runaway youth experience difficulty in both the primary and secondary socializing institutions *prior* to their leaving home. Indeed, difficult as their family life might seem, becoming a runaway places them in a still more difficult and unknown status, that is, that of being an illegal alien, a stateless person. Thus, it seems unlikely that a youth would have seriously considered leaving his home, school, and friends unless he were already in difficulty in several areas of his life.

Peer groups are extremely important sources of identity and direction for most adolescents. Runaway youth cut themselves loose from stable, home-abiding friends when they leave home. So it does not seem surprising to find that runaways tend to have friends and siblings who are also runaways. Running away was not a socially isolated action. Most runaways reported runaway episodes by their peers—friends, classmates, siblings and other relatives—as can be seen in the following table (2.33).

TABLE 2.33: Runaways in Peer Group, by Runaway Type

	Sisters	Brothers	Relatives	Classmates	Friends
Victim	41%	56%	60%	76%	95%
Exile	50%	18%	37%	63%	84%
Rebel	37%	32%	41%	72%	75%
Fugitive	50%	39%	35%	65%	90%
Refugee	45%	51%	55%	70%	84%
Immigrant	32%	40%	49%	73%	88%

A very high percentage of all types were acquainted with other runaways in their peer and sibling groups. Thus, among these various runaway types, the runaway act itself is "normal," conforming behavior (that is, runaways' significant others are also likely to be runaways). They can find an affinity with those of their peers and siblings who are also relatively loosely connected to the primary and secondary socialization institutions. Together these runaways form a social network of transient youth.

We feel this finding has implications for services, in that running away is greatly influenced by peer group membership. Such a finding suggests that group work methods with runaway-prone youth might be helpful. It also suggests that friends and adolescent siblings of runaways may constitute a special prevention problem for school or family counseling. All adolescents live in a peer world that gives them direction, identity, and social reality. Such group membership is far stronger than parental ties during late adolescence. Perhaps work should be done with high-risk groups in schools and neighborhoods, or within families that have runaway children. Such runaway prevention services, or alternative "runaway terminals" might have high service payoff.

Such psychological factors as peer group identity are very crucial for runaway youth. They seek friends and support from other runaways. Yet our subjects told us of their fear and distrust of other runaways, and about half believe runaways "rip off" other runaways. Many runaways report they have been "ripped off" while on the road (see the following table 2.34).

TABLE 2.34: Perception and Experience of "Rip-Off," by Runaway Type

	Think Runaways Rip Off Others	Think Runaways Rip Off Runaways	Have Been Ripped Off
Victim	81%	48%	45%
Exile	79%	47%	67%
Rebel	82%	40%	19%
Fugitive	94%	74%	26%
Refugee	83%	56%	30%
Immigrant	88%	47%	52%

Fugitives are most suspicious, most prone to feel that runaways rip off other people and other runaways. Exiles are more likely to report having been "ripped off" (67 percent) than other runaways, with fewest rebels reporting they were ripped off (19 percent). Thus, the runaways are telling of their fears and experiences on the streets, and such fears may pose the need for certain

types of services to protect runaway youth from harm during the
runaway episode.

This fear of the road and the types of experience that befall
runaways were evidenced in many of the things runaways reported.
For example, some runaways reported bad experiences while hitchhiking, and some said they would warn other runaways *not* to
hitchhike, as seen in the following table (2.35).

**TABLE 2.35: Reports of Bad Hitchhiking Experiences and Intention to
Warn Others not to Hitchhike, by Runaway Type**

	Bad Hitchhiking Experience	Warn Others Not To Hitchhike
Victim	41%	26%
Exile	32%	53%
Rebel	34%	25%
Fugitive	30%	20%
Refugee	20%	36%
Immigrant	29%	39%

Thus, some fear of the road is evidenced by all runaways, with
victims reporting the largest percentage of bad hitchhiking experiences, and refugees the least amount. A striking aspect of the table
is the lack of correlation between the incidence of bad hitchhiking
experiences and a disposition to warn others. For example, a larger proportion of victims than of exiles had bad experiences, but
the latter were much more prone to warn others.

The delinquent activities of runaway youth are the source of
much concern to several agencies of society. As we have noted,
many runaways were already labeled as "juvenile delinquents," so
that running away was only one small process in an already deviant
career. When a runaway enters an illegal alien status (particularly
when complicated by an additional label of "undesirable alien,"
that is, "delinquent"), he finds few options for survival other than
illegitimate survival strategies, such as are offered in the "underground" world of the hustlers, pimps, dope dealers, and petty criminals. About one-fourth of the runaways stated they depended
primarily on delinquent acts to support themselves while "on the
run," but many more told us they occasionally obtained survival
needs, when necessary, in one or more of the following ways.

Immigrants were more independent, had their own resources,
or were able to work, obtain free food, and so on, than other
types of runaways. Exiles were most likely, and refugees least likely to panhandle. Exiles, victims, and refugees were most likely to

TABLE 2.36: Survival Strategies, by Runaway Type

	Own Supplies	Work	Free Food	Panhandle	Prosti- tute	Deal Drugs	Steal
Victim	53%	24%	83%	55%	31%	83%	76%
Exile	50%	20%	67%	74%	16%	92%	15%
Rebel	56%	10%	67%	36%	16%	71%	44%
Fugitive	30%	13%	71%	55%	20%	54%	46%
Refugee	29%	5%	35%	21%	28%	85%	33%
Immigrant	81%	24%	64%	68%	15%	59%	52%

*Table covers multiple responses and does not add up to 100%.

deal drugs, but, in fact, most runaways reported occasionally deal-ing in drugs in order to survive. Victims (31 percent) were most likely to engage in prostitution. Occasional resort to prostitution cut across sex lines. In fact, as shown earlier, when the survival ex-pedients were tabulated by sex (Table 2.13), about one-fourth of the girls and one-fifth of the boys sold sexual services.

Victims were also the most likely to steal (76 percent) while exiles were the least likely (15 percent) to report that they engaged in stealing as an occasional means of support.

Thus, the runaways' fear and distrust of the formal agents of society may indeed be rooted in reality, given the "underground" life-style destined by the structured lack of other legitimate op-tions for survival. These are the circumstances to which youth communes and counterculture agencies have tried to respond with their "loose" networks of service.

CHAPTER 3

Parents of Runaways

The stereotype of a parent of a runaway is that of a concerned father and mother, frantic with worry about their child's absence, looking everywhere for the child, calling everyone for help, including the police.

In Los Angeles, for example, a firm specializes in tracing "absconders," and in an interview with us, the manager told us that one type of customer for these absconder services consisted of parents who sought runaway youth. He described these customers as white, upper middle class, two-parent families seeking a teenage daughter who had apparently run off with an unknown "boy friend." Many such parents feared for their child's life and wanted the child returned, whatever the cost.

Interviews with police departments in both Los Angeles and the San Francisco Bay Area revealed that they, too, received frequent calls and visits from desperate parents seeking their runaway daughters, essentially the same type of parents the private firm saw.

Parents who are seen by social agencies also seem to fit the pattern described by police and professional tracers of missing persons.

The dynamics of parent-child interactions which led to an adolescent jumping from "the frying pan into the fire," that is, to leave home for the uncertainties of the street, is an important factor in any attempt to forestall or serve runaways.

Among our subjects, as previously noted, only two-thirds ran away from a parents' home. Among those who did, only 36 percent felt their parents would have actually reported their absence to the police.

What types of parent-child relationships did our runaway sample report?

Many child development studies have shown the importance of a stable early childhood. Two-thirds of our runaway subjects' homes had been "broken" before they were 12 years of age, and three-fourths of those had lost one or both natural parents at least five years previous to the runaway episode. A very high proportion of these runaway children, compared to the general population, had lost one or both parents by death: 4 percent had lost the mother, 15 percent a father, and 2 percent both. Some of the fathers had been killed in Vietnam.

The residential mobility of these runaway youth prior to the age of 12 was very high: only 17 percent reported residential stability. Those in the other 83 percent reported *an average of four residential changes during their first 12 years.* This high mobility creates a number of serious social problems for a child—it means a lack of territoriality, loss of stable peer group, and a loss of school identity. A child grows up feeling "transient," without roots, without stable significant others, and this, combined with a lack of a stable family life, could indeed produce a group of "wanderers and vagabonds" who feel they have no home, belong to no one and to no place. Severe identity problems, a sense of anomie, and a sociopathic outlook on life could well occur, given these contingencies.

The sociodemographic backgrounds of these runaways' families seem to point to a general lack of stability, to a breakdown in communication networks and open the question of serious identity crises for the young persons growing up in such families.

A number of studies show that children can survive very difficult structural deficits, even such deficits as broken homes, poverty, working mothers, residential mobility, and so on, if they have strong supportive relationships within the family. Granted such structural deficits make such supportive relationships more problematic, nevertheless, thousands of children who endure poverty, broken homes, and other problems reach maturity without serious handicaps. What is the quality of the relationship within the families of our runaway subjects?

We first asked how well the parents "understood" the subject. Over one-fourth felt their parents understood them well or fairly well, while three-fourths indicated a lack of parental understanding, with one-third saying their parents did not understand them at all, indicating a high degree of breakdown in parent-child communication.

We have previously reported the high incidence of poor intrafamily relationships among our runaways (see Tables 2.5 and 2.11). Here, we look at the specific nature of these abrasive relationships.

Forty-four percent of the runaways stated that their parents treated them worse than other parents treated their children, revealing a deep sense of injustice and distrust toward their parents, adding to the difficulties they must resolve. Over three-fourths of the runaways complained that their parents were strict—perhaps raising questions about a more popular notion that the parents of runaways have been "too permissive" with their children. Nearly three-fourths of the subjects indicated a strong sense of parental injustice, stating that their parents were likely to "falsely blame" them for action of which they were innocent, showing a great deal of distrust within the family.

One-half of the runaway subjects reported they felt their parents had neglected them in some form. The type of neglect, among those who reported parental neglect, is stated in the following table.

TABLE 3.1: Types of Parental Neglect Perceived by Runaways
(N=107)

No interest	47%
No supervision	31%
No care, no time	14%
Overcontrol	7%

One-half of the runaways indicated that they felt neglected by their parents, and these feelings presented psychological stress to the adolescent.

Even more serious is the previously reported fact that *48 percent of the runaways indicated that their parents had abused them in some form* (see Tables 2.12 and 2.28).

The deeply ingrained feelings of child neglect and abuse among one-half of these runaway subjects seem to indicate a psychological rupture between parent and child. In fact, one-fifth of the subjects stated that their parents had so physically abused them as to "hurt them badly," while 11 percent reported that other family members had "hurt them badly."

Children of alcoholic parents are known to have difficult experiences. *Forty-one percent of the runaways we interviewed reported that one or both of their parents have a problem with alcohol.*

Further, 17 percent of the runaways reported that one or both parents had a serious drug problem.

These parental difficulties with alcohol and drugs add to the multiproblems facing the runaway youth, as well as the social workers who attempt to serve them.

One-half of the runaways contacted someone "back home" during the runaway episode. Of those, one-half contacted a parent, 16 percent a sibling, while the rest contacted a friend or relative. The reasons given for the contact are indicated in Table 3.2.

TABLE 3.2: Runaways' Reasons for Contacting Home
(N=110)

Let them know I was ok	30%
Let them know where I was	10%
Find out what was happening	16%
To straighten out a problem	4%
To get money	2%
To come home	4%
Required to make contact	36%

As can be seen (Table 3.2), when contact was made, it was involuntarily made in one-third of the cases, and only 8 percent of the contacts were made to arrange a return home or to "straighten out the problem"—again pointing up the breakdown in the emotional ties between parents and child.

Among the half who *did not* contact anyone "back home" the reasons given by the runaway were as follows (Table 3.3):

TABLE 3.3: Runaways' Reasons for not Contacting Home
(N=105)

Didn't care about them	39%
Fearful of outcome	27%
No one there to call	20%
No one cares about me	7%
Not ready, vindictive	7%

These bitter and sad responses make explicit the dynamics of running away felt by at least one-half of the subjects—they didn't care about anyone "back home" (39 percent); they were afraid of being "turned in" (27 percent); they had no one to call (20 percent); they felt no one in their family cared about them (7 percent); they weren't "ready—still angry" (7 percent).

These are indeed serious parent-child ruptures, and make further contact difficult and complicated.

Among those who had run away previously, but who had returned to their parents' home from a last episode (N=83), we asked why they returned home. The runaways' answers were as follows (Table 3.4):

As can be seen, over one-half returned home from a previous runaway episode because they had been "forced to" or convinced to return by the authorities who had picked them up while on the run. These were involuntary returns, and they didn't seem to resolve any of the problems.

TABLE 3.4: Runaways' Reasons for Returning Home

"Captured"–forced to return	34%
Just went home	34%
Was convinced to return	18%
"Down and out"–broke	7%
Adventure was over	7%

We posed the situation of the runaway's potential return home, and asked each subject how he would be received if he should return home. The responses were as follows (Table 3.5):

TABLE 3.5: Reception at Home, as Seen by Runaways
(N=215)

Welcome	47%
Can't imagine	22%
Punished	20%
Ignored	11%

One-half of the runaways again indicated complete alienation and estrangement from their families, saying they would be punished or ignored or that they could not picture a reception by their parents. *Only 47 percent of the runaways felt their families would welcome their return.*

One further question probed the parent-child relationship as perceived by the runaways. We asked, "If you went home, what would you do?" One-fourth stated they would run away again.

We can clearly see that for many of our subjects, the parent-child relationship has been seriously ruptured, and it is questionable if a return home would solve such serious difficulties. In one-half of the cases, however, work could be done to help heal the ruptured parent-child relationship.

We attempted to interview parents from each type of runaway situation. We encountered great difficulty in finding parents who would consent to discuss their children's runaway episodes with us. Since we were dependent upon volunteers, we could only obtain selected subjects who would face the painful situation. Thus, our parental interviews are only illustrative, and are not intended to be representative of runaway parents' perspective in general. We were able to obtain interviews with 38 parents of runaways.

The interviews with parents of the victim runaways were obtained from three anonymous mothers who were in two different programs for alcoholism treatment. These mothers reported the struggles they had with their adolescent children and the general home atmosphere of violence and abuse that applied not only to the parent-child relationships, but to husband-wife relationships as well. One informant told us of how her husband (her adolescent daughter's stepfather) regularly engaged in sexual intercourse with her daughter with her covert knowledge. The daughter ran away from home on several occasions, always being returned by the social agencies. The stepfather and mother both drank heavily, and the adolescent children were left "to shift for themselves." The runaway daughter finally married a sailor and never again returned home. The mother, now sober and divorced, feels that the trouble and conflict in the home was due to the heavy drinking and that this caused all members of her family to suffer greatly. This parent's view of child abuse is closely substantiated by the other parents, all of whom feel the runaway episodes were a child's natural response to an intolerable home situation.

All three of these parent interviews were painful experiences for the informants, and all felt they had, in some sense, failed their children. All blamed drugs or alcohol use for their child abuse practices.

The exile parent was also found in an ex-alcoholism program. Only one such parent volunteered for an interview. This woman told us she "threw out" three of her adolescent children during a bout of heavy drinking and while in a fit of temper. She always regretted the incident and immediately after the child left tried in a number of ways to get the child to return home. This type of behavior became rather common until eventually after multiple-kick-outs, her children, one by one, found alternative living arrangements with relatives or friends and refused to return. She, too, feels that the "kicking out of the kids" was a function of her own illness and that there was an intolerable family life for all members of her family.

The rebel parents were somewhat easier to locate, and we were able to interview 11 of them. These parents felt their children were unruly and out of control, refusing to abide by their wishes. Some of these parents had felt the discipline problem had been present for several years, other parents tended to feel their adolescent had gotten "out of control" because of bad friends. They were particularly upset about the problems of drug use and sexual behavior. One parent told us of filing charges of incorrigibility against a son because of his aggressive and rebellious nature. All parents seemed to feel that their runaway child *had* to change his behavior in order to return to their good graces; no interviewed parents of rebel runaways indicated any willingness to change *their*

attitudes. Fathers were more firm, but mothers were also very upset about their children's "bad behavior" and refusal "to mind."
They buttressed their complaints by pointing out that their child's
school situation was further evidence of his or her "bad conduct."
They said the school couldn't do anything with the runaway either.
Despite their concern about discipline and control, parents of rebel runaways usually sent money to the child, or heard from him.
Often their children would return home, only to leave again after
the longstanding quarrels erupted. They looked forward to hand-
ing the runaway over to other forces, such as marriage, the milita-
ry, or juvenile court.

Parents of fugitive runaways were found among probation officers' and school counselors' cases. Seven parents volunteered to
be interviewed. All were concerned about their child's involvement
with authorities and expressed great ambivalence about his or her
behavior. On one hand, they disliked the child's drug dealing,
fighting, vandalism, or other activities that led to his legal status
(on probation), but on the other hand, they indicated concern
about the various injustices the court or the school put upon their
child. They felt that running was a reasonable response on their
child's part to avoid institutionalization, although they felt helpless about how to make him or her "behave." In two cases, the parent was on public assistance, and other children in the family had
also been classified as juvenile delinquents. When their runaway returned, they failed to notify "authorities," but remained helpless
in the face of his or her troubles.

The refugee runaways were represented by social workers
who had supervised placement or "treatment" of runaways in foster homes or institutions. Two social workers who specialized in
adolescent foster home placements were interviewed. Both told us
of problems in finding adequate placement for black or Chicano
adolescents and their disappointment about these clients running
away from these hard-to-find homes. They felt the runaway episode was an indication of these adolescents' general difficulty in
adapting to life and that flight from the problem was symptomatic
of their serious personality disorders. Running away was also viewed as a sign of "untreatability" of the particular client. They
seemed to feel such runaways were in need of a more structured situation where their self-destructive behavior could be better controlled.

Immigrant parents were found through ads placed in local
newspapers. Fourteen such parents were interviewed. Five of the
families were on welfare or disability payments, the families were
large, and the socioeconomic status low. They felt their child had

been disappointed or unsuccessful in school, and had gone away with friends to look for work or to "see the country." They felt their runaway children were old enough or "big enough" to take care of themselves, and since they had been bored and restless at home, running away seemed like a reasonable choice. Often these children returned for "visits," before they were off again to become "tourists."

Nine sets of parents of immigrant runaways were from a more affluent background, and were certain their runaways were in a "phase" and would return to go on to school or take jobs when they could find them. Five of these parents were stepparents who really had little concern about the runaway, feeling they had done all they could for the adolescent and now the rest was "up to him (or her)."

Parents of runaways, in general, appeared bewildered, disappointed, or exhausted with the problems of their adolescent runaway. Perhaps his or her leaving was, in some way, a relief, although it would be shameful to admit such a feeling.

SUMMARY: PART I

In summary, the findings indicate the necessity for a differential policy aimed at different needs as those needs are expressed in the vocabulary of motives by the runaway. It is clear from the data that runaways exist at considerable peril, and leave home generally because the situation is no longer tolerable. Even less tolerable is the situation of the state-raised child who is institutionalized or in a foster home. Institutionalization has proved to be destructive in large numbers of cases where delinquent careers start with an institutional definition of a status offense as a delinquent act. Lastly, the risks are even greater for runaways who cannot rely on any socially supportive assistance once they have decided to leave home. One only has to ask the runaways themselves to discover the insecurities of being on the run.

Yet the problem remains that not all runaways run from the same kind of situation. Consequently, they tend to look for different strategies for survival according to the typology we constructed, and they are in need of different types of service.

Victims

Victims fled out of fear of abuse and/or assault. More than two-thirds of them were from broken homes or foster homes. They reported a high incidence of alcoholic or drug abuse in their homes. Nearly one-third were on probation. A relatively high proportion of them were ethnic minority females.

The interviews with parents of victims lent considerable evidence to support the argument that a policy of remanding the runaway to the control of the parents is only setting the stage for a repeat of the episode. Many parents admitted that physical abuse of their adolescents, although they do not call it abuse, was their only mechanism of control. More than one-third of female victims (15 out of 42) left home because of sexual molestation by the father or stepfather. Plainly, it would be a mistake to return a female to a home that she left to escape incest. Nor does placement in prison seem just under these circumstances. Such a person may first require psychological counseling before the appropriate social action could be taken. Additional measures of support might be required that would guarantee their continued schooling or vocational training.

Exiles

A majority of these youth, who felt they were expelled by their families, came from homes with single parents or a stepfather. They came from families where alcohol and drug abuse were common and experienced considerable problems at school, with many instances of expulsion or other disciplinary measures. The majority also had problems with the law prior to leaving home.

Parent interviews indicated a sense of exasperation with their inability to cope with adolescent behavior, but unwillingness to place the child in an institution. They seemed at the point of washing their hands of the responsibility of raising these children and at the same time certain that they would be better off outside the house on their own.

In some cases servicing of exiles could be facilitated by parent counseling or training in communication techniques. There were clearly examples of exile runaways where a reconciliation between parent and the youth could be negotiated. Where banishment was final, social services would have to provide almost everything basic to survival.

Rebels

Rebels left home because of authority struggles with their parents. They evidenced considerable degrees of dependence on the family, but seemed unable to reconcile conflicts on their own. Their families were more intact than those of victims or exiles, and many came from families where the father was a white-collar worker. The majority were expelled from school or had dropped out. Trouble with the law was not as great as in the case of victims or exiles.

Parent counseling in this situation could very well bring many rebels back home.

Fugitives

Fugitives ran from feared retribution for some transgression. Only 5 percent ran from homes where both parents were still together. Most were males. Only 5 percent were still in school. Drugs and alcohol were very common at home, as were troubles with the law. They had strong peer group affinities with other runaways.

The fugitive was fleeing from a specific, perceived threat. Appropriate services to fugitives might be agency support and counseling. Diversion programs would certainly be important in an attempt to short-circuit a strong tendency toward delinquent careers.

Refugees

Almost all refugees had fled from institutions or foster homes (only 2 percent were with both natural parents). Some of these were actually running back home. They had already been provided with society's "services"—foster home placements or institutionalization—and they were overtly rejecting these "services" by runing from them. The efficacy of just giving them more of the same seems dubious, and this raises questions about the social effectiveness of foster home placement and institutionalization.

Immigrants

This type appeared at the opposite end of the spectrum from the victim. This group exhibited the greatest degree of independence. They came primarily from intact families in which fathers held blue-collar jobs and mothers acted as homemakers. Relatively large proportions of the white and native American runaways in our sample were in this category.

In general, immigrants were running toward something as opposed to fleeing from something. Their situations were not necessarily intolerable or even unpleasant. Rather, their home environment didn't afford the independence valued by this group.

As an indication of their degree of independence and maturity, the immigrants were not as likely as the other types to have siblings or relatives who have run away. Furthermore, although more than half of the immigrants reported dropping out of school, expulsion or suspension was relatively infrequent. This is another indication that these individuals are decisive and act on their decisions, as distinct from troublesome youth rejected by others. Consistent with views of their capabilities, immigrants were the runaways more likely to leave with their own funds or to locate jobs to sustain their needs while on the run. Because they were less likely to engage in illegal means for survival, they were not apprehended as frequently as the others.

Service implications for this type appear to be relatively straightforward. As a group, the immigrants would benefit from programs geared toward helping them establish economic self-sufficiency. Job training, employment opportunities, and housing accommodations seem appropriate for their particular needs.

Interviews with parents of these runaways indicated that, in many cases, the immigrants left with their parents' consent. In addition to moral support, some of the parents interviewed confessed to giving their sons or daughters financial assistance. In such cases, the "runaway act" was seen as a positive step toward adulthood rather than as a reaction against the parent or home environment. Contacts between the immigrants and their families were frequently maintained, with little of the animosity or sense of guilt manifested in other runaways' relations with their parents.

In sum, various motivations for running away suggest different social service needs. One would not send a victim back to an abusing parent without some intervening services. The rebel would require services of a family counseling type, given the open authority struggle between the child and the parent. The exile who has been ejected from the home requires resettlement, rather than a futile trip "back" without any change in the situation.

The fugitive is already in flight from the legal authorities and would likely resist and distrust traditional social services, as would the refugee, who is in flight from some type of social service, that is, alternative placement, which sent him on the run.

Immigrants appear to be most likely to have emancipated themselves, and seem to be precocious adults, needing jobs, status, adult identities, and a chance to "make it" on their own.

All such differential service needs must be considered if any impact is to be made by social services to runaway youth.

INTRODUCTION TO PART II

In Part I we have described how runaways are illegal aliens in their own land. Although they may leave home for different reasons that lead to different needs, they still face the uncertain and problematic role of an illegal or stateless person.

Yet the laws also provide for social services to runaways, irrespective of their illegal status. This presents the runaway and his family with a classic contradiction—on one hand society rejects him, on the other hand, society makes some attempt to serve him while he is illegally abroad in the land. This ambivalence creates a climate of inconsistency and uncertainty in which these adolescent youth must find their way.

In Part II of this study, we attempt to examine the "services" available to runaways, both from formal and informal asocial networks in our society. We begin with a description of how runaways view social services. We then present an analysis of ways in which runaways are served by four types of social agencies (public, private, diversion, and counterculture) based upon an in-depth organizational analysis of eight agencies at the two West Coast runaway terminals (the Los Angeles and San Francisco Bay areas). We next turn to a national survey of social agency professionals who exert a significant influence on the making of policy for runaways and play a decisive role in implementing such policy. We examine their perceptions of the types of runaways, of the needs of runaways, and of the services available to runaways. The instrument used in the national survey was also employed in a regional survey of social agencies, involved with runaways, in Los Angeles and San Francisco. We thus obtained a three-dimensional view: of the eight local agencies studied in depth, of a representative national agency sample, and of a regional sample that was more comprehensive than our eight local agencies.

Do social workers view runaway problems the same way all over the country, or was our study limited by geography or the uniqueness of the runaways we studied? Can we generalize about the runaway issues faced by social agencies?

How well do social agencies meet the needs of runaways, and how much of the total runaway population do they serve? If they do not adequately serve or do not serve the entire spectrum of runaways, what other social networks provide runaways with support and identity? What is the world of the runaway, both within the formal and informal structures of society? How well does the "service" function of the legal agencies offset or mitigate the conflictual situation created by the legal status laws which impact upon the underage runaway?

These are the basic questions that we explore in Part II.

CHAPTER 4

Runaways' Views of Social Services

We asked all the interviewed runaways a question about their general knowledge of, and attitudes toward, formal social agencies, asking them to list "helpful or appealing" agencies that served runaways. *Over half (55 percent) did not list any agency* as being either helpful or appealing. Nearly one-third (32 percent) listed free clinics, crash pads or counterculture agencies, while 8 percent listed a public agency, 3 percent gave a private agency, and 3 percent mentioned a law enforcement or diversion agency as being helpful. *In sum, only 14 percent of these runaway subjects felt that any form of a formal social agency would be either helpful or appealing to runaways,* turning (if at all) to counterculture agencies.

But, what is the extent of these runaways' actual knowledge of social service agencies? If they know of the existence of specific agencies, how likely are they to use these services? In order to gather such data, we asked each subject about a series of specific social agencies as possible sources of help. Each subject was first asked if he or she *knew* if that specific agency was available to serve runaways and second, had he or she ever *used* the services of that agency. The responses are shown in the following table (4.1).

Earlier in this study, we have noted that many of the subjects appear to be "chronic" runaways—that is, they have run away many times, have been "on the road," often for extended periods of time, and might be thought to be quite sophisticated about the runaway scene and knowledgeable about all types of resources.

It seems quite surprising that so few of our subjects, even those most "sophisticated" runaways, "knew" of agencies which serve runaways. The distribution of knowledge ranged from 15 percent who knew about the food stamp program to a high of 48 percent who knew about free clinics. The best known runaway services are free clinics, drug clinics, crash pads, churches, social workers, and police departments, although all were known by less than *one-half* of the sample (48-43 percent). Those programs least well known as serving runaways were the food stamp program, public

TABLE 4.1: Runaways' Knowledge and Use of Specific Resources Reputed
to Serve Runaways
(N=209)

Specific Resources	Knowledge of	Use of	% of Use by Those Who Knew
Crash pads	43%	21%	49%
Free food projects	33%	22%	67%
National Runaway Switchboard	24%	2%	8%
Local switchboards	34%	19%	56%
Drop-in centers	25%	14%	56%
Social workers	43%	19%	44%
Churches	43%	21%	49%
Travelers Aid	21%	11%	50%
Runaway shelters	20%	20%	100%
Free clinics	48%	27%	56%
Legal aid services	21%	8%	38%
Hospitals	36%	18%	50%
Food stamp programs	15%	10%	67%
Public welfare	19%	4%	21%
Drug clinics	45%	5%	11%
Probation department	34%	8%	24%
Police department	44%	18%	41%

welfare agencies, *runaway shelters,* and Traveler's Aid (all known by less than 20 percent of our sample).

In terms of runaways actually using services, we found even lower proportions. The most frequently used agencies were free clinics, free food projects, crash pads, churches, and runaway shelters (27 percent ot 20 percent of all subjects). The least frequently used resources were the National Runaway Switchboard, drug clinics, welfare agencies, and probation departments (less than 5 percent of our sample used these resources).

Even when runaways *knew* of potential service agencies, the percent of runaways who actually utilized such services varied widely. While only 20 percent of the runaways knew about runaway shelters, all who knew about them used them. The same trend was present for free food projects and food stamp programs. In such situations, it would appear that these types of services should be more widely advertised, since runaways appear to be able to trust these and to use them for needed shelter and food while on the road. Note that these are services within the counterculture world—free, unrestrained, and dealing with basic needs.

One runaway girl symbolized this need for us when she told us that her idea of an ideal runaway agency would be "an empty house and a full 'fridge'."

Public agencies fared poorly in terms of either knowledge of or use by runaways. But runaways, in general, simply are not informed as to the potential services available. This is again the result of the double bind of being, on one hand, an illegal alien, and on the other hand, being eligible for public social services.

These findings suggest important conclusions: (1) that agencies responsible for meeting the social service needs of runaways need to develop a wider informational network if they are to be utilized by needy runaways; (2) that the critics who feel that society is offering so many resources that children are enticed to "run away" are obviously not correct, since so few even "sophisticated" runaways know and use social agencies that are supposedly available as resources for runaway youth; and (3) that there is an inherent contradiction about the runaways' legal status (being an "illegal alien") and still being "eligible" for social services, albeit having to be handled as a *runaway* and risk forcible detention and return home as a price for "services."

As a solution to these "double bind" situations, runaway youth rely on their own resources, on friends, relatives, and their own "hustling" ability to provide for themselves. Only when they are "picked up" or in some type of serious trouble do they come into contact with the official social or law enforcement agencies.

We asked them about the reasons they didn't use the social agencies, and 59 percent stated that they "distrusted" the agencies, while 27 percent stated that they knew nothing about them. Seven percent felt that the agencies didn't have what they needed, while 4 percent stated they had negative experiences or bureaucratic "hassles" in the past. We asked if they could tell us which agencies put youth off, and 59 percent could not answer that question since they claimed no knowledge of such service.

TABLE 4.2: Runaways: Listing of Agencies that "Put Youth Off"

No response	59%
Law enforcement agencies	19%
Public agencies	10%
Private agencies	4%
Counterculture agencies	4%
Diversion agencies	3%

As can be seen (Table 4.2), the two public systems, law enforcement and public welfare, were seen as the two agencies most likely to put youth off, while counterculture and diversion agencies appear to have the best reputation among our subjects.

Thus, social agencies that purport to serve runaways appear to be serving only a few, and most of those on an involuntary basis, placing the illegal alien in a "double bind," that is, if he seeks help, he risks "detention and return" to that which he considers to be an untenable situation.

We asked these runaways what adult they would contact, if they felt it would be necessary to turn to someone for help, and one-half could not think of any adult to turn to! Again, such findings point out the alienation of many of our runaway subjects. Only slightly more than one-third (37 percent) stated they would contact either their parents or another relative if necessary to seek help from an adult. Only 14 percent stated they would turn to a social worker, counselor, religious or probation worker, that is, formal sources of potential help.

We specified the type of help needed as medical and asked our subjects who they would turn to for medical help. Thirty percent could think of no one to turn to if they were sick, while one-fourth stated they would turn to a free clinic, and 15 percent mentioned the hospital as a source of health services.

Seventeen percent of our sample told us that, at some point, they needed help with their drug problems. We asked them where they went for help with their drug problems, and 44 percent of those who needed help said to no one, or to casual acquaintances on the street. Twenty-two percent turned for help with their drug problems to some religious group or religious counselor. Only 16 percent turned for drug help to a drug program or other counselor.

As can be seen, even when faced with specific health or drug problems, our runaway subjects tended not to turn to formal agencies for help, but rather looked to counterculture or interpersonal networks for assistance.

CHAPTER 5

An Organizational Analysis of Eight Social Agencies that Serve Runaways

Turning to social agencies and the services they offer to runaway youth, we again confront the contradiction in the perceptions of runaways as "illegal aliens" and as disturbed children in need of help, as antisocial transgressors, and as social victims. This contradiction breeds ambivalence in the attitude and behavior of social agencies that are supposed to service runaways.

The present policy toward runaways, under the Title XX revisions, is that services may be given without income or referral eligibility requirements. However, the broadening of Title XX regulations regarding runaways as a class does not alter state laws and rules that define the runaways' status as illegal. Do agencies report these "illegal aliens" to the court or "deport" them to their families? The answers are determined by state law, which may confound the apparent intent of Title XX.

The implications of the above emerge from our investigation of the present status of social services to runaway youth. In this investigation we studied eight social agencies in the San Francisco and Los Angeles areas, California's two major urban centers. We deliberately selected four types of agencies: two are established and conventional, except that one type is public and the other private; the other two types—diversion and counterculture agencies—are emergent. We chose one agency of each type in the two areas. (See appendix for profiles of the eight agencies.) Diversion agencies are adjuncts of juvenile court systems; they are used to divert runaway youth from incarceration into a social service or counseling situation more responsive to the cause of their being adrift in society. Juvenile justice systems have come under heavy attack from many quarters for their treatment of incorrigible or status offenders such as runaway youth. Lerman's study (1970) of the institutionalization experiences of youthful offenders, "Child Convicts," found over one-half of all incarcerated youth were serving time for noncriminal offenses (such as running away from home). Since that time, a number of strategies have emerged within the criminal justice system to decriminalize such youth. Diversion programs are one result of this trend.

On the other hand, out of the ferment of the sixties, the "love-ins" in the Haight district of San Francisco and elsewhere, a series of alternative service systems began to take shape. The Diggers in San Francisco provided free food and lodging to many young people who flooded the West Coast. To meet their needs a series of counterculture, self-help groups formed. One of these became "Huckleberry House" in San Francisco, a place for runaways. These counterculture groups took many forms, from communal crash pads to more formal agencies founded by churches or concerned individuals and groups. Two of these counterculture agencies were included in this study.

For purposes of this study, we conducted an analysis of the organizational patterns, definitions, services and ideologies of four types of agencies. Our methods were those of the field study; that is, we visited these agencies and talked with administrators, supervisors, and staff about their services to runaways. Basically, we were interested in how they defined runaways, how they viewed their needs, and what services they gave them. If they were not able to adequately serve the runaways (in their own view), we looked for the barriers to service, both external and internal.

We observed these eight agencies and studied their services to runaway youth over a nine-month period. We interviewed many of the staff, both informally and formally. We developed an interview guide for formal interviews with nine agency administrators, 17 supervisors of social services, and 20 social service workers throughout all eight agencies. After nine months of study, a number of observations emerged:

1. Social agencies of all types serve only a very few of the actual runaway population, and when they do so, it is because of unique or special problems other than that of running away, for example, pregnancy, drug use, venereal disease, accidents, encounters with the law.

2. Most runaway youth served by social agencies are "multi-problem" children and are often wards of the juvenile court as well.

3. Social agencies find their services are generally inadequate or inappropriate for a large percentage of the runaway youth they do serve.

4. Most social workers do not view the runaway youth as a "special category;" rather they view him or her as a disturbed or

abused child not unlike other youth in their caseloads, albeit one they are not especially equipped to serve.

5. Services given runaway youth by social agencies are often brief contact services, are not followed up, and may result in either return of the youth to his or her family, or placement with a social control agency, such as a diversion program or juvenile hall.

6. The legal status of runaway youth is ambiguous, and nearly all social agencies deal with the police or courts in working out treatment plans for runaways. "Treatment" can only follow legal disclosure and sanction—the runaway must be "labeled" and adjudicated before he can be served.

These general findings hold for all agencies irrespective of type under study, to a greater or lesser degree.

Of all agencies in our society, the law enforcement system remains the largest, most powerful and most likely agency to come into contact with the runaway. Thus, we developed a separate study of the juvenile justice system to cover this area. However, in this chapter, we are reporting only on our organizational study of eight social agencies, which were carefully selected after screening a large number of social agencies of all types because they were reported to be those most sensitive to serving runaway youth.

EIGHT SOCIAL AGENCIES SERVING RUNAWAYS

We now take a closeup look at the eight agencies and the services they offer. These are, by category:

Public agencies—the Los Angeles Department of Public Social Services and the Alameda County Welfare Department (both of which clients often call "welfare").

Private agencies—Hillsides, a residential treatment center in the Los Angeles area, and San Francisco Traveler's Aid.

Diversion agencies—Way Home, a counseling center in Los Angeles, and Charila House, a residential center in San Francisco.

Counterculture agencies—1736 House in the Los Angeles area and Huckleberry House in San Francisco.

THE PUBLIC AGENCIES

The Los Angeles County Department of Public Social Services and the Alameda County Welfare Department are large public agencies under the direction of the supervisors of the two counties. They are the official welfare agencies in their counties, operating under federal, state, and county regulations. Each has the primary responsibility for developing, under all of these regulations, the official program of the county to meet the welfare needs of its citizens. These are important agencies, in view of Title XX's recent inclusion of social services to runaways as a class. The public agencies carry the weight of the other side of the contradiction in our society, which involves the structural ambivalence toward runaways. The public agencies are responsible for social services to aid these "illegal alien" runaways. What are the service-delivery systems that could carry out such a task?

Specialized services for children, including runaways, are organized as the Children's Services Division. In Alameda County these services are centralized. In Los Angeles County, much larger both in population and geography, the Metro North district office, situated in a section just northwest of the Los Angeles Civic Center, was selected for study.

The Children's Services Division in both agencies provides broad-based services to youth with serious protection or placement needs, whether or not families meet the usual financial eligibility requirements. There is no charge for service. However, placement costs would be evaluated with relation to family income and commitments, with parents paying part of the cost if determined financially able.

Intake tends to be a formal and time-consuming process. Referrals may come from community agencies, including the police, from citizens concerned about the welfare of children, or from families requesting service on their own behalf. The emphasis is upon crisis intervention with relatively brief service and referral. However, families are served as long as children are thought to be in danger; placements made by the county worker are supervised throughout their duration; and dependent children served as long as the court retains supervision.

Service to Runaways

A separate service category for runaways does not exist in the public agency services. Therefore, at present no young people are seen and categorized as *runaways* by the public agencies. No estimates are available of the number of runaways seen in either public agency. Some youngsters are known to have run away from their homes, foster care placements, and juvenile institutions; this fact is noted in the case narrative, but not recorded statistically. Undoubtedly, agency personnel would not always know about brief runaway episodes when youngsters are living at home, and possibly not about some brief episodes of placed children.

Running away is seen as symptomatic behavior, and workers tend to treat it as an indication of family malfunction and individual distress. Referral is often made to other community agencies when more extended or intensive counseling is indicated.

Since running away is categorized as illegal behavior, public agency workers are under constraint to see that such youngsters are returned to the supervision of their parent or other appropriate adult immediately. In fact, particularly with youth 16 and 17, many workers would attempt to negotiate some arrangement that would be at least minimally satisfactory to the youth, rather than stressing immediate return. Since pregnancy is not infrequently associated with runaway behavior among teenage girls, it is significant that pregnant girls or young mothers 16 and over can sometimes be aided as a separate family unit, on occasion resolving some of the tensions which may have led to the runaway episode. Such girls may well require medical services which can be provided often with the assistance of Medi-Cal (the California name for welfare-related medical assistance).

Perhaps more frequently than young people are aware, serious medical needs can be met, and required parental consents negotiated with substantial mediating service by the workers.

Perhaps the most difficult kind of service to get is that related to the meeting of day-to-day needs for food and shelter and a little pocket money, if runaways are not willing to return home.

Most of the counseling done with runaways is on either side of the runaway episode, when young people and their parents are living under the same roof, but having difficulty with personal and family problems or with patterns of growing up and independence-control problems. Usually such counseling occurs in the protective service area, where there is some issue of child neglect or abuse, often within a public welfare family.

Some runaways are also seen for placement, some placed as a result of repetitive runaway episodes, which lead to a judgment of incorrigibility or lack of effective parental control. Some children also are runaways from placements. In all of these cases, the department records would treat the runaway episode as an item in the case narrative, but not as a statistically recorded item.

Since the majority of public welfare clients require income maintenance services, the runaway seen by the agency is likely to come from a poor family. Since statistics are not kept for runaways as a category, the only available information is impressionistic. Approximately equal proportions of boys and girls are said to be seen. Workers vary in their perception of the predominant age of runaways between the categories of 13-15 and 16-17. Workers were not willing to estimate ethnic proportions of the runaways seen.

Staffing Patterns

The staffing patterns of the agencies are closely guided by regulations supervised by the Civil Service Commissions. Positions are defined in writing, together with duties, classifications, qualifications, and other circumstances.

In the child services series, college graduation is required for the basic professional level. Graduate work and experience are both valued, especially the master's degree in social work. In recent years some positions have come to require, or give extra credit for, fluency in languages of major ethnic populations in the county.

With the partial exception of affirmative action plans mandated by law and regulation, positions are required to be filled without regard to sex or ethnic considerations. Within established limits of the earliest time that one could complete educational and experience requirements in the child services series, and a conventional retirement age, age integration of staff is common. With increased unemployment and increased competition for suitable jobs at college graduate level, staff turnover has decreased sharply, increasing workers' length of service, and probably, eventually, the average age of staff, and probably also affecting the rhythm of affirmative action program changes.

Barriers to Service

The *external barrier* to service to runaways most often noted is that of the legal situation. Although runaway youth are no longer defined as having violated law by absenting themselves from the supervision of those legally entitled to that supervision, public agencies are still required to return the youth to parents or guardians. Runaway services may be viewed by youth as partly punitive in nature.

Closely related are the social and community perceptions surrounding runaways, which characterize them as "bad" and "troublesome" and view services to them by a public agency as encouraging behavior that law and community opinion strongly desire to eliminate. Also included is the stigma attached to receiving service from the welfare agency.

No budget category exists specifically for runaways, although the revised Title XX allows for such services without establishing eligibility. While budget for staffing is available under other headings to serve youngsters who may have running away as one of the behavioral symptoms of other distresses, there is little flexibility in meeting emergent survival needs of youngsters in the midst of a runaway episode.

Public agency staff feel that the lack of sufficient funding is a barrier to service of clients in general and runaways in particular.

Many also see the cultural diversity of the community as an external barrier to service. Although this could also be viewed as an internal barrier, in terms of the agencies' need for firmer plans for coping with the diversity which exists, in a large urban area the wide diversity, not only of ethnic groups, but of groups of all kinds with different languages, mores, and expectations on a variety of subjects does constitute a difficult problem for agencies to cope with, particularly with regard to runaways who have no place to go.

Two *internal barriers* to services to runaways are lack of staff and lack of money budgeted to serve runaways. While lack of money is primarily an external barrier, the agency may have some flexibility that might be used to provide at least some money for identified needs of runaways, some money to be used flexibly for unbudgeted emergencies.

Many public agency workers feel that their agencies lack credibility with runaway youth who are potential clients, due to the illegal status of runaways and the lack of flexibility and immediate resources as well as the cumbersome bureaucratic system.

ESTABLISHED PRIVATE AGENCIES: TRAVELER'S AID AND HILLSIDES

Traveler's Aid in San Francisco and Hillsides, a residential treatment center in Pasadena, near Los Angeles, reflect the great diversity that exists among private agencies that may serve runaways in these two large urban areas. They are similar, however, in that each has been in its community for over 50 years, and each has a strong commitment to social work as the core discipline out of which service is developed. Both are thought to represent in some fashion the "old-line, established" social service agencies in their communities, although both try to be in the forefront of service with the most current and well-regarded social work approaches to their respective clients. All professional staff have masters' degrees in social work.

Traveler's Aid has developed a wide variety of services in air and bus terminals, in its office near Market Street, and "on the streets." These services are available to runaways as well as a large group of other "transients." Hillsides, growing out of an earlier Episcopal Church concern for orphans, has in recent years become a residential treatment center for moderately disturbed children, some of whom are runaways.

Primary Service Mission of the Agency

The service mission of Traveler's Aid is quite varied, the unifying factor being service to transients and newcomers, those in the area less than 45 days.

Counseling services are basic to the mission of the agency. It also deals with a wide range of client advocacy issues, the need for which workers encounter servicing their clients. Counseling services are, as a rule, relatively brief, seldom more than three visits. Referrals are given when indicated and available. The agency is very much aware of areas in which needs exceed the availability of services in the community.

Limited assistance is available to meet survival needs for food, shelter, and transportation. Scrip and tokens are given for nearby hotels, restaurants, and for bus travel locally. Beyond two or three days, clients still needing this kind of assistance are referred to other agencies.

The service mission of Hillsides, in contrast, is quite specific: residential treatment services for 55 youngsters age 7 to 13 at the time of intake. Average length of stay is nine months to a year. With the services of social workers and house parents, the aim is really a therapeutic community. Psychiatric consultation is available, as are the services of an educational therapist who works with those youngsters who are not ready to participate in the program of neighborhood schools, which most residents attend, or who are experiencing a temporary emotional or behavioral crisis.

Service to Runaways

Traveler's Aid is aware of seeing a substantial number of runaways, though it has not kept a statistical record of runaways by category. It did have a record that 7 percent of clients seen in 1973-74 were under the age of 18, including both runaways and the children of transient families. Since a total of 65,074 were seen in that year, 4,555 were under 18. Of the total, 61,074 were seen by volunteers for information and referral, still leaving 4,000 seen by the social work staff for somewhat more extended service.

They see youth who report a wide range of family problems and difficulties with schools and police. Some young people ask help in returning to their families, which the agency is often able to provide. Others ask help to stay in the city, refusing to return home. Parental consent must be obtained for Traveler's Aid to offer scrip for an overnight hotel stay. If youngsters are not willing to contact parents, referrals are made to more informally structured community resources. Young people sometimes request additional counseling and are seen at the office for relatively short-term service.

The agency is very interested in the development of community resources to meet the survival needs of youngsters away from home. It has been interested in, and contributed to, the formation of a halfway house, and also of Huckleberry House.

Hillsides serves runaways as it serves all its residents, through a total program of residential treatment. Though it has no special category for runaways, about one-third to one-half of its residents have had runaway episodes, either from their own homes, from foster care, or from Hillsides itself, although running away seldom is the presenting problem. Some youngsters run away repeatedly, although the average age of the population is young for such behavior. Sometimes children are placed at Hillsides because of a history of running away; other children run for the first time, distressed over institutional placement.

Particularly with the young runaways, the behavior is seen as clearly symptomatic. Some children run as a result of personal and family distress; some are angry at not getting something they think they need; some run away from a specific conflict; others run as an assertion of independence. When parents are separated, it is not uncommon for children to run from one to the other. In the case of children running away from Hillsides, some run back home others just run away, doubting they can count on any adult to be dependable in meeting their needs.

Counseling incident to running away, then, concentrates on themes of developing trust and learning to deal with conflict more directly.

The major funding source for Traveler's Aid (76 percent) is the Bay Area United Way. Another 18 percent comes from capital funds and investments; 5 percent is from current contributions. Additional funds in the budget would allow for expansion of the program in some very helpful ways, particularly in the area of services to runaways.

At Hillsides, since nearly all children are placed by the county, most of the funds come from the county programs making the placements, approximately 80-85 percent. The other 15-20 percent of the budget is contributed by private donors. Medi-Cal meets the medical needs of children. Cost per child is computed at $1,013 per month.

Legal constrictions are the greatest barrier to adequate services to runaways. Three of four workers were aware of a feeling that in the community Traveler's Aid is viewed as an "establishment" agency, and that some clients both runaways and minorities in general, may not seek services from it because of that.

Service Outcomes

Outcomes of services to runaways at Traveler's Aid are often seen as problematic when youth do not wish to go home. Appropriate referrals are insufficient in the community; many are seen with whom more needs to be done, but cannot be done. Huck's and other "counterculture" agencies to whom referrals are made do not report service outcomes in order to maintain client confidentiality.

Hillsides tends to see outcomes in terms of a youngster being "ready to leave" and return home or to homelike foster care. Termination evaluations take into account the opinions of social work and cottage staff, children, their parents, and often a psychiatric consultant. Foster home placements for children released from Hillsides are supervised by the staff.

Placement at Hillsides may be terminated for some youngsters because of behavior that indicates that the agency simply cannot make progress with them; this might be repeated running away or grossly disruptive behavior, coupled with psychiatrically oriented diagnosis.

Recommendations

Traveler's Aid workers thought there should be a specific program for runaways in the agency; all thought that the emergency needs of runaways should be met and would like to do so in their agency for those who come to them. Housing and food were seen as urgent needs which, when not met, left youth open to exploitive adults. "Advocacy" was seen as a need, someone to go to bat for a youngster in specific situations, as well as to intervene with the community to see that the common needs of youth are met. A need was seen for a drop-in center, and possibly a van from which to operate an outreach program.

Workers at Hillsides deal with a relatively stable population in placement. All workers saw running away in this context as symptomatic of other problems, and none thought that a runaway category would be useful at their agency. Some workers thought there should be programs in the community to meet the needs of runaways.

DIVERSION AGENCIES: CHARILA FOUNDATION AND THE WAY HOME

Charila Foundation in San Francisco and Way Home in Van Nuys, near Los Angeles, have in common the fact that they are innovative new programs receiving substantial funding from juvenile justice diversion programs. Their contrast shows the range of service available under such programs: Charila is a residential treatment center, and Way Home is an outpatient counseling center.

Charila House is composed of three houses with residential facilities for nine girls each. The residents are girls between 15 and 18, for the most part, although under certain circumstances a girl might stay through age 10. All staff have either professional or college degrees.

Way Home sees itself as a nontraditional counseling center with an emphasis upon the problems of the family, particularly those of parents and children. A variety of approaches is used and clients are seen as individuals, families, and groups.

Five or six staff interviewed indicated master's degrees in counseling-related fields. All interviewed were white, evenly distributed between men and women. The age range is about 25 to 50.

Primary Service Mission

Charila's primary service mission is to be a residential treatment center for disturbed adolescent girls. Staff members speak of a "therapeutic milieu." Girls are asked to commit themselves to a stay of at least a year. Eighty percent are placed by the probation department.

Way Home sees its primary service mission as being a community counseling clinic, where individuals and families come to work out personal or interpersonal problems. Way Home works with approximately 400 clients a year, predominantly white, middle-class residents of the surrounding community, and among these some are runaways.

The program has a hot line component, always available, but clients are encouraged to come by appointment except in emergencies.

Service to Runaways

Charila's program is focused on the 27 girls in residence, so that it is not actively involved in service to youth during runaway episodes. However, most of its residents have run away at some time. Running away is viewed as symptomatic, and treatment focuses on helping clients to feel secure with caring people and to learn how to resolve conflict without running away from it.

Way Home offers only counseling services. If a runaway came to it during the runaway episode, it would be able to offer counsel since its intake process is simple and quick. It would not have services related to "survival needs." Since some runaways are experiencing family or personal problems whose resolution would encourage them to return home, counseling is a relevant service.

In addition, Way Home has been given a grant to do a substantial amount of juvenile justice diversion work; close to 15 percent of its funding for the next year will come from that source.

At Charila, 90 percent of funding comes from fees paid by probation and other county agencies for service to placed girls. An additional 5 percent is raised from contributions, and the girls raise the other 5 percent through a variety of small fund raising activities. All of the budget is geared to the residential program, and none is set aside for direct services to runaways.

At Way Home, most of the funds are received from fees paid by clients. The average cost computed for a counseling session is $9.50. Clients with lower incomes are served on a sliding fee scale.

Workers at Way Home were concerned about the legal problems of seeing young people without parental consent. They felt that this was a problem not only with regard to counseling runaways, but also for young people still living at home who might have problems they weren't ready to discuss with their parents.

Others mentioned external barriers in terms of relationships with other community agencies, feeling that some more traditional agencies disliked their having developed such a diverse program so rapidly. As a consequence, these agencies were not inclined to refer runaways to Way Home.

Recommendations

Charila staff did not feel it was appropriate to have a separate service category for runaways, either at their agency or at agencies in general. All saw running away as symptomatic behavior, to be dealt with to the extent possible by encouraging trust and the willingness to face conflicts and resolve them in the family. However, several of the staff interviewed saw the need for places where survival needs and counseling could be provided for youth "on the run."

At Way Home most workers saw running away as symptomatic and thought that the most needed service was counseling. Some workers thought their agency should have a special program to serve runaways. Workers focused on the need for what one called "an escape hatch," a place where youngsters could stay safely un-til they were ready to return home or find some other more per-manent resolution to the problem which caused them to run. Some saw value in a long-term residential center, while some thought an outreach worker in the agency would be useful in iden-tifying problems before youngsters actually left home.

COUNTERCULTURE AGENCIES: HUCKLEBERRY HOUSE AND 1736 HOUSE

Huckleberry House in San Francisco and 1736 House in Hermosa Beach, near Los Angeles,* both grew out of community concern about the need for "a place to be" for runaways. "1736" came to be known by its street address. Huck's signaled its purpose by adopting the name of the most famous runaway in American liter-ature. Each "set up shop" 24 hours a day in an old house in a neighborhood frequented by young people, staffing with people involved in its formation, mostly with social work backgrounds.

Primary Service Mission: Service to Runaways

Both Huckleberry House and 1736 were organized with the mission of serving runaways. As drop-in centers, open 24 hours a day, they found that young people who "drop in" are not all run-aways. Since their intake policy is free, accommodating to the ex-tent possible all young people who come in, as well as parents who come seeking counsel about their children, both plan to continue to serve in this way. Both find that while an occasional runaway comes from far away, most of their walk-in clients are local young people. Intake tends to be an easy process, with records taken in-formally.

Both offer some services to meet the "survival needs" of youth "on the run." Both provide food when needed and a few beds for short stays. Over 50 percent of Huck's clients stay at least one night.

"Someone to talk to" is seen as a primary need for youth who come to both agencies, so that counseling and referral are two of the major service available at each. Personal and family counsel-ing is available and is thought to be an important part of the pro-gram. Areas of legal and medical services and job counseling are seen as important to many.

Both agencies had substantial information about clients seen. Huck's has seen a few more youth each year (1972: 503; 1973: 520; 1974: 559). Their ages ranged from 12 to 18, but two-thirds

---

*As powerful evidence of the lack of formal services to runaways it is important to note that 1736 House is the only runaway-specific agency in all of the Los Angeles area—a major terminal for runaway youth from all over the country.

were 15 and 16. Sixty-two percent defined themselves as runaways. Sixty-two percent came from families in the greater San Francisco Bay area. Girls constituted 58 percent of the clients; boys, 42 percent. Ethnically, clients were 62.1 percent Anglo, 18.4 percent black, 13.1 percent Latino-Chicano, and 6.1 percent "other," mostly Asian. Parents are also seen.

1736 reports that in the 11 months from May 16, 1974 to April 16, 1975, 564 persons received service, including those under 18, young adults, and parents. Some services were brief. Only 31 clients were seen from outside of Southern California, including 25 from out of state. Services included 403 nights' lodging, 986 meals. Among 170 persons under 18 that were seen, age breakdowns were: 10 and under—10; 11 to 13—9; 14 to 15—65; 16 to 17—86. An additional 91 were 18 to 20; 103 were in their twenties. Sixty-four adults over 30 were seen, including some up to 80. The ages of 75 clients were not known. Ninety-seven, or 57 percent of those under 18, were runaways.

It seems clear, then, that a walk-in agency known to be willing to serve runaways will serve some runaways among those who walk in. Huck's served 62 percent and 1736, 57 percent of their under-18 clients who were runaways, but these are not very large numbers given the number of runaways on the street. It also seems clear that a number of youth not presently on the run will come in for service; among them are likely to be some who have considered running, or who have done so in the past and might again.

At Huck's the staff is predominantly young, interethnic, and fairly balanced between men and women. A variety of opinions on many issues are represented, and there is an effort to operate by consensus. Several of the staff members have Bachelor of Arts degrees, but education is not currently a requirement for employment. Personality factors and experience are thought to be very important. In addition to salary, all staff members are given $600 yearly for educational experiences or individual therapy.

At 1736, there are only six staff members, working a variety of hours, part-time and full-time, paid and unpaid. They are predominantly young and white (as is the neighborhood they serve), and divided between men and women.

There are no formal educational requirements, personality, interest, and experience being viewed as major relevant factors. At least one staff member has a Bachelor of Arts degree.

Budget

At Huck's the budget is about $10,000 a month. About 15-20 percent goes for direct services to clients, the remainder to rent, operating expenses, and salaries. It has received some money from church and community sources, including the United Bay Area Crusade, but most of its funding has come from county, state, and federal sources, through grants relating to drug programs, as well as juvenile justice diversion programs, and services to runaways.

The 1736 budget is only about $1,200 a month. Rental of the house is regularly provided by its sponsoring church, as is food. Operating expenses and salaries are dependent on contributions from church and community people, including the time donated by volunteers.

Neither agency charges a fee for service, feeling that this kind of service must not have cost barriers.

External barriers to service noted at Huck's most vehemently were lack of sufficient and dependable funding, mentioned by everyone, and legal problems with runaways' status, mentioned by four out of five workers interviewed. Some also saw some social and community barriers, such as a variety of interagency conflicts and negative community feelings about runaways. Some noted awareness that Huck's was not trusted by all ethnic and "third world" groups. However, most workers thought the agency had credibility with young people generally, and that problems with parents were personal rather than ethnic.

At 1736, the only external barrier upon which everyone agreed was the severe lack of stable sources of financing. The legal barrier was also important, in terms of defining running away as an illegal act. The agency seems to be able to encourage understanding on the part of youth that they should at least let their parents know where they are, and on the part of parents to give the youth some time to work through problems, rather than demanding immediate return.

Since clients are free to come and go at both agencies, they do not always stay until all of the problems seem resolved. Having gone, however, they are free to return if they wish. Many continue to come to counseling even after any emergent shelter need is over. To some, the available service to meet the survival need is the major question.

Recommendations

Workers at Huck's recommended more beds for emergency needs, as well as a longer term halfway house. They also recommended more work with parents, including parent groups, and more ongoing groups for youth. Another recommendation was that young clients be trained to help other youth who come in.

At 1736, workers saw a need for peer counseling, a Spanish-speaking worker, groups for parents, a limited term halfway house, job counseling, and more public information about programs set up to help runaways.

Workers in both agencies thought that running away should not be a separate category for service in the sense of excluding others from any available services, but many felt that during the runaway episode, young people had needs not usually shared by others, which urgently needed to be met.

ORGANIZATIONAL ANALYSIS: WORKERS' VIEW OF SERVICE DELIVERY SYSTEMS

We now turn to a series of analytical questions that were posed to workers in the agencies described above with the aim of contrasting or comparing services to runaways by the several agencies, and their perception of runaway needs and the barriers to meeting these needs.

The first organizational issue we explored was how runaways come to the various social agencies. How do they learn of the agency, how are they referred or recruited or find the intake door to that particular agency?

Since, as we have hypothesized, runaways may be seen as "illegal aliens," the most common door to social agencies appears to be involuntary, that is, the runaway is "sent" to one or more of the social agencies. Within the eight agencies studied, runaway youths' initial contact with a social agency usually resulted from a previous encounter with police.

Counterculture agencies may be more of an exception to this finding since they are more likely to see youth who are seeking help or coming as a result of a friend's recommendation, although referrals from the judicial/welfare system were also common.

The intensity of the judicial-agency liaison relationship varies from the direct Los Angeles Department of Public Social Services judicial contact to less frequent judicial referral of runaways to Huckleberry House.

Another counterculture agency, 1736 House (Hermosa Beach) seems to value its level of credibility with both youth and adults. The 1736 staff feels that it has good relationships with the police and stresses the importance of working with the system without losing sight of its primary responsibility to the runaway youth.

Contact with the runaway in the two public agencies studied (DPSS and Alameda County Welfare Department) is within a former legal context. Youth who receive services here fall into the legal categories of "dependent" or "delinquent," and judicial referral is typical.

Other referral sources mentioned by public agency staff were schools, law referral system, foster parents, hospitals, friends or self-referral—however, the initial referral was usually made by the police.

Similarly, judicial referrals are also typical for diversion programs. The two studied were Charila Foundation, San Francisco, and the Way Home, Van Nuys (San Fernando Valley, Los Angeles).

Diversion is the process of keeping a child from entering into the juvenile justice system. Juveniles in such programs usually have been picked up by the police or sheriff's departments on a first offense or nonserious criminal offense, and are given the alternative of becoming involved with a community counseling program. Under such a program, the youth's offense does not go on record, and his parents receive counseling services. Diversion referrals may come from police, sheriff's, or probation departments.

Next in frequency of referral contact with the judicial system are the private established agencies. Two such agencies, Traveler's Aid of San Francisco and Hillsides Episcopal Home for Children, were studied.

Over all, it appears from the above survey that the law enforcement system continues to be the primary recruitment and referral source for these various types of social agencies in their service to runaways.

SOCIAL AGENCY WORKERS' VIEW OF THE RUNAWAY

We felt that the way agency workers viewed runaways was an important factor in understanding the service patterns. We asked the agency workers about the reasons children ran away from home. Workers responded with multiple reasons, and we present them in the following table:

TABLE 5.1: Agency Workers' Perceptions of the Cause of Running Away, by Type of Agency
(N=46)

Reasons	Public Agency	Private Agency	Diversion	Counter- culture
Family problems	81%	88%	100%	88%
Personal problems	88%	100%	67%	88%
Child in trouble	63%	66%	50%	44%
Seeking adventure	19%	33%	8%	33%

As can be seen (Table 5.1), most agency workers viewed the runaway causes as being complicated, centered in both the child and his family, and involving serious emotional problems.

All these agencies seem to agree that a runaway youth is running from some serious family difficulty, but only in a few instances do these agencies offer family-centered counseling.

Our next organizational question was about the tools available to social agencies to serve runaways. Under this heading, we first examined the staffs—their training, experience, and commitment to serving runaways.

SOCIAL AGENCY STAFF SERVING RUNAWAYS

There is a clear difference between the professional background of staffs that work with runaways in the counterculture agencies and the staffs of all other agencies.

Agencies, other than counterculture, make specific academic requirements of staff. The following table compares the professional backgrounds of the workers we interviewd at the public and private agencies.

TABLE 5.2: Social Agency Workers' Professional Qualifications, by Type of Social Agency
(N=46)

	Public	Private	Diversion	Counter-culture
Graduate professional	6%	56%	50%	—
Undergraduate	88%	—	25%	33%
Para-professional	—	44%	25%	44%
Volunteer	6%	—	—	11%
No particular training	—	—	—	11%
Total	100%	100%	100%	100%

As can be seen (Table 5.2), the counterculture agencies are more likely to rely on persons without "professional" training in serving runaways, while most other agencies' employees are college-educated or professionally trained in social work.

In our interviews with the workers in the eight agencies, we selected those who were reported to have the greatest knowledge of, or policy input into, services to runaways. In the following table we present the positions held in the agency by the workers interviewed regarding runaway services.

TABLE 5.3: Social Agency Workers' Position within Agency,
by Type of Agency
(N=46)

Position	Public	Private	Diversion	Counter-culture
Administrative	6%	33%	33%	11%
Supervisory	56%	45%	9%	33%
Direct Service	38%	22%	58%	55%
Total	100%	100%	100%	100%

As can be seen (Table 5.3), most workers who were interviewed were giving direct services to runaways, particularly in the diversion and counterculture agencies.

We asked these social workers if they felt their agency should provide additional services to runaways and their affirmative responses are shown in Table 5.4.

TABLE 5.4: Agency Workers' Affirmation of Need for Additional Services
to Runaways, by Type of Agnecy
(N=46)

Public agency	69%
Private agency	44%
Diversion agency	75%
Counterculture agency	66%

Thus, except for those in the private agencies, a decisive majority of the agency workers indicated that additional services were needed in their agencies in order to adequately serve runaway youth.

SERVICES NEEDED BY AND PROVIDED TO RUNAWAYS

We then asked social agency workers about how they saw the "needs" of runaway youth and the services they felt were lacking.

Social agency workers all seemed to recognize the many problems and dangers faced by runaway youth. The responses to need-assessment questions were classified into support services (food, shelter, money, transportation) and emotional support (counseling, residential treatment, return to their family, and so on). In the following table, the social agency workers' assessment of the principal needs of runaway youth is presented.

**TABLE 5.5: Runaway Needs as Perceived by Agency Workers,
by Type of Agency
(N=46)**

Type of Agency	Support Services	Emotional Services	Total
Public agencies	39%	61%	100%
Private agencies	33%	67%	100%
Diversion agencies	41%	59%	100%
Counterculture agencies	25%	75%	100%

*Many social workers, of course, saw a need for both support and emotional services;
the table indicates which type of service need they saw as primary.

As can be seen (Table 5.5), most of the agency workers saw
the emotional problems as the primary service focus for runaway
youth, although support services were viewed as the more crucial
needs by approximately one-third of the respondents.

We then asked the agency workers about the types of services
given to runaways by their agency, classifying the responses into
support and emotional services. These responses are reported in
Table 5.6.

**TABLE 5.6: Agency Workers' View of Type of Services Given Runaways,
by Type of Agency*
(N=46)**

	Basic Support Services	Emotional Support Services
Public agencies	40%	60%
Private agencies	32%	68%
Diversion agencies	33%	67%
Counterculture agencies	43%	57%

*Again, it needs to be understood that many workers saw their agencies as providing
both support and emotional services. The table indicates which type of servcies was,
in their view, preponderant.

As can be seen (Table 5.6), the counterculture agencies are
most likely to provide support services, while private and diversion
agencies provide counseling and treatment services.

These broad categories of needs and services were further analyzed to get at the specific service patterns we found within each
of the social agencies.

Agencies serving runaways provide a variety of services that can be further broken down into the following categories: life support (housing, food, medical care, and so on), counseling (personal and vocational), referral, legal (protective services, child placement, court referral), and services designed to facilitate the runaway's return home. There is one "other" category including job information, recreational activities, offering counsel to parents, and follow-up services.

Since youth under 18, who receive temporary housing, must first consent to agency notification of parents, this presents those youth who don't want parental conflict with a dilemma, and they are often without a place to sleep. Certain services are available without parental consent, although all agencies stress parental involvement as a significant component of their counseling program.

In comparing and contrasting services among agencies, one can begin by looking at the legally sanctioned service orientation of LA-DPSS and the Alameda County Welfare Department. These agencies offer services in all categories mentioned above, but each service is structured by legal guidelines. Therefore, what can be done for a runaway is open to little flexibility—and given according to the category the youth falls within: dependent, juvenile offender, AFDC, medical care case, and so on.

The private agencies generally tend to develop such administrative or professionalized structures that immediate, walk-in help for runaways is not available. These agencies do not serve significant numbers of runaways; rather they serve adolescents with emotional and personal problems, most of whom are not runaways. Running away is treated as a symptom of a more deeply ingrained problem, and the treatment is largely conventional "casework treatment" a youth group setting, or in a crisis-oriented casework encounter. Both private agencies studied work closely with the legal system.

The two countercultural agencies (Huck's and 1736) do attempt to provide an open and receptive atmosphere for runaways, and differ from the more formal agencies by informal intake procedures, lack of eligibility formalities or fees, ability to meet some survival needs as emergent, show tolerance for openly expressed differences, and seem to show consideration to work with youth, parents, and police and to "buy time" for conflict resolution. These agency services seem innovative and closer to some of the perceived needs of runaway youth.

FUNDS FOR SOCIAL AGENCY SERVICES TO RUNAWAYS

The second major tool available to social agencies is the funding of relevant programs.

The description of the various funding bases of the agencies was sought, but in addition, we attempted to get some type of cost-per-runaway, or cost-per-runaway service. We were unable to obtain fiscal data, or case accounting data in any format that would permit such analysis.

The fact is that social agencies, like most human service agencies, do not run according to cost-accounting or management-by-objectives guidelines. These are not businesses—they do not see money per se as leading to direct "profit or loss," and, hence, their accounting systems do not reflect production or consumer-oriented figures. Rather, each agency pools its total funding and attempts to cover a wide range of services. Most of them do not have separate services for runaways, which further compounded the difficulty of estimating cost-effectiveness in services to runaways.

After looking for fiscal accounting and costs of runaway services in all the eight agencies, one impression emerges—that all agencies feel they are short of funds, that their caseloads are too large, and their services too few. The private agencies all seem to expend a great deal of time, energy, and thought in fund-raising, and many workers indicated that the fiscal instability of their agency, indeed its very survival, was the major problem of that agency.

RUNAWAYS AS A SEPARATE SERVICE CATEGORY

We asked the social agency workers if they thought runaways should be assigned as a special service category, and we present the data in the following table (5.7).

TABLE 5.7: Percentage of Social Agency Workers who thought Runaways
Should be a Separate Category, by Type of Agency
(N=46)

Type of Agency	%
Public agency	13%
Private agency	22%
Diversion agency	17%
Counterculture agency	22%

Workers seem to feel that runaways are actually exhibiting more serious behavior than running away and should be seen as "disturbed children," not simply as runaways. Many also indicated that they felt their agency was not an appropriate service facility to meet the "true" needs of runaways, while other workers felt that further "labeling" of these youth might add to their social adjustment difficulties, and that they should not therefore have a special service category.

It is of interest to learn that social workers did not wish to develop specialized services for runaways, but rather advocated continuation, either within their agency or other agencies, or a broad range of social services for young people.

We analyzed the responses of agency staff members regarding providing separate services in three major areas. That is, we were concerned as to whether these agency workers would advise separate runaway programs in (a) their own agency, (b) social service agencies in general, or (c) the agencies that comprise the juvenile justice system. In that way, we attempted to cover all aspects of their general understanding about separate runaway programs.

At the Agency Represented

A great majority of the staff members interviewed felt that runaway behavior should not be treated as a separate category for the purpose of providing services at their agencies, and certainly there was a belief expressed by an even greater majority that there was a need to decriminalize the runaway act. Typical expressions were: "Runaways should not be treated punitively"; "A child who runs away has no business being involved in the court system. His family or social problems have nothing to do with the criminal justice system"; "Kids shouldn't be associated with the criminal justice system. Their parents should be called in!"

Other responses exhibited a concern over needed alternatives in these cases: "There should be family crisis units instead of a juvenile hall placement"; "Kids who come from bad family situations should be separated from those who are truly delinquent, and they should be referred to diversion or family counseling programs."

Those interviewed who felt that runaways should not be treated separately expressed the following ideas: "It would reinforce labeling a problem (runaway) which is part of a larger context"; "It would be too difficult to provide separate services"; "It is necessary to view the treatment of juveniles in an overall sense."

The reasons given for a negative answer to a separate runaway category usually involved the perception of runaway behavior as a symptom that could not be treated adequately without considering other problems involved: "Everyone has the potential to run away, and in treatment one must deal with the family as a whole. We try to look at the whole spectrum of behavior and family background"; "Children are not nomads by nature…the act of running away is symptomatic and must be treated as such"; "All of the kids who run away have individual needs, and to group them together for providing services is handling it at a surface level."

There were only a few "yes" answers to this part of the question: "Runaways should be treated separately at this agency because their needs are different"; "We should increase service for runaways here in order to provide them with short-term housing and legal advice."

At Social Service Agencies in General

Although most of the individuals interviewed felt that runaways should not be considered as a separate category for the purpose of providing services at their own agencies, many did believe that this distinction should be made at other community agencies serving youth. Comments were: "Especially in the case of a chronic runaway, there need to be people who have developed skills and know of resources specifically for this problem"; "Although the emotional crisis may be the same as in another case, this child's actions are different and the ways of dealing with them must also be different"; "Yes. In the sense that running away is a crisis situation, this makes immediate services and great attempts to involve the family, a crucial component for effective treatment"; "Runaways are people who have nowhere to go and who don't fit. There must be places for them to stay that are geared to their needs."

Most of the beliefs expressed in relation to a negative answer to this part of the question resembled those stated previously, in response to the same question about the interviewee's own agency: "No, because running away is always symptomatic of an inability to cope with a situation. More attention should be paid to a global view of the family"; "Running away is only the presenting problem."

Other individuals interviewed expressed their beliefs in terms of the needs, not just of runaways, but of all minors: "Special services are needed in general for people under age 18"; "Laws should be clarified and changed so as not to necessitate separate treatment for juveniles who run away."

Within the Juvenile Justice System

In terms of considering runaways as a separate category for the purpose of providing services, a majority of the agency staff members interviewed felt that within the juvenile justice system, distinctions should be made. However, they felt that distinction should not lead to a "criminal status" but were unclear as to alternatives.

LAW ENFORCEMENT VIEWS THE RUNAWAY

At this juncture it might be helpful to interject the law enforcement viewpoint. We interviewed law enforcement officers in both
the Los Angeles and the San Francisco Bay Areas, and generally
they agreed that runaway behavior should be decriminalized, but
provided few suggestions for alternative modes of service. There
was a nearly unanimous opinion that running away is primarily
caused by family problems, that most of the initial law enforcement contact with a runaway case occurs through parental phone
calls to police, and that whenever possible a diversionary program
is preferable to the traditional juvenile justice system.

Juvenile officers generally saw runaway behavior as a minor
offense with very serious potential. Youth picked up on other offenses such as shoplifting, drinking, drug-related offenses, or so on,
will usually be charged with the more serious criminal behavior,
though they might also be classifiable runaways.

In both areas, the emphasis of most juvenile officers was on
returning the youth to his/her home, though there was some reali-
zation that in some cases the need would be better met by referral
to an appropriate agency.

Two-thirds of the agency workers we interviewed said they
generally refer runaways to the police when it is not possible to
send them back to their parents. Since police tend to refer runaways to social agencies when appropriate, the result is that the
runaway is sometimes shunted back and forth when the home situation is seen as intolerable.

COMMUNITY RELATIONS

All agencies report difficulties in community relations; however,
the intensity varies. This is of intense concern to DPSS and Alameda Welfare. They report a lack of positive support with all community agencies.

Both public agencies feel they fill a need in the community
that no other agencies provide for, but possibly some of their difficulty in relating to other agencies stems from the legal restrictions under which they must work. The resulting procedural structure and rigidity in philosophical approach impair a good working
relationship with other community resources.

On the other hand, the counterculture agencies have difficulty in maintaining good relationship in the community for the opposite reason. Their lack of procedural structure and their flexi-

bility with regard to treatment of runaways is the source of problems in relating to other social agencies or agencies of social control. This is more descriptive of Huck's problem than that of 1736 House, since the latter, as part of its basic philosophy, makes a conscious effort to be cooperative in order to maintain strong, positive community ties.

The private agencies had differing reports with fewer common feelings about their community relationships. Traveler's Aid reported that it sometimes had difficult or inadequate relationships with other community agencies, but felt it was well known in the San Francisco area and was utilized by many agencies. Hillsides felt that its relationships with police, schools, public and private agencies, and with individuals were good but that it needed more visibility in the neighborhood. Aware of the problem, personnel are making efforts to increase public awareness.

The diversion agencies both support good community relations in general with only occasional individual problems with members of the police force or other social agencies.

All the agencies interviewed believed they would benefit from stronger, more positive community ties, and all had some either ongoing or planned activity to create better understanding and cooperation.

BARRIERS TO ADEQUATE AGENCY SERVICES TO RUNAWAYS

If the public and private social agencies are not serving significant numbers of runaways, or if these services are unappealing, irrelevant, or ineffectual, what are the barriers to agency services to runaways?

We asked agency workers about both the internal agency barriers and the external barriers to runaway services.

Each worker gave a number of responses. Table 5.8 presents the percentage of workers who gave each type of response. (The table (5.8) does not add up to 100 percent, since each response is tabulated separately, and reflects multiple responses by the workers.)

Internal barriers to adequate services to runaways most frequently mentioned were too few staff and fiscal limitations. Physical and organizational barriers were the next most frequently mentioned, while staff and ideological conflict about runaway services ranked third as an interior-agency barrier.

TABLE 5.8: Agency Workers' Perception of Internal Barriers to Services for Runaways, by Type of Agency

Barriers	Public	Private	Diversion	Counter-culture
Too few staff	94%	100%	25%	44%
Wrong type of staff	44%	56%	16%	22%
Administration	50%	—	58%	22%
Board inaction	13%	11%	33%	33%
Organizational flow	81%	22%	50%	44%
Internal conflict	38%	33%	33%	77%
Ideological conflict	69%	22%	8%	66%
Physical limits	69%	66%	75%	66%
Fiscal inadequacy	94%	55%	92%	88%

There were several other barriers that were cited: inadequate staff and heavy caseloads, insufficient counseling resources, legal restrictions, inadequate crisis residential facilities, lack of adequate referrals, and philosophical differences with supervising agency.

All social agencies feel a shortage of staff and funds. We feel the internal staff and ideological conflicts are reflections of the lack of clarity as to what type of services *actually* would successfully aid the runaway. There is considerable evidence from all "experts" that there is a good deal of ambivalence about just what could and should be done to help runaways within a social agency structure.

In terms of working with problems of the runaway, some staff members expressed a feeling of being "locked in"—by a structure, program outline, legislative requirements, bureaucratic requirements, or by political considerations or a lack of adequate finances. Other interviewees expressed the belief that their agency was doing everything necessary to work adequately with the problems of the runaway. All interviewees were receptive when asked

TABLE 5.9: Agency Workers' Perception of External Barriers to Services for Runaways, by Type of Agency

External Barriers	Public	Private	Diversion	Counter-culture
Social-community	69%	33%	17%	44%
Fiscal indemnity	63%	66%	83%	88%
Cultural conflicts	63%	44%	25%	44%
Legal problems	88%	44%	50%	66%

to express their ideas in the form of recommendations for services and programs, on both a practical and an ideal level.

We classified the respondents' answers to the question regarding external barriers to services, and these are noted in Table 5.9.

As can be seen (Table 5.9), the fiscal restraints are ranked as the most serious external barrier to adequate runaway services. The legal status of runaways with relation to the ability of the agency to deliver services to runaways is the second most serious external barrier. Social, community, and cultural conflicts are also viewed as external barriers to runaway services.

SUMMARY

This chapter was based on interviews with 46 individuals who work in eight agencies in two cities. Each of the agency representatives interviewed shared with us his or her knowledge, feelings, and beliefs in response to verbal questions that also asked for recommendations concerning specific aspects of treatment services for runaways. There are some implications for policy change within the responses given, as well as many recommendations and ideas for the implementation of additional youth services.

CHAPTER 6

Attitudes of Social Agency Workers Toward Runaways: A National and Regional Survey

In order to gain a more comprehensive understanding of the nature and scope of the runaway situation from the perspective of social agencies and to unearth what efforts and steps are being made to deal with the problem, the Institute for Scientific Analysis conducted a series of three surveys, which supplemented our concentrated study of eight social agencies, described in the preceding chapter.

The first sample was comprised of participants in three regional conferences on runaway youth, sponsored by the Office of Youth Development and the Social and Rehabilitation Service of the Department of Health, Education, and Welfare. The first conference was held in Monterey, California, on October 6-9; the second at Kansas City, Kansas, on October 28-31, and the final meeting in Columbia, Maryland, on November 13-16, all in 1974. A questionnaire dealing with runaway services, client characteristics and views concerning the extent and severity of the runaway phenomenon, was administered at each of the three conferences by the Institute for Scientific Analysis research staff.

A total of 164 persons representing public and private agencies and projects or programs attended the three conferences. A wide variety of interests were represented, ranging from law enforcement and judicial agencies at one extreme, through private programs such as Traveler's Aid and the Red Cross or PTA, to privately run facilities such as runaway houses or shelters and "free clinics" at the other extreme.

In all, 39 states and the District of Columbia were represented in the sample. States not represented in the "conference sample" were Connecticut, Georgia, Kansas, Mississippi, New Mexico, Oregon, South Carolina, South Dakota, Tennessee, Vermont, and Wyoming. Nearly 80 percent of those attending the conferences completed the questionnaire.

A questionnaire identical to the one presented at the regional conferences, but with a few added questions, was mailed to a randomly selected sample of local agencies in Los Angeles and San Francisco in July 1975 to determine the current views of program people in this sector and to compare these views with the conference sample.

A total of 45 questionnaires was returned in the local sample; 18 from Los Angeles agencies and 27 from the agencies in San Francisco, representing an approximate 50 percent rate of response.

In our third survey, the identical questionnaire used with both the conference sample and the local agencies sample was mailed to 93 agencies from the membership roster of the National Network of Runaway Services across the United States. It was hoped that the responses of those agencies in the national network would attest to the reliability of the findings of the previous two surveys and substantiate the generalizability of our findings.

Forty-five questionnaires were returned from our initial network mailing, representing a 48 percent rate of response. Because of the manner in which our three samples were drawn and the close correlation between respondents' answers in the three samples, we are reasonably confident that our findings are indeed generalizable.

FINDINGS

The following section will deal with some of the information collected, beginning with agency views of the severity and nature of the runaway problem, the profile of the typical runaway client seen, and conclude with some data on the types of services rendered in the agencies.

First, as can be seen in the table (6.1) below, there was near-unanimity among respondents from all three samples that the runaway problem was not temporary, and close to half of the respondents in each sample believed the problem was likely to grow.

Respondents were asked to designate the most serious problems confronted by runaways, to estimate the effectiveness of cur-

TABLE 6.1: Nature of Runaway Problem, as Seen by
Three Social Agency Samples

Nature of Problem	Regional Conferences % (N=133)	Local Sample % (N=45)	National Network % (N=45)
Temporary	2%	7%	2%
Lasting	45%	51%	49%
Likely to increase	47%	40%	48%
No opinion	6%	2%	1%

rent programs and the extent of their utilization by runaways, and to specify "barriers" to successful service delivery. Responses showed that most agreed that survival was the most serious problem while exploitation and legal problems were next in frequency of mention; most thought that very little official assistance was available to runaways, and it was little sought by runaways in need. Reasons cited for nonutilization of services included lack of publicity and the runaways' fear or suspicion of official agencies; and most cited inadequate funding as the principal "barrier" to successful service delivery. Other "barriers" listed were bureaucratic red tape and the illegal status of the runaway, the latter inhibiting application for services and their delivery. Finally, it was noted that few agencies are devoted exclusively to runaways, making a response to their distinct needs more difficult.

RUNAWAY CHARACTERISTICS

All respondent agencies were asked to describe the typical runaway youth served, on the basis of age, sex, race, socioeconomic status, legal status, drug abuse, geography, length of time on the run, and point of origin.

In terms of demographic variables an overwhelming majority of the respondents agreed upon the profile of the "typical" runaway seen, as follows:

age—approximately two-thirds agreed the typical client fell into the 13-15 age bracket;

sex—more than half indicated that female clients outnumbered males;

race—between four-fifths (regional conference sample) and more than nine-tenths (national network sample) agreed that the largest group of runaway clients was white;

socioeconomic status—a substantial majority held that the typical runaway came from a moderate income family.

Table 6.2 indicates the frequency and distribution of responses with respect to the typical runaway characteristics just discussed.

The consistency in respondents' views was maintained with respect to the legal status and alcohol and drug use of runaway clientele. Most (from two-thirds of the regional conferences sample to 97.5 percent of the national network sample) believed that their typical runaway client was not in trouble with the law, except for his runaway status. A significantly smaller proportion, but still a majority of those who expressed an opinion on the matter, said the typical runaway client was not engaged in drug or alcohol abuse. Responses to questions about these issues are indicated in the Table 6.3.

TABLE 6.2: Demographic Characteristics of "Typical" Runaway Client, as Seen by Three Social Agency Samples

	Regional Conferences 5 (N=133)	Local Sample % (N=45)	National Network % (N=45)
AGE			
12 or less	9%	—	—
13-15 yrs.	62%	69%	72%
16 +	29%	31%	28%
SEX			
Male	11%	23%	7%
Female	54%	57%	68%
Equal	35%	20%	25%
RACE			
White	81%	82%	95%
Native American	2%	6%	—
Chicano	1%	6%	2%
Black	3%	3%	2%
Other	13%	3%	—
SOCIOECONOMIC STATUS			
Low income	19%	25%	16%
Moderate	80%	67%	84%
High income	1%	8%	—

TABLE 6.3: Legal and Narcotic Involvement of "Typical" Runaway Client, as Seen by Three Social Agency Samples

	Regional Conferences % (N=133)	Local Sample % (N=45)	National Network % (N=45)
Legal Trouble			
Yes	23%	4%	2.5%
No	66%	71%	97.5%
Don't know	11%	24%	—
Drug or Alcohol Abuse			
Yes	38%	33%	30%
No	47%	42%	70%
Don't know	16%	24%	—

Respondents from all three agency samples also gave consistent responses to questions about the runaway clients' length of time on the run, and the kind of living situation from which they ran. Between 66 percent (local sample) and 100 percent (national network sample) held that the typical runaway client had been on the run for a month or less (see Table 6.4). A clear majority of the local and national network samples, and almost half (46 percent) of the regional conference sample held that runaways from "broken homes" were typical. However, a sizable minority in all three samples (between one-fifth and one-third) thought the typical runaway client came from a home with both parents present. (see Table 6.5).

TABLE 6.4: Length of Time on the Run by "Typical" Runaway Client, as Seen by Three Social Agency Samples

	Regional Conferences % (N=133)	Local Sample % (N=45)	National Network % (N=45)
One week	39%	22%	69%
One month	33%	44%	31%
One-six months	10%	9%	—
Don't know	18%	24%	—

TABLE 6.5: Home Situation of "Typical" Runaway Client, as Seen by Three Social Agency Samples

	Regional Conferences % (N=133)	Local Sample % (N=45)	National Network % (N-45)
Natural parents	30%	21%	32%
Broken homes	46%	59%	60%
Other	25%	21%	9%

This concludes our section on the agencies' perception of the "typical" runaway. Based on their individual experiences and clientele we noted a high degree of uniformity in responses pointing to a general profile of the "typical" runaway utilizing agency resources as: female, white, 13 to 15 years of age, from a moderate income level and broken home, on the run less than one month, with no serious drug or alcohol involvement, and no trouble with the law.

RUNAWAY TYPOLOGIES

In the survey instrument, six main runaway types were delineated, based on our findings from our runaway interviews, and then presented to the agencies in our three samples so they could rank them as to frequency seen.

The six types were described as follows:

1. *Independent* youth seeking autonomy or venturesome youth.
2. Youth with *psychological problems.*
3. Youth with *family problems,* including those neglected, abandoned, or abused.
4. *Delinquent* youth.
5. *Pushout* youth, forced to leave home as a result of economic conditions, pregnancy, and so on.
6. *In hiding* (youth on the run from law enforcement agents or pressures of school, and so on.)

As shown in the following table (6.6), the "youth with family problems, including neglected, abandoned, or abused children" received an overwhelming majority vote as the most frequently seen type: 59 percent of the conference sample, 61 percent of the local sample, and 89 percent of the national network sample.

TABLE 6.6: Prevalence of Runaway Types Seen, by Three Agency Samples

	Regional Conferences % (N=131)	Local Sample % (N=45)	National Network % (N=45)
Independent youth	12%	8%	9%
Psychological problems	11%	11%	—
Family problems	59%	61%	89%
Delinquent youth	6%	11%	—
Pushout	7%	5%	2%
In hiding	3%	5%	—
Other	2%	—	—

When these same six types were ranked by our three samples according to the seriousness of the problem they posed, there was some disagreement. However, in all three samples the youth with family problems was the most serious concern: 52 percent of the conference sample, 49 percent of the local sample, and 40 percent of the national network sample. The youth with psychological problems followed by order of seriousness. See table 6.7.

It would seem from our responses, which are based on agency workers' experiences with runaway youth, that the treatment priorities should be placed with the youth with family problems. He represents the most prevalent and most serious type. Clearly the programs aimed at this target group would receive majority support and endorsement from the agencies and achieve maximum impact. Another suggested component, according to our data, is psychological counseling, as psychological problems rank second on the "seriousness" scale.

TABLE 6.7: Perception of which Runaway Type Seen Presents the Most Serious Problems, by Three Social Agency Samples*

	Regional Conferences % (N=133)	Local Sample % (N=45)	National Network % (N=45)
Independent youth	3%	5%	9%
Psychological problems	36%	33%	40%
Family problems	52%	49%	40%
Delinquent	21%	36%	29%
Pushout	28%	22%	40%
In hiding	21%	29%	38%
Other	9%	—	—

*Because more than one type was rated as "most serious" or perhaps because respondents tried to convey the concept that the most serious problem was posed by a combination of the listed characteristics (for example, a youth with *both* family and psychological problems, who is also delinquent) the columns, when added, exceed 100 percent.

SERVICE DELIVERY

In our agency survey, we invited respondents to check, from a list of possible service components, those services featured in their individual programs. Our tabulations revealed that counseling and referral were among the most common services provided by the agencies with survival services, that is, food, clothing and shelter, next in order of prevalence.

Least common program components were financial assistance, education alternatives, and residential treatment. What a preliminary analysis of service suggests is that crisis intervention is the main thrust. The runaway problem is being dealt with on an emergency basis, and as a result little is done by the agencies to aid in the establishment of viable and alternative life styles by the runaways.

Table 6.8 gives a breakdown of service components provided by the agencies in our three samples.

TYPE OF AGENCY AND SOURCE OF CLIENT

The major source of runaway clients, as Table 6.9 indicates, varied among our three samples.

In the samples composed of agencies attending the three regional runaway conferences and those from the national network roster, we broke down the responses by type of program, namely private, semiprivate, and public or governmental.* The data indicated pronounced differences. Of the public agencies, almost 50 percent reported receiving runaway referrals from law enforcement agencies or the judicial system as opposed to the private or semiprivate sector in which clients come primarily as walk-ins or referrals from other sources. This finding would seem to corroborate reports that few runaways seek out public agencies for help. (See Table 6.10).

TABLE 6.8: Agency Service Categories, by Three Social Agency Samples

Service Category	*Regional Conferences % (N=89)	Local Sample % (N=45)	National Network % (N=45)
Shelter	64%	38%	93%
Food	65%	40%	89%
Financial aid	43%	29%	36%
Individual counseling	73%	49%	89%
Group counseling	65%	49%	89%
Family counseling	71%	69%	96%
Legal counseling	57%	49%	73%
Vocational counseling	44%	40%	67%
Family planning	37%	42%	60%
Drug/alcohol counseling	62%	58%	82%
Hotline/switchboard	38%	33%	71%
Referral	70%	33%	71%
Residential treatment	—	33%	47%
Educational alternative	—	—	2%
Medical assistance	—	42%	56%
Drop-in facility	48%	42%	69%
Placement assistance	—	56%	84%
Other	21%	6%	36%

*This question was added after the conference at Monterey, hence the smaller number of responses. Again, because of multiple answers by respondents, totals exceed 100 percent.

TABLE 6.9: Major Source of Runaway Clientele, by Three Social Agency Samples*

	Regional Conferences % (N=133)	Local Sample % (N=45)	National Network % (N=45)
Walk-in	34%	27%	51%
Law enforcement	39%	22%	18%
Social service	20%	17%	29%
Other	20%	13%	24%

*Multiple answers given, hence totals exceed 100 percent.

TABLE 6.10: Source of Clients, by Type of Agency
in Regional Conference Sample

	Private % (N=56)	Semi-Private % (N=48)	Public % (N=68)
Walk-in	41%	25%	15%
Law enforcement	16%	19%	49%
Social services	13%	23%	12%
Other	29%	21%	16%
Don't know	2%	13%	9%

INFLUENCE OF THE "EXPERTS" ON RUNAWAY POLICY

The participants in the three regional conferences on the runaway problem—professional social workers, agency personnel, and law enforcement officials—are regarded as the "experts" in the field. Indeed, this is why they were invited to the conferences by the sponsoring federal agencies. Their "expertise" was to be tapped for the formulation of policies and programs, which they, in the main, would implement. In addition to serving as counselors to the officially empowered makers of policy, these experts also appeared in the role of advocates for the runaways. Patently, the runaways, even if they were inclined to speak for themselves, lack the status, organization, and power to exert any significant influence on the political processes that shape policy. Their parents also do not constitute a recognizable pressure group, and are, moreover, either among the powerless layers of society, or are so inhibited by guilt or a sense of their own inadequacy in relation to their runaway children that they could serve but poorly as their advocates. As a consequence, this vacuum is filled by the "experts" in the sociopolitical arena.

On both these counts, as counselors and advocates, the "experts," who deal directly with the runaway problem, also become a "pressure group" to influence policy. We have already described their perceptions of the runaway problem; now we examine their capacities and activities to influence and implement policy.

The regional conferences had been designed to assist HEW in developing guidelines, programs, and strategies for the federal role in meeting the runaway problem. However, conferences can produce effects beyond those specifically intended by their designers. Among other things, a conference can be a learning experience for its participants. This is especially true when the conference deals

*Examples of the three types are: Private—runaway houses, free clinics, and so on; Semi-Private—YMCA, Red Cross, Traveler's Aid, other large private agencies; Public or Government—Welfare, Probation, and Courts. (Refers to asterisk on p. 109)

with a highly controversial subject, or perhaps a newly emerging problem, for which standard solutions do not apply and in relation to which the participants have varying levels of experience and varying orientations.

Six months after the three conferences, each participant was asked about his/her subsequent "pressure group" activities in relation to the runaway problem to test two general hypotheses: (1) One potential effect of the conferences could be to maximize a "knowledge transfer" function, with payoffs in an increase in activity, and (2) not all attendants profited equally or engaged in the same amount of post-conference activity. Here one might expect that local influence and the extent of the local power base would decisively affect subsequent levels of contacts and activities.

Methods

To investigate these matters a followup questionnaire was mailed to 133 conference participants. In all, 97 subjects or about 74 percent of the sample returned this questionnaire. Responses to this questionnaire supplied the data for this segment of our study.

Findings

Looking at those who returned our questionnaire, it is apparent that a wide variety of persons concerned with the runaway problem were brought together at the conferences—ranging from public agency people to alternative service people and including various experts in the field as well as local community leaders.

One important consideration in assessing the local effect of the conferences involves the relative influence of the individual participant and the influence of his or her agency locally. The more influential he or she is, and the more influential the agency or project represented, presumably the more effective they should be in applying their gained knowledge, and the more active they should be on their return. To measure personal influence, respondents were asked, "As an interested party who is involved with runaways—how would you describe your position vis a vis formation of runaway policy and progress in *your community?*" Their responses are tabulated below (table 6.11).

Just about one-third of the sample (32 percent) reported having *primary responsibility* or a great deal of influence, with all others indicating lesser amounts of personal influence.

When asked to evaluate the relative influence of their program or agency in their respective communities, as shown in Table 6.12, over 40 percent reported a *great deal of influence* locally.

TABLE 6.11: Personal Influence on Runaway Policy Locally, as Seen by Regional Conference Sample

Little or no influence	6%
Some input	40%
Minor responsibility	21%
Primary responsibility	32%
Total	100%

TABLE 6.12: Respondent's Agency or Program Influence on Runaway Policy Locally, as Seen by Regional Conference Sample

Little or none	5%
Very little	6%
Some influence	45%
Great deal of influence	43%
Total	100%

In summary, it would seem that the bulk of the sample were middle-management people with slight or limited personal influence who represent organizations with either *moderate* or *great* degrees of influence locally in matters concerning runaway policy.

Significantly, when asked to name those organizations or agencies that play the *most important* roles locally, a majority of the respondents mentioned the local law enforcement or criminal justice agencies, such as the courts or probation departments. Some 90 mentions of this sort were made with the next most popular grouping being the various public social service agencies with some 75 mentions, and finally 50 references were made to private agencies of various sorts.

This preponderance of "criminal justice" agencies mentioned as the "most influential" local organizations seems to corroborate the felt need among conference attendants for "decriminalization" of this runaway phenomenon.

POSTCONFERENCE ACTIVITIES

One measure used to evaluate changes in local activity and involvement following attendance at these conferences was a series of queries about personal contacts stemming directly from attending each conference. Four specific areas of contact were covered: (1) legislative, (2) immediate agency superiors, (3) heads of other agencies, and (4) key community leaders, plus one miscellaneous unspecified others category.

As seen in Table 6.13 responses ranged from a high of 71 percent reporting contact with *other agency* heads, to 66 percent having contact with their own superiors and 50 percent contacting key community leaders, followed by about 30 percent having contact with legislators or others. This would seem to indicate at least a moderate range of increased activity resulting from the conferences and tends to corroborate the hypothesis concerning learning effects of such conferences leading to new activities.

At the same time, in response to another measure of activity (see table 6.14), 50 percent of the sample reported developing "new relations with other programs" and 41 percent reported initiating "meetings." At the other extreme, at least 15 to 16 percent of the sample reported developing "new programs" or "redesigning or changing old programs" as a result of attending the conferences. Clearly again, this seems to demonstrate that some measure of increased activity and interest derived from the conferences.

TABLE 6.13: Personal Contact Resulting from Regional Runaway Conference as Reported by Conference Sample

Legislators	30%
Immediate superiors	66%
Other agency heads	71%
Key community leaders	51%
Others	31%

TABLE 6.14: Additional Activities Resulting from Regional Runaway Conference as Reported by Conference Sample (N=97)

Submitted reports with recommendation	26%
Initiated meetings	41%
Developed new programs	17%
Submitted new proposals	25%
Developed new relations with other agencies	51%
Redesigned or changed program	17%
Other	16%

Consistent with our second hypothesis, these increased levels of local contacts and runaway-related activities did not seem to be equally distributed throughout the sample. For example, when respondents are separated on the basis of their self-reported levels of influence, as shown in Table 6.15, it can be seen the most influential are more likely to report contact with legislators. Over 57 percent of those individuals reporting primary responsibility for runaway policy personally in their respective locales, also report contact with legislators as a direct result of attending these conferences. This compares to only 39 percent of the total sample reporting such legislative contacts.

A striking correlation could also be noted between increased levels of other activities resulting from the conference and the degree of influence possessed by the respondent's agency, as can be seen in Table 6.16.

TABLE 6.15: Contact with Legislators, by Degree of Personal Influence, as Reported by Regional Conference Sample

| Legislative Contact | Degree of Influence | | | |
	Little* % (N=31)	Minor % (N=21)	Primary % (N=26)	Total % (N=78)**
Yes	39%	14%	58%	39%
No	61%	86%	42%	62%
Total	100%	100%	100%	100%

*Those reporting "little or no influence" are combined with the "some input" category to form the "little" influence category.
**Nineteen subjects were excluded due to incomplete responses to these questions.

TABLE 6.16: New Runaway Program Efforts, by Degree of Agency Influence, as Reported by Regional Conference Sample

| Type of Activity | Agency Influence | | | |
	Little % (N=45)	Some % (N=21)	Much % (N=31)	Total % (N=47)
Submitted reports	9%	25%	33%	27%
Initiated meetings	18%	34%	52%	40%
Developed new programs	–	11%	26%	17%
Submitted new proposals	18%	17%	33%	23%
Developed new relations	18%	53%	57%	51%
Redesigned or changed program	9%	14%	24%	18%
Implemented anything	9%	11%	26%	18%

CONCLUSIONS

In summary, samples representing local agencies in San Francisco and Los Angeles, the national network of agencies serving runaways, and a group of agencies invited to attend three regional conferences on the runaway phenomenon, gave strikingly similar responses to a wide range of questions about runaways and the services they receive. Although the three samples were drawn at different times within a two-year period, all characterized their "typical" runaway client as: female, aged 13-15, white, from a moderate-income family. Furthermore, she was characterized as not having a serious drug or alcohol problem and as being on the run from a broken home, usually less than one month, when first seen by the agencies. The majority of the agencies perceived the major problems of the runaway in terms of survival needs and consequently stressed program components, such as food, short-term shelter, counseling, and referral services to meet these needs. A preliminary analysis suggests that the thrust of agency services is toward treatment of the runaway as a transitory problem, in that service appears to be basically of a temporary nature. Perhaps future research might be directed at examining alternative programs offering such things as continuing education and job training as a means of dealing with the older population of runaway youth.

Our follow-up study of the conference participants has presented some preliminary evidence, to the effect that the conferences stimulated local efforts to deal with the runaway problem by (a) increasing coordination between agencies, (b) introducing new programs, purposes, and (c) changing and revising current programs. In addition, the extent of these local efforts was found to be related to the amount of influence wielded by the participants as measured by self-reports—with the more influential respondents indicating more such activities and contacts.

This extra dividend or result of the fact-finding conferences and the clues as to how to achieve even more effectiveness or impact seem worthy of further investigation and more complete study than was possible in this project. One major suggestion might be that conference attendants should be selected from "influentials" rather than from middle management—particularly if the "experts" or "influentials" might be expected to develop a *pressure group* or to implement new actions in behalf of runaways.

It would also seem that should further study replicate these findings, designers of future conferences might well profit from studying these effects and allowing for such consequences in their planning process.

CHAPTER 7

The Underground Life: How They Survive

The runaway who does not seek the services of social agencies traverses a labyrinthine jungle which for many becomes like the rites of passage on their way to adulthood. Those who leave home for extended periods almost immediately face the basic problem of survival, and to survive means to fulfill the most elementary needs of food, shelter, and travel on a daily basis. Burdened with the status of an "illegal alien," without protection and without rights, the runaway is often obliged to turn to deviant behavior in order to weave his way through the intricate passages and blind alleys of the urban maze. Their choice of behavior reveals a pattern based on the vocabulatory motives that spells out the real consequences of how *they* view their situation.

Work, illegal according to the child labor laws, is no longer an alternative for the runaway who cannot pass for the legal age. So now the child who would be found in the coal mines of West Virginia in an earlier period, waits for a pick-up on the "Meat Line" on the Sunset Boulevards throughout the country. Is it not the common irony that the reforms of one generation create the moral issues for the generations that follow?

Many runaways "pass" their test during the "rites" on the road toward adulthood and leave behind that experience as they pass on to greater challenges. They enter permanent occupations, professions, or higher education and a transformation of their social roles. For others the "rites of passage" is life itself, it is what life is all about, and the artifices acquired during the runaway episode are part of a continuum of behavior patterns followed in adulthood.

Once committed to detention the minor is apt to follow a self-fulfilling prophecy and become a "habitual" delinquent and a graduate criminal. Running away has often been defined in research studies as a part of delinquent syndromes and criminal behavior (Foster 1962). Such studies may suffer from a statistical bias, however, since the research is generally conducted with institutionalized children. A large percentage of runaways are never captured, melting into the countless faces in the city streets until they are of legal age or they return home.

The purpose of this chapter is to analyze those runaways who really never make extended use of the social agencies available to them. These runaways are the majority by far, accounting for more than 70 percent of all runaways in this study. But the different life-styles adopted by each reflect the differences in their motives for leaving home and their self-images. Of course, behavior has a certain fluidity that defies prediction, yet the presence of definable archetypes that represent different patterns of behavior is also undeniable. Ranging from degrees of dependency to degrees of independence outlined in the Typology section, it is reasonable to suppose that the consequences of these motives will also reflect different choices on how to survive on the run. But in one sense all runaways are in the general category of the "illegal alien," and their choices are structurally limited. Delinquent and deviant behavior necessarily runs high among all those who cannot legally work for a living.

An astoundingly high percentage of all runaways admitted to dealing drugs or stealing in order to meet their survival needs at some time during the run. Victims were the most likely to steal for their source of food. A few runaways reported to us quite candidly how they operated as a team, shop lifting in supermarkets and large department stores. Some operations were based on a simple method of boosting while the partner distracted store clerks. Others were sophisticated con games that required at least one who could lay down a good rap. It could be done alone or in teams and involved boosting expensive items from a large department store and returning them to the complaint window to demand a refund.

The exiles were most prone to deal drugs according to our typological breakdown of the data, 92 percent of them supporting themselves by occasionally selling on the streets or in the schools. The usual system entailed acquiring prescriptions from willing doctors, filling them at a local pharmacy, and selling them at a profit at local schools where they mixed easily with the population. In Venice we heard reports of one doctor who prescribed a morphine-based drug known as Dilotta, given ordinarily to terminal cancer patients. The drug is more addictive than heroin since it comes pure from the pharmaceutical company, and addicts soon develop a habit that must be satisfied frequently. Runaways barely into adolescence showed great familiarity with the drug culture and seemed to have no trouble melting into its loose and transient fraternity.

Another significant minority were being kept by someone or had gone into prostitution. The fugitive types were most likely to find themselves in such arrangements. "Being kept" usually meant a place to sleep in exchange for sexual favors, many of which were exacted by homosexuals or older men. The informal sexual contract often began by making a casual pick-up on the strip in Hollywood or on Market Street in San Francisco or on Telegraph Avenue in Berkeley where certain corners are designated as the "Meat Rack." Almost every major city has some such location where the young runaway is apt to make a contact. Another system frequently used by young females was to develop a "rap" after being picked up hitchhiking. Frequently this was nothing more than using their feminine roles on a "captive" audience to panhandle. Others used it as a means to pick up a "John" to sell sexual services.

However, some runaways were befriended by older persons who "took them in," offering shelter and food out of a concern and interest in these youngsters. Transient friendship patterns were found during hitchhiking. Other youngsters were "being kept" by some relatives or former friends' relatives.

The independently inclined runaways were less apt to steal, deal drugs, or get caught in some sexual trap out of necessity. The immigrants, for instance, were more likely to have their own money while on the run than the more dependent victims, refugees, or exiles. It was evident from our interviews that the immigrant runaways had greater experience at "making it" on the streets and were more likely to be competent runaways. They were more knowledgeable about the services that were available to runaways and how to get them. They also seemed to know their way around the counterculture centers where they could get help without answering any questions. It also appeared that it was the white youth who knew best the free services available, such as the free clinic, the crash pads, and free food outlets.

As was indicated in our examination of "seen" and "unseen" runaways (Chapter 1), most runaways did not turn to agencies for help either because they did not know about them or because they distrusted them. We now present thumbnail sketches of runaways trying to "make it" on their own.

PROFILES ON SIX TYPES OF RUNAWAYS

The following "characters" are drawn from the interviews in each of the six motive types. These are representative cases selected from each type. Pseudonyms are used, but the "cast" is real; their stories are personal, but not unique. The runaways' experiences are commonplace for the youth who seek a way to "make it" on the streets.

The Victim

Melissa was 15 at the time we interviewed her. She had been on the road six months since she left Seattle, Washington, in the middle of the school year. She hitchhiked to San Franisco where her sister lives, but the trip down from Seattle reinforced her self-image of the victimized youth. She was raped by an older man on her second night out and was molested several times afterwards before she reached her sister's home. Among the runaways, 85 percent reported sexual abuse while hitchhiking. The high incidence of sexual offenses against them is coincidental with the fact that the majority in the victim typology are female and come from homes where physical abuse and incest run high in the vocabulary of motives for leaving home. Melissa came from such a home.

Her fears of sexual abuse by men dominated her adolescent years. She reported being raped by her father when she was 14, and a few days before she went "on the run" he beat her after she came home late one night. She related how he ripped her clothes in a violent binge, put his finger inside her vagina, and accused her of being a "slut and a whore."

Melissa found that life at her sister's home was not much better. The constant feuds in which she was embroiled convinced her she would do just as well on the streets. Melissa's behavior was typical of the victim runaways who were much more prone to seek aid from their friends and relatives than the immigrants. Sixty-two percent of the victims sought such help, as opposed to 50 percent of the emancipated who were more inclined to seek independent sources of income. But Melissa found that her early maturity made it easier to find a job in a restaurant in contrast to most juveniles of her typology. Only 23 percent of the victims worked during the run; a majority panhandled to get by. Melissa had tried her hand at begging for a few days before she found a job, but discovered that hustlers and pimps were constantly propositioning her to enter prostitution. Melissa avoided close associations, even with her own peer group; her experience on the run was that other runaways were just as likely to rip her off as were the street hustlers and older men. Eighty-one percent of the victim types believed that runaways rip off others. Very high percentages of victims dealt in drugs (83 percent) or engaged in petty theft (76 percent). Victims who used social agencies turned most often to the church, the free clinic, and the shelter house.

Burdened with the highest degree of dependency, the victim runaways seemed much more likely candidates to turn to delinquent or deviant behavior as a means of surviving than the immigrants who were already beginning to seek out a way to melt inconspicuously into society. Victims had a difficult time remaining free; more than 60 percent were captured by the police.

The Exile

At 16 Kelli was thrown out of the house by her mother who could not cope with Kelli's unmanageable behavior. She tried living with her father for a while, but found the responsibility of having to care for an alcoholic too great a burden and left to try and make it on her own. She continued going to school in the same area as her family, but didn't see much of them. She lived in various roommate arrangements for the next two years, but several times attempted to return to her father's or grandparents' home when her economic resources dried up. Like Melissa, Kelli came from a working-class family. Her principal source of income was selling drugs, which was consistent with her type; an astounding 92 percent of exiles dealt drugs.

Kelli's system was neatly organized and indicated the degree to which she was socialized into the drug culture. Her system entailed sexual favors for doctors in exchange for prescriptions, which she filled and sold to connections in the neighborhood and at the high school. Kelli incidentally confessed to being sexually indifferent to men in general; it was simply a business negotiation. As a consequence of her drug dealing she found it unnecessary to steal, which was again consistent with her type; only 15 percent of the exiles resorted to theft. But 28 percent said that they were "kept" by someone during their experience on the road.

The greatest "hassles" for Kelli and the exiles came from hustlers, police, and people who picked them up while hitchhiking. A majority of the exiles reported trouble with the police, mostly for delinquent behavior. Eighty percent of the exiles reported going to friends and relatives during their runaway episode. Twenty percent worked, and nearly three-quarters said they had panhandled during the run. The majority of the exiles were also like Kelli in that they were female and had not been captured up to the time that we interviewed them.

The Rebel

Bobby ran the gambit of hassles at home: drunken fights between his parents, arguments over his right to do the things he wanted to do, and humiliating scenes in front of his friends. He left— but he regrets it. Bobby has a younger brother he hopes to return for some day. He is not sure he will stay, but he hopes he can work it out. If not, he's going to take his younger brother and split for the wild yonder, never to return.

Bobby did a lot of panhandling (only one-third of his typology did the same) and counterculture bum hopping that included community living and free food handouts. Bobby worked in a communally run fruit and vegetable storefront in Venice where his work was exchanged for free food and floor space to sleep on. Two-thirds of the rebels found a regular free food source similar to Bobby's. On the side he dealt drugs, selling a lid of marijuana several times a month to make ends meet. More than two-thirds of the rebels dealt in drugs.

Rebels found their greatest hassles with hustlers, older men, and other runaways. Bobby said dope dealers were the only ones ever to give him trouble, but of course there was also the ever-present fear of a police arrest.

A large percentage of the rebels (80 percent) said they had problems with homosexuals or, in the case of females, reported sexual molestation while hitchhiking. Only 17 percent reported that they were kept by anyone in exchange for sexual or other favors.

Rebels are most likely to be detained and returned to their homes, where the parent-child "hassles" continue.

The Fugitive

The fugitives are in a transitional category. They have yet to sever their dependent ties to the family, but on the other hand see themselves as fugitives on the run from something unpleasant. Angela's case was unique in the general run of fugitive types. She was stopped by police while hitchhiking in Palo Alto on her way home from school. As the daughter of a well-known political activist, Angela was known to the police. They asked to look through her purse; she refused to allow them, whereupon they accused her of carrying a gun. Angela stuck by what she considered her right not to be searched without legal cause, and the police released her. Upon arriving home, she was told by her mother that the police were coming to the house at five o'clock to talk to her. The mother, fearing they might arrest Angela, suggested that she leave for a while. Angela agreed and went to her father's house and later to her aunt's. When the police came to the house and were told by the mother that Angela had left, they threatened to have her classified as a runaway.

A week later the mother entered the hospital, the police came to the house and took Angela's brother and sister to juvenile hall on grounds of negligence. When Angela learned of this she fled to San Francisco in order to avoid incarceration. Angela believed that the harassment of her family by the police was due to the political activity in which her mother was involved.

Her case was similar to that of most fugitives in that she fled from a perceived threat of institutional incarceration, but she differed in that she had her mother's backing. During the run on the road the fugitives said they had less trouble with sexual molestation and more problems with being turned in to the police. The majority of the fugitive kids were captured.

The Refugee

Mike and his younger brother ran from a Baptist home for children where they frequently suffered corporal punishment. They first went home, but following a declaration by their parents that they would be sent back to the "school," Mike and his brother took to the road. Mike's parents were fundamentalists in their religious beliefs and expected their children to observe the Biblical law as a daily routine. Mike had no sense of what his parents felt for him or his brother; he only knew that the rules were many and the concessions to convention few. Mike rebelled against the restrictions of the religious school like most refugee runaways who went on the run either from an institution or a foster home.

The majority of refugee runaways had trouble with the law, and 34 percent of them said that these troubles are what led them to run away in the first place. Delinquent patterns were high for those who already had been committed for either a status offense or for some delinquent behavior.

Only 5 percent of the refugees worked to support themselves while 85 percent dealt in drugs. For Mike smoking cigarettes was a delinquent adventure which indicated he had not yet been socialized into the drug culture. Free food was only a small portion of the refugee's regular source of food (about one-third); only 21 percent panhandled. Mike supported himself by panhandling; he reported making as much as $30 or $40 a day. Mike's biggest hassles on the road came from hustlers and older men, which was consistent with what most other refugees reported. Their problems stemmed from people turning them in to the police. A higher percentage of refugees than of ther other types reported being kept by someone either in exchange for sexual favors or through some other arrangement. A little more than one-third told of such informal contracts.

The Immigrant

The young immigrant runaway has made his break from the family bonds. The rites of passage for the immigrant are an adventure to reach out for independence. David was one of the runaways we interviewed who indicated his leaving home had more to do with his desire to pursue a career than problems with his parents. Hassles at home were commonplace, but David thought of himself as a musician and living at home wasn't developing his skills or making the necessary contacts with other musicians to get into a rock group. He also didn't like living in the cold winters of Minnesota and decided to leave for California after he saved $300. The immigrant runaways distinguished themselves from all other runaways in the marked habit of planning their run in advance; 71 percent of the immigrants had their own money before they left home.

The immigrants seemed to move with greater ease and more experience. They knew where to look for services they wanted. David reported that he survived mostly on free food handouts and food stamps, which were easily obtainable in California.

Most of the immigrants were able to elude capture and remained free to make their own roles of precocious adulthood.

THE WAY IT WAS

Among some of the runaways we interviewed, especially the older "chronic" runaways, we encountered memories or second-hand stories of the halcyon days of the counterculture, when a variety of informal or "underground" services were available to youth on the run. Those days are gone, but it is not simply an indulgence in vicarious nostalgia to report what we learned about them from interviews with our subjects and from other sources as well. Something useful about serving runaways may be gleaned from the countercultural institutions that proliferated in the 1960s.

The Diggers, for example, are now a folk legend. In collaboration with other groups in San Francisco's Haight-Ashbury district, the "hippie" mecca in the late 1960s, the Diggers established an autonomous network of social services to provide free food and lodging, free music, free clothing, free LSD and marijuana, a free medical clinic—and free love. The Diggers seemed to have surmounted the problem of other agencies in making their presence known to youthful nomads. Their slogans—"Need a place to crash? You've got it!" and "Do Free"—caught on. Their free crash pads were jammed every night—while a more conventional shelter house nearby was virtually empty. Their daily free food offerings at 4 p.m. in Golden Gate Park attracted a vast clientele. There was no red tape, no intake process to secure these services. The Diggers were then part of a larger sense of community that typified the Haight-Ashbury district in that age of "love-ins" and "flower children." They met survival needs—but they also offered much more. Their young clients did not fear being turned into the police, or being pressured to return to their parents.

The Communication Company, an informal ideological organ of the Diggers, managed to combine its publication services to the Haight-Ashbury community with other services that met specific needs of runaways (as well as older itinerant youth). The Communication Company offered free printing and distribution of handbills and leaflets to the youth of the Haight-Ashbury streets. The leaflets were usually announcements of coming events, warnings about bad drugs, and sometimes included highly literate political agitation urging youths to form "revolutionary gangs." The facilities were provided by a writer with a predilection for young boys—"puppies" as he called them. This 33-year-old man had rented an apartment in the Haight-Ashbury district with the proceeds from a successful novel. Youths who joined the Communication Company could learn printing and writing skills. They were housed and fed and were expected to distribute handbills on the streets after each printing. As the Haight-Ashbury turned sour the founder of the Communication Company ran out of money. In the words of its founder, this runaway service agency "drowned in catshit and dirty dishes."

The underground press was another counterculture development that provided sustenance and support for runaways. Organized along traditional private enterprise lines, the weekly underground papers needed cheap labor for production and news vendors for distribution. Many of such "employee," were recruited from the transient youth population. Apprenticeships were available to those who sought entry into this area of journalism, provided they were willing to work for practically nothing. Many runaways met their minimum needs by hawking underground newspapers on the sidewalks of San Francisco, Berkeley, and Los Angeles.

Some underground newspapers tried to provide sleeping facilities and even occasional meals to the runaways (and others) whose labor went into the enterprise. One Los Angeles publication allowed kids who worked there to sleep in its office. This paper had the rule that no one could sleep in the office but this was subject to the anarchistic prescription that no one was allowed to enforce any of the rules.

Other, less savory ventures also cropped up and "served" runaway youth. The Charles Manson family is a notorious example. But the "family"—an informal collective in which housing and food were shared—was not an uncommon phenomenon in less destructive guises. These families were also part of the informal social network to which runaways could sometimes turn for help.

The youth counterculture was succeeded and to some extent replaced by a variety of religious sects, some of them very deviant by traditional standards. The Jesus Freaks and the Children of God adhere to chiliastic versions of Christian theology, but the Hare Krishna Movement, the Divine Light Mission, and the followers of Reverend Sun Moon have adopted Far Eastern spiritual approaches to make a general appeal to young people. It is unclear just how many runaway youths may have joined these religious faiths, but recurrent stories of irate parents who have been refused access to their children indicate that these monastic innovations have absorbed some members of the runaway population.

Taking the Hare Krishnas as an example, we see that initiates undergo a period of seclusion from their former selves and may be sent to a region far away from their homes. Their heads are shaved, they are given a new name, and are then sent out to reach new converts or put to work in the organization's incense factory or elsewhere. Hare Krishna thus perpetuates the counterculture industry tradition, using converts to sell literature or beg alms on the streets or to manufacture the products that are sold by sect members.

All these sects have mobilized the desires of youth to change the world into religious channels. Sun Moon claims that his worshippers will one day control the world. The Children of God have preserved some of the youth counterculture's militancy and antagonism toward the established political order. In general, these religious groups have a mission of salvation and offer ascetic programs that are neither as exploitative nor as damaging as some of the other nonmandated groups.

It is beyond our purview to examine what happened to the counterculture, to its institutions and publications, or to analyze why it happened. Nor did we undertake a serious examination or analysis of religious sects that attract—and serve—some runaways.

It seemed to us, however, that there should be an awareness of such alternatives among those responsible for public policy with respect to runaways. In one sense these alternatives may be seen as a reproach to the more conventional agencies and the gap that exists between them and their prospective clients. In another sense, these alternatives seem to be related to the "illegal alien" status of runaways, which prompts runaways to seek succor from institutions that are beyond the conventional pale, and hence are not associated with the legal system. Finally, these nonconformist agencies do exert an attraction to a segment of runaway youth, and it might well be worthwhile to investigate the elements that make up this attraction. This suggests an area for further inquiry.

CHAPTER 8

Runaway Utilization
of Social Services

As pointed out in Chapter 3, service and resource utilization by the sample of runaways was quite limited. To review briefly, overall only about 27 percent had used any source of services, with the highest rates of observed use involving counterculture sources as contrasted with the public agencies and programs.

In part, this avoidance of service sources on the part of runaways was due to a widespread lack of knowledge about existing facilities. At the same time a high degree of mistrust and/or fear of detainment was associated with the avoidance of many public sources of assistance.

In this section we shall go a step further and examine how different sources of services are utilized by different types of runaways. The most common users and least common users of each of 17 different service sources will be described in the following section along with some discussion of these findings.

FREE CLINICS

Employing the typology developed in this study and beginning with the free clinic, with its informality and variety of services and its close identification with the counterculture, we see in Table 8.1 that the exiles and the immigrants make the greatest use of free clinics—some 42 and 46 percent respectively. Rebels and refugees make the least use of these agencies—13 percent and 12 percent.

To the extent that free clinics are located near middle-class areas and are known best to the middle-class runaway, we would expect our sample of refugees to make less use of these facilities since they tend to be working-class in background (including welfare cases). In addition, it should be noted that refugees also reported less knowledge of such facilities, which may account for their less extensive use of free clinics. There is also some evidence suggesting that exiles are very street-wise individuals who rely on a wide variety of resources including coping by means of work, panhandling, or selling dope to survive. As we shall see in following sections, rebels, as a group, tend to be underrepresented at all the various sources of runaway services.

POLICE DEPARTMENTS

Contacts with local police departments were most common among exiles (32 percent) and fugitives (35 percent)—the latter presumably because of their greater involvement with criminal activity. Police contact was reportedly least common for victims (10 percent) and immigrants (10 percent), with the latter group being older runaways with relatively little criminal involvement in their backgrounds. Of course, the illegal status of the runaway in general probably precludes greater use of these facilities as it does with other law enforcement agencies such as probation departments. In any case, about half the sample, regardless of type, reported no knowledge of police services.

PROBATION DEPARTMENTS

Conversely, victims displayed the highest frequency (17 percent) of contact with probation agencies, not unexpectedly, in view of the high incidence of child abuse and neglect in their family setting. Also predictably, the fugitives, or delinquent runaways, placed second (10 percent) in the rate of contact with probation. The remaining types all displayed lower rates of contact of this kind. Roughly two-thirds of the runaways, regardless of type, reported not knowing of runaway services offered by the probation department.

SHELTER HOUSES

These private sources dealing in short-term housing and other survival services were most employed by victims (31 percent) and fugitives (30 percent). Both groups would seem to need this type of service most. Exiles and rebels use these facilities least—only 11 and 9 percent respectively.

LEGAL AID SERVICES

Rates of contact with such programs tended to be so low overall—some 8 percent—that little variation was noted among types. What little variation existed tended to suggest that victims and immigrants made slightly more use of such services than did the other runaway types. Victims became involved with legal aid perhaps because of foster home placement, adoption, and the like. More research is needed to clarify the nature of these relationships. Roughly three-fourths of all runaway types reported no knowledge of legal aid services.

CRASH PADS

Moving on to the use of crash pads or those informal, countercul-ture facilities featuring short-term survival services, we see in Table 8.1 that the immigrant type displays the highest use of crash pads (39 percent), while at the other extreme, rebels report the least use of this type of facility—only 6 percent. All other types fall somewhere between these two extremes. Immigrants reported having the most knowledge about such facilities, so presumably it is not surprising they should use them most. Rebels conversely had the highest rate of ignorance about the existence of crash pads and hence the lowest rate of usage.

HOSPITALS

Exiles were most prone to use public hospital facilites; one-third of them did so. The exile, having little fear of returning home, presumably would feel most free to use such public facilties, as compared to groups like the refugees who are fleeing foster homes or the like and who fear being caught. In addition, the exiles, as a type, displayed the least degree of collective ignorance about public hospitals while refugees displayed one of the highest rates—some 79 percent.

FREE FOOD PROJECTS

The use of private free food outlets is most prevalent among the exiles—with nearly half reporting such contact while on the run. At the other extreme, relatively few rebels (9 percent) or refugees (2 percent) use such programs, which is due in part to less knowledge and access to such programs. Two other groups, immigrants (34 percent) and fugitives (37 percent), also reported using these projects extensively, but less so than the exiles. Exiles also were most knowledgeable about these projects, again demonstrating their greater street wisdom, with refugees reporting the least knowledge.

TRAVELER'S AID

The traditional source of help for the traveler in trouble is Traveler's Aid, with offices at all the larger centers of travel. Use of these facilities is relatively low among runaways in general. Lack of knowledge concerning these services is widespread among runaways. For such a large and seemingly well-established program, this amount of collective ignorance is surprising. Among those who do use these services, exiles tend to be the main users (26 percent), while the other groups, particularly victims, who need different kinds of help than those offered by Traveler's Aid, use it rarely.

This low rate of utilization is accompanied by a correspondingly high rate of ignorance—some 78 percent overall report not knowing of Traveler's Aid services.

CHURCH PROGRAMS

Utilization of church services by runaways was noticeably greatest among victims (31 percent) and least pronounced for the immigrants (15 percent). One of the highest use figures—26 percent—was recorded for exiles, who also displayed the least ignorance of church services, with only some 39 percent reporting no knowledge of church programs for runaways.

THE NATIONAL RUNAWAY SWITCHBOARD

The least used and least known resource noted in this study was the National Runaway Switchboard or Hotline, as it is sometimes called. Only 2 percent of the sample reported using it and nearly two-thirds stated they had no knowledge of its existence. With so few reporting any use, there could be no appreciable variation from type to type. All groups seemed nearly equally ignorant of this resource.

LOCAL SWITCHBOARDS

The local switchboards are appreciably better known than is the national Hotline. They are also used much more extensively, with the immigrants tending to be the most common users (36 percent) and the refugees the least common users (5 percent). This parallels almost exactly their respective degrees of knowledge of the facility. Some 86 percent of the refugees reported no knowledge such local switchboards, as compared to 47 percent of the immigrants. It may be reasonably assumed that the greater use of local switchboards, as opposed to the national Hotline, is related to the tendency of most runaways to stay fairly close to home.

SOCIAL WORKERS

Social workers as possible sources of help are not utilized extensively by the runaway population. Only refugees displayed an appreciable rate of usage (36 percent), probably because of their status as people without families, many of whom are running from institutions or foster homes. Not surprisingly, refugees also recorded the least ignorance of these sorts of services—only 33 percent had no knowledge of these efforts.

FOOD STAMPS

The use of the Food Stamp program was also not widespread. It is noteworthy that rebels had the least contact—none reported any use of food stamps. At the other extreme, 16 percent of the fugitives reported some use of these resources. There was relatively little variation in the proportions who knew nothing of this program—some 80 to 85 percent generally.

WELFARE

Welfare programs were also rarely used. Lack of knowledge did seem to account for some of the rather low rates of usage noted overall—some 4 percent of the sample indicated they used some welfare services. Rates of use by the various types of runaways ranged from 0 to 7 percent, with no one group displaying any great degree of use. (Of the eight runaways who reported some use of welfare services, only four considered the contact helpful.)

DROP-IN CENTERS

The reader will note in Table 8.2 that knowledge of such counter-culture or informal facilities is rather limited, with nearly three-fourths of the sample reporting no knowledge of "drop-in centers." Nevertheless, usage rates varied from 7 to 20 percent, with victims reporting the lowest degree of use and immigrants the highest rate. Victims displayed the most ignorance in this area—some 82 percent had no knowledge of such programs.

DRUG-ABUSE CLINICS

The lack of use of drug clinics does not seem to stem primarily from a lack of knowledge that they exist. Fugitives clearly display the highest rate of use (16 percent), and this perhaps suggests one aspect of their difficulties with the law. None of the others displayed this high a rate of contact. Fugitives also displayed the least ignorance concerning these facilities—only 32 percent had no knowledge of such services.

SUMMARY AND DISCUSSION

In summary, then, it should be noted that while only a minority of runaways used the various services available, certain runaway types tend to be found disproportionately at one type of service and not at another. For example, the immigrant is never reported among the greater users of *public* and formal *private* resources, but instead is found to resort most often to the *counterculture* sources of help.

Two groups, the rebels and the refugees, are practically never seen in any great numbers at *any* facilities or programs, either public or counterculture. These two groups would thus seem to be the most *unserved* types of runaways.

On the other hand, victims and exiles are frequently high users of both public and counterculture facilities, with fugitives tending to be slightly more frequent users of the counterculture services.

This differential usage of programs and services suggests that the public agencies and the established private agencies would primarily serve exiles, victims, and fugitives, with relatively little contact with rebels, refugees, and immigrants.

This would seem to check with the earlier results of a survey of programs, which noted that "independent runaways seeking independence"—a definition which corresponds closely with our immigrant types—are least often seen by the sample of agencies surveyed. Conversely, the refugee type or foster home child is seen in large numbers only in the public sector as one might expect.

SUMMARY: PART II

In this section we have described the ways runaways view social agencies and the formal and informal social services that runaway youth use while "on the road." As can be seen, the formal agencies serve only some 4 to 18 percent of the runaways, and generally only those who come to their attention because of other types of problems, for example, illness or pregnancy, or because of police pickup and referral. Some are treated as psychiatric cases, some are given protective services or placements, and most are counseled and returned home, if possible.

Thus, while Title XX allows public agencies to give "social services" to runaways as a class, without additional eligibility requirements, we found this to be an inadequate counterbalance to the crushing weight of the runaways' illegal status. The contradiction between being an illegal alien and being "serviced" is a very great one, and is reflected differently in the lives of runaways, who are running away for a variety of reasons.

We also examined the attitudes and functions of social agencies and their personnel vis a vis runaways. A panoramic, nationwide survey was made possible through interviews with persons attending three federally sponsored regional conferences of professionals who deal with runaways. The findings of a more focused and more probing study of eight social agencies in the San Francisco and Los Angeles areas were also reported in this section. These eight agencies were divided into four categories: public, private, diversion, and counterculture. A sizable majority of personnel in all the agencies, except the private ones, agreed their agencies should provide more services to runaways. A majority of the agency personnel cited lack of funds as a barrier to servicing runaways, but in the private agency sector the proportion was 55 percent, whereas it ranged from 88 to 94 percent in the other sectors.

Most of the respondents in our national agency survey agreed that inadequate funding was the principal barrier to adequate service to runaways. They saw survival as the most serious problem of runaways, using the term primarily in its elementary food-and-shelter sense, but also blanketing emotional needs under the heading of survival. The national survey also produced a striking consensus on the "typical" runaway: a white girl, 13 to 15 years of age, from a middle-income family, who had been away from home for a relatively short time, was not in trouble with the law, but could not cope with intrafamily problems. Most agency workers conceded that few runaways sought their help, and those that did received little for their effort.

We examined the runaways' life outside the formal social service network, and discussed how different types of runaways struggle to survive as illegal aliens on the hostile and dangerous streets, depending on casual contacts with pick-ups, hitchhiking "friends," hustlers, pimps, and other deviant people.

Differential use of and contact with the existing social services and programs was noted with respect to the various runaway types delineated. In general two runaway types—the rebel and the refugee—were consistently the least likely to report use of any given service facility and hence must be regarded as the "least" served types observed. Immigrants, on the other hand, frequently reported using the counterculture facilities available, while avoiding the public sector.

These and other findings lead directly to the next subject of discussion: the implications of these facts for future runaway policy vis a vis services.

TABLE 8.1: USE OF PROGRAM SERVICES, BY RUNAWAY TYPES*

	Victim (N=42)	Exile (N=19)	Rebel (N=32)	Fugitive (N=20)	Refugee (N=43)	Immigrant (N=59)
Free clinic	21%	42%	13%	30%	12%	46%
Shelter houses	31	11	9	30	14	22
Police dept.	10	32	19	35	23	10
Probation dept.	17	5	6	10	7	3
Legal aid	12	11	0	5	5	12
Crash pads	17	21	6	25	12	39
Hospitals	12	32	9	20	9	25
Free food	17	47	9	37	2	34
Travelers Aid	2	26	13	16	7	12
Churches	31	26	19	21	19	15
National swtchb'rd	0	0	0	0	5	5
Local switchboard	14	26	7	33	5	36
Social workers	12	16	17	16	36	14
Food stamps	12	5	0	16	14	14
Welfare	7	0	0	5	2	5
Drop-in centers	7	16	10	16	12	20
Drug clinics	10	0	3	16	0	5

TABLE 8.2: IGNORANCE OF PROGRAM SERVICES,
BY RUNAWAY TYPES*

	Victim (N=42)	Exile (N=19)	Rebel (N=32)	Fugitive (N=20)	Refugee (N=43)	Immigrant (N=59)
Free clinic	53%	47%	36%	65%	67%	38%
Shelter houses	58	53	56	65	65	41
Police dept.	60	53	47	55	56	60
Probation dept.	58	68	74	63	65	69
Legal aid	74	79	81	63	86	75
Crash pads	63	33	70	63	65	36
Hospitals	61	42	60	68	79	59
Free food	71	44	72	56	84	51
Travelers Aid	80	74	75	74	84	77
Churches	61	39	55	47	67	53
National swtchb'rd	93	78	71	63	81	67
Local switchboard	63	63	67	59	86	47
Social workers	58	72	46	63	33	62
Food stamps	90	89	73	83	83	85
Welfare	82	94	73	89	74	80
Drop-in centers	82	63	66	78	77	70
Drug clinics	63	61	52	32	69	39

*In both tables not all subjects responded to each item, and percentages are on number of responses to each item.

CHAPTER 9

A Discussion of the Findings

Policies aimed at aiding runaway youth must deal with the inherent contradiction between the law embodied in Title XX of the Social Security Act asserting permission for public welfare social agencies to serve runaways and law requiring parental permission before such services can be provided. This structural ambivalence is evident in the inconsistency and confusion of policies impacting upon public agencies, which find themselves obliged to administer some compensatory social action, even though the legal status of the client renders provision of the service problematic.

The definition of a runaway does not easily acquire universal agreement and varies according to the social context of the period. Thus, in a period when the country still had a frontier, the runaway would more likely be accepted as simply a young pioneer. The modern argument for extending the wardship over the adolescent coincided with the passage of child labor laws and compulsory school attendance. It has been widely advocated since the passage of child protection legislation that a prolonged apprenticeship into adulthood is necessary where the complexities of a post-industrial society are too great to negotiate without a guardian. Along with this theory is the analogous concept that if the parent cannot raise the child, the state must. But the unique "youth boom" of the 60s and the early 70s produced immense strains on the public institutions that assumed responsibility for unsupervised youth.

To complicate matters further, the institution of the family is under great strain in a period when the ceremonial vows of marriage have merely symbolic significance. The U.S. Census Bureau has recently acknowledged this changing family structure in pointing out the increased number of single-parent families and remarried parents. The increased number of runaways is merely symptomatic of the larger social problem.

Despite stated goals of decriminalization of the so-called "status offenses," which include runaways, the fact remains that there is a great ambivalence in both law and practice in terms of runaways. Some segments of society are concerned about runaways as potential dangers to the social order, while another segment offers "social services" to youth on the run.

While the estimate of the number of runaways in the two large West Coast terminals we studied ranges from a few hundred to a few thousand, the fact is that only a handful of agencies give *any* services to runaway youth. Only a few "beds" exist for youthful transients, no matter how many federal grants, studies, books, or publicity drives have emerged from these locales. The Runaway Youth Act of 1974 provided very modest amounts of funds, distributed to each state for runaway services, and these funds are doled out to agencies that deliver relatively short-term counseling or respite programs. We attack this major social problem in a piecemeal fashion within the legal contradiction that exists in most state laws.

Runaways, as a class, are only a tip of a much larger socialization problem evidenced in every high school in the nation—the struggle by adolescent youth to find meaning and purpose in their lives. The runaway incident can be viewed as one act of many indicating the presence of a socialization gap between the parent and the child, the school and the child, and many other societal forces and the child.

The adolescent faces conflicting norms and expectations at every level of his world. Most adolescents manage to find their way through these changes and discontinuities and proceed into a pattern of class-aligned life-styles. Others, buffeted by such discontinuities and lack of stability at home, in the family, the neighborhood, the media, react in ways detrimental to their own futures. They fail to find continuous support in the home, where parents themselves are caught up in great pressures of change and discontinuity—economic, social, and emotional. They fail to find adequate supports and continuities in school systems, torn by the winds of change and conflict. They seek identity and meaning from friends equally buffeted by and reactive to the discontinuities of life. Changing sexual mores add confusion to already chaotic life-styles. Excitement and adventure are found in action—often mindless and disorderly. The social control forces of the secondary institutions label and channel such "maladaptive" adolescents into deviant careers—that of the delinquent, the poor student, the dropout, the disobedient child, the sexually promiscuous person, and so on. The combination of actions and labels tends to form a continuous social career—and the running away incidents are only one part of further discontinuities. Once running away from home and school becomes routinized, the adventure of the road, despite its dangers, develops a challenge and a meaning of its own, and the socialization into a deviant career is completed.

Our data shows that this deviant status constitutes a problem for individual runaways. They are afraid of the police, afraid to seek help at formal agencies, afraid to trust others for fear of betrayal, and so on. Data from social service agencies also establish that delivery problems are created by the runaway's illegal status. The social service agencies must notify parents and police in order to provide services to underage youth.

Thus, it would seem that laws affecting adolescents' legal rights and status must be changed if society is serious about helping runaway youth. Not only state laws that label runaways as status offenders, but also laws regarding compulsory education, child labor, and so on, need to be changed if society wishes to resolve the contradiction faced by many adolescents.

The other side of the runaways' contradiction is that official public agencies propose to offer social services to these youth, services that place the runaway in jeopardy of involuntary detention, control, and return to the very situation from which he or she has fled. Parents are often not a party to such agency intervention or services. Only the runaway is handled, packaged, and shipped. The findings show that only a relatively few runaways obtain social services, because of their ignorance of service availability and because of their fear of entrapment should such services be sought. Only when in dire emergency need or "captured" does a runaway get into contact with social service agencies. Our data show that informal sources of help are much more likely to be used than the formal ones. Furthermore, we found that formal social services to runaways were often in areas not central to the runaways' survival needs. Most runaway services are geared to individual work. They do not address the larger social issues facing young people in this society.

The narrowness of the social service perspective was evident in answers to a series of questions we raised with both runaway youth and social agency workers. We asked both groups to describe an "ideal social service program" such that it would meet the needs of the runaway.

Agency worker responses were as follows: a place with counselors who are sensitive to the needs of youth; a private group home with a small number of residents, family counseling; a complete change of environment (nonurban); a place for anybody, not just runaways or people under age 18; a place that allows kids freedom for self-motivated and self-regulated growth; and many places in the city geared to meet the different geographical, cultural, and ethnic needs.

Some of the more descriptive responses were expressed as follows:

"Centers would be set up in different cultural neighborhoods, with an educational as well as live-in component. The school would have an extensive program. Residents would acquire a skill, develop a positive mental attitude about themselves. There would be no involvement with the juvenile court. Another component would include training residents (who could be kids or parents) to work with new clients, and eventually the group would set up a place in the country to serve as a long-term residential treatment facility."

"I would set up a big house at the beach where runaways could feel free to come. There would always be someone there to relate to. The kid could stay there as long as necessary. It would be perfectly safe, and a person could be comfortable doing whatever he does best with people. It would be a place where people can *play*—too many people have lost the ability to play."

"It needs to be an official place where a runaway has alternatives besides just to keep running or go to juvenile hall. A social service workers would come there and help get the family back together."

"A kid should have a 'time out' place to go. This would be for children who have a tendency to run. These kids need a person to go to and a place to go to talk about feelings and to have someone listen. It must be an objective person who is warm and receptive. Someone at the place will talk with the kid and his parents so that he doesn't have to go home to the same situation he left."

"I would set up a cross-country network of alternative living situations, not bound by state regulations where any kid from any state can stay."

"I would want a group home for kids with problems, not exclusively for runaways. There would be a short-term facility for transients, plus a general residential treatment, diversion program."

"I would use many decentralized agencies which share responsibilities but give different services to different kinds of kids: crisis center; hotline; legal staff; and long-term housing. There might be a variety of housing arrangements available, such as group homes; foster homes with good, interested, and trained families; a cooperative apartment house with house managers who are sympathetic to runaways whose parents won't help. There would also be money available, a special travel emergency fund to help send those kids home whose parents can't afford it."

"A place which is open and accepting, but with some real solid structure. Learning opportunities there would include helping the kid learn how to use the system to meet his own needs."

"A place in a nonviolent community with proximity to other young people, but to straight people, too. A physical facility that is informal, warm and small."

We asked runaway youth to describe "what type of set-up (they) would like to see as the ideal place to go to while on the run." We asked each runaway subject to describe the elements of an "ideal agency" which would serve him and best meet his needs. The responses are listed below:

TABLE 9.1: Features of the "Ideal" Agency to Serve Runaways, as Described by Runaways* (N=215)

Ideal Agency Would	%
Offer free food and shelter	58%
Be free from outside interference	47%
Be safe from the law	40%
Have an understanding staff	38%
Have staff who were able to "relate"	37%
Would have voluntary participation	36%
Would have recreation facilities	26%
Place would be a "nonagency"	25%

*Table contains multiple responses; does not add up to 100%.

As can be seen (Table 9.1), runaways seem to be seeking support without controls, yet some seek for the understanding and "help" of others. This "ideal place" could only exist in a society where the basic legal contradictions between control and service had been resolved. At the same time, while runaways seek "freedom" and no bureaucratic structures, they also seek relationship and understanding on a voluntary basis.

Although few runaways mentioned family counseling as a crucial treatment component, those few felt that emotional support should be part of an ideal agency. Again, the responses indicated a distrust of the establishment and authority, situations most were fleeing from. There was an emphasis placed upon sensitive counselors who have an ability to relate to the runaways' problems. It is interesting to note that this same element sought in counselors by the runaways was used in counterculture and informal agencies as a staffing criterion, as opposed to the formal agencies which imposed credential requirements for staff counselors. The runaways' perceptions of the staff in the "ideal agency" were revealed in the following interview comments: "counselors who had been through the same experiences, same trips could really help," "a place to go with people who have done it before [and can] give you views," "people who understand runaways and assist in coping with problems…feel free to speak, take time to rap with kids—free communication."

In addition to whatever type of services offered in the agencies, runaways felt that the climate within the agency was important. Invariably they mentioned, "freedom to come and go," "where nobody hassles you about curfew," "atmosphere of freedom and trust," "room to breathe," "harmony in house," "just like home without the hasslement," and "a mellow place" as ideal environments for runaway service agencies.

Based upon such suggestions, it would seem there is a need to provide alternative service patterns for adolescents moving around in the world. Other countries have encouraged legitimate travel for young people by creating hostels and wayside services, by allowing young people to spend time as "tourists" in their own land. For example, under innovative programs sponsored by the Canadian government, it became possible for restless youth to be given stipends to spend time traveling across Canada, stopping to work or to learn at selected hostels. It was felt such a youth-touring program legitimatized the searching behavior of youth and gave each youth a broad perspective about his own homeland. Thus, these adolescents were better prepared to choose the place and the type of life they wanted with a sense of the diversity and options open to them.

Such an open legitimate approach to school dropouts, runaways, or "delinquents" might resolve the inherent legal and social contradiction the runaway youth and those who would serve him now face.

APPENDIX I

Research Methodology: Formation of The Runaway Youth and Agency Samples

Introduction

The present research has been guided by the premise that only by examining runaway youth in their natural life circumstances can we best understand their perspectives, their struggles, their goals, and solutions. To achieve such understanding we entered the world of the runaway at several levels, including the social agencies which serve runaways and their families, the juvenile justice system, and the largely unexplored street scene.

Selection of the Runaway Sample: The Unseen

Concurrent with our research efforts to identify the major runaway service agencies in the San Francisco Bay and Los Angeles areas, the staff conducted an intensive campaign to locate and contact others who informally serve runaways. Through our contacts in runaway service centers, free clinics, and community switchboards, we were able to cultivate a network of anthropological-type informants. Included in this network were outreach street workers, runaway service providers, key persons in crash pads and communes, former runaways, and street people. The informant system served several important functions.

First, and most significantly, the development of our informant system served to establish the credibility of our research staff and to spread the word among possibly apprehensive runaways that the interviews were "safe," that is, that the interviews were confidential and that the youth would not be jeopardized by them.

Second, by enlisting the aid of these informants, we were able to conduct preliminary screenings of all prospective subjects not referred by agencies. These key informants and former runaways were able to test the veracity of each subject's stories informally, prior to referring the youth to our project. One Berkeley informant detected two youth who purported to be runaways but turned out to be local residents living at home who hoped to earn money from a feigned interview. Thus, we are fairly confident that the "unseen" runaways interviewed were genuinely on the run and were not impostors. The street informant network provided a rich and continual source for identifying street runaways and recruiting them into the project. Youth were much more likely to openly participate in the research if they learned of us from someone they related to and trusted.

Once runaway youth were recruited into our research, we concentrated on creating an atmosphere of trust and understanding. The prior reference by our informants, who were trusted by the runaways, facilitated establishment of rapport between the staff and the subjects. A team of eight field interviewers in San Francisco and six in Los Angeles, nearly all former runaways with research experience, was trained in the administration of our elaborate field protocol. Since the runaway population represents a wide range of ethnic and social-class backgrounds, every possible effort was extended to pair similar backgrounds between subjects and field staff during the actual interviewing. In addition, because of the large and increasing proportion of females among runaways, more than one-half of the field staff were women (60 percent). Only in rare instances, when the most appropriate interviewers were on assignment and the youth was leaving the area, were we forced to violate this approach. The average age of our field staff was 26 years, with 35 being the upper limit and 18 the lowest. The ethnic composition of the field research staff was four blacks, four Chicanos, four Caucasians, and two Asian-Americans. Thus, to ensure the recruitment of subjects and the validity of the data collected, field researchers were selected because they were all familiar with the world of the runaway and could establish rapport with subjects.

In addition to our informant system, we sought entry into another, less well explored network of services available to runaways. Entering the realm of the unofficial runaway service provider is not a simple task as many of these people operate in direct violation of laws relating to minors. Those who offer runaways employment are subject to prosecution for violation of child labor laws. Those who provide shelter face the possibility of prosecution for harboring a runaway. Those who engage runaway youth in sexual activities are contributing to the delinquency of a minor. This list of possible criminal charges is not meant to be exhaustive, but rather to indicate the protective veil of secrecy which tends to surround these unofficial providers. This was the situation initially encountered. Many service providers recognized the significance of our research and lent their support. As we made further contacts with counterculture ventures, and as they grew to trust our staff (realizing that the research was completely confidential and that no one would be directly identified in any reports), we were further taken into their confidence. Within a matter of two weeks staff had been invited to no less than three unofficial "foster homes," that is, crash pads, in San Francisco and Los Angeles. We were also invited to a religious commune in San Francisco, which was the home of several runaways.

One proprietor of a Bay Area "foster home" for runaways and other troubled youth was eventually hired, trained, and assigned to interview the runaways living there.

SAMPLING TECHNIQUES

Recruiting the "Unseen" Sample: Field Method

Several sampling procedures employed concomitantly throughout the conduct of our research deserve illumination. Initially, field interviewers were stationed at various runaway congregation centers in San Francisco's Tenderloin and Haight-Ashbury districts, on Berkeley's Telegraph Avenue, and at Hermosa Beach and Hollywood Boulevard in Los Angeles. Other interviewers were stationed at various runaway and youth serving programs throughout the Bay Area and Los Angeles, including Huckleberry House and the Haight-Ashbury Free Clinic in San Francisco, and the Coffee Cellar and the Free Church in Berkeley, and 1736 House in Los Angeles.

This field method provided the opportunity to become acquainted with street people and street workers in the area and to gain their confidence. It was not long after our field workers let it be known that they were interested in conducting "safe" interviews with runaways scene inhabitants.

Snowball Sampling

Once some runaways were identified, interviewed, and paid, they were asked to identify or contact other youth who were on the run and might be willing to participate in our research. This technique, commonly known as snowball sampling, has repeatedly proven its efficacy in identifying subjects from deviant or otherwise closed societies, and was the second major sampling technique employed in the study. A preliminary screening interview was conducted with each "snowball sampled" youth to verify the claim that he or she was actually on the run. Through field placement of interviewers, the help of their informants, and snowball sampling, we were able to contact 35 percent (73) of the entire sample in a relatively short time.

At these field sites, youth were approached and introduced to the project. They were told that the federal study was designed to explore the reasons that young people offer for running away from home and their experiences while on the run in an attempt to understand more fully the world of the runaway. Emphasis was placed on the applied nature of the research, namely, that social policy and programs for runaways were in the making and that relevant strategies can be designed most effectively with the input of the client population. The study would give 200 youth an opportunity to express their opinions concerning the nature of the American family, and the juvenile justice system, to relate their travel experiences, and to comment on the availability and utilization of social service. All this, they were told, would be communicated to program planners and social policy leaders in Washington.

If the possibility of having their voices heard and of impacting upon social policy failed to motivate their participation, there was also the $10 payment in exchange for a two-hour interview. All youth received the money for their participation. All participation was voluntary, and they were advised of their option not to respond to any questions which they deemed too personal or potentially incriminating. Complete confidentiality and anonymity were assured prior to the interview.

THE PERSISTENT PROBLEM OF IMPOSTORS: AN EFFECTIVE STRATEGY FOR MANAGING THE PROBLEM

Anticipating potential sources of abuse and misrepresentation is critical to assuring that they are kept to a minimum. Recognizing this problem at the outset, we took precautions to reduce or eliminate this potential source of faulty data. The problem of dealing with impostors arose only for the "unseen" sample of runaways, those not served by any formal agency. For obvious reasons, the youth referred by social agencies did not present such problems. These youth were bona fide runaways as evidenced by police reports, parents' reports, and in-depth interviews with agency staff. Therefore, we are confident that all youth referred from the eight agencies were in fact runaways.

In selecting our "unseen" sample, we operationalized a *five-pronged screening approach,* which served both to identify impostors and to test the veracity of our subjects. As indicated above, the initial screening generally took place when our street informants sounded out a potential subject. Our informants were generally familiar with the youth's circumstances. For example, two informants know of people who regularly housed runaways, and this knowledge proved to be productive in locating our sample. The second level of screening occurred when a member of our research staff made initial contact with the youth. Each interviewer would engage each potential interviewee in a brief but insightful discussion about his/her recent experiences as a runaway, focusing on street life, reasons for leaving home, point of departure, places visited, time on the run, and so on. In addition, the interviewer would test any information learned and relayed by our street informants.

Nearly all of our trained interviewers were former runaways and were familiar with life on the streets for youth in flight. We recruited field workers who understood the world view of runaways, who would be sensitive to the needs of these youth, and who would, by virtue of their experience, be in a position to intuitively perceive the veracity of a youth's story. This was the third screening device.

The fourth data quality control device consisted of a series of questions built into the field instrument for cross-validation. These items concerned the number of runaway episodes, their duration, distance traveled, amount of money required to survive, and so on. Several questions were repeated at different points in the interview to check for logical responses and consistency.

The final internal precaution in our five-pronged approach to avoid misrepresentation by nonrunaways was that we would permit only one snowball referral from any runaway interviewed. This eliminated the danger of having the youth refer all of his/her brothers, sisters, and friends.

We are concerned to point out two potentially serious consequences of widespread notification that subjects will receive remuneration for participation in research generally, and particularly with regard to recruitment of unknown populations. We dealt with these hazards as we confronted them. The first, and most readily apparent problem was that of representation by youth that they were runaways when in fact they were not. The second problem was less apparent, but no less important as it affects the quality of data. Here, the problem stems not from prefabrication of several runaway experiences, but rather from exaggeration or "popularization" of these experiences. This problem has long plagued field researchers. Essentially, the subject interprets his/her role as an actor in a play. The script is tailored to fit audience interest. In our project, where it was known the research focused, in part, on the runaway experience, there was a real danger that runaways would be tempted to exaggerate, to make their story more interesting (or more impressive) by improving upon the truth.

In a curious way, the $10 payment could also, at times, serve as an incentive to exaggerate or dramatize. This occurred when a subject felt he/she should give the interviewer his/her "money's worth," and if the true story did not seem to be "worth," and if the true story did not seem to be "worth" $10, something extra was thrown in.

If at any level of screening an informant, an interviewer had the *mere suspicion* that the youth was not a bona fide runaway, the interview was terminated. It was considered that under such circumstances the possibility of collecting erroneous data was hardly worth the risk. Since there was an abundance of youth on the streets who had in fact run away from home, the substitution could readily be made. Four youth purporting to be runaways fell into this questionable group and were not interviewed.

Although it is true that even the most advanced screening measures will not foil the cunning and determined youth, we feel that the preventive measures outlined above offered the greatest protection and ensured that the level of data abuse was kept to a minimum.

An unanticipated problem arose regarding the payment to subjects, but it was minor and easily rectified. In one agency that we studied, the administrative staff regarded the payment of money to be contrary to its treatment approach and thought that it positively rewarded antisocial behavior which the staff was trying to affect. When it was explained that these youth were being compensated for their time and information about a social world that is relatively unknown, all objections to payment faded.

THE SAMPLE

To avoid seasonal fluctuations in the rate of runaways served by the various social agencies, our methodology required the collection of all youth data within the same time frame. Youth were referred by agency personnel to our project shortly after intake, and with few exceptions, every runaway served by these programs during the time frame voluntarily participated in the study. The number of youth participating in the research project was, therefore, a direct outcome of the size of the runaway population each agency serves. Our research was designed to collect data on a minimum of 20 youth at each of the four service networks in the San Francisco and Los Angeles areas, or to collect data at each site within a three-month period, whichever came first. In some agencies, notably the San Francisco diversion and counterculture agencies, runaway caseloads were high enough to permit collection of data on more than 20 youth in a relatively short time. In other agencies, such as San Francisco's Traveler's Aid, 1736 House, and The Way Home, however, the catchment population was not as heavy. All of the runaway youth seen by the staff of these agencies were contacted by our field staff during the data collection phase of the research.

PROTECTION OF SUBJECT CONFIDENTIALITY

To ensure that project staff maintained the highest standards of professional ethics in the protection of human subjects, monthly project reports were submitted to the SAC Policy Review Committee, and two meetings of the group were held with the principal investigator.

If the youth volunteered to participate in our study, he/she was given a consent form to read and complete. Field workers took extreme care to ensure that each youth fully understood the consent form and its implications. The gist of this easy-to-read document was that participation was purely voluntary, that the youth was not forfeiting any of his/her rights by participating, that the subject was free not to respond to any questions that seemed too personal or potentially incriminating, and that $10 would be paid for the interview. Before, during, and after the signing of the consent form, each youth was instructed that all data collected would be for research purposes only and that no names or identifiable characteristics would appear on any field protocol or in anything we wrote. All of these procedures have been systematically carried out without exception. For those youth who were living at home or who were the legal charges of programs, the consent forms were first signed by the parent or legal guardian and countersigned by the youth before a field session was conducted.

SELECTION OF THE SOCIAL SERVICE AGENCIES

During the formative months of our research, June-July 1974, staff in both Los Angeles and San Francisco devoted considerable effort to identifying all social service agencies which offer assistance to runaway youth. Contact was made with all such agencies. We then analyzed the runaway-serving networks in both areas to distinguish the important from the marginal service agencies. Once the primary youth serving agencies were identified, we began intensive field study at each site. Researchers were assigned to each agency or program. They made frequent visits to the sites, conducted formal and informal in-depth interviews with nine administrators, 17 agency supervisors, and 20 direct line staff across all eight agencies. We interviewed all available administrative and supervisory staff and a random selection of line staff employed for more than eight months. We observed these eight agencies, and analyzed their services to runaways over a period of nine months.

An analysis of the various types of agencies serving runaways outside of the juvenile justice setting revealed the following categories, the public welfare sector, private service agencies, diversion programs, and counterculture programs.

Public Welfare

Public welfare agencies are designed to service a wide variety of social needs of the community. We selected for study the public welfare departments in Alameda and Los Angeles counties. Field workers were assigned to observe and interview staff in both locations. For purposes of optimizing the sample selection process within the welfare department, three primary service units within the Children's Protective Services Division were selected, since that is where the agency was most likely to see runaways. These included the Foster Care Placement Unit, Children's Investigation Unit, and the Children's Dependency Unit in each location. These units were selected because of their focus on services to youth and their reported familiarity with runaway youth who are served by the department. Given the large number of foster home failures (many are evidenced by episodes of absconding) this division seemed to offer the most promise for locating our sample. Two of the three units in Alameda County are comprised of seven workers each, while the third unit (Child Dependency) has approximately 25 workers. The staff distribution in the Los Angeles division was comparable. Throughout the data collection phase, only 13 runaways came to the attention of the Alameda County workers. Two of these youth were not seen by our field staff because their parents or legal guardians failed to grant their consent. Otherwise, all runaways seen by this division, during the time frame participated in our research. At the outset, we were informed by staff at the Child Services division in the Los Angeles office that they served as many as 12 runaways per month. During the three months of research, however, a total of 18 youth were served by the department and interviewed by our staff.

The Private Sector

In San Francisco, there was little difficulty in selecting a private social service agency in contact with youth, many of them on the run. Traveler's Aid has a long and celebrated history of serving the city's transient population and others in need. Traveler's Aid has historically maintained outreach posts at bus depots, train stations, and airports where it was likely to encounter runaways. Amicable cooperative relations were readily developed between research staff and the agency. We encountered some difficulty, however, in selecting the Los Angeles private agency, and for that matter, with the diversion and counterculture agencies as well. Two important limitations emerged. Our initial and subsequent efforts to locate agencies serving runaways proved that there was a dearth of such services in the Los Angeles area. We found this situation to be rather perplexing since the popular press has depicted the "Strip" and local beaches as heavily populated by runaways. Indeed, our research indicates that to a large extent this picture is accurate, yet there were few agencies providing any direct services to these transients. Additionally, those agencies that we contacted that served youth reported that they did not see runaways in any appreciable numbers to justify their cooperation and participation in our research. We found that we had greater success recruiting runaway youth than the agencies supposedly designed to service their needs.

Hillsides Episcopal Home for Children was finally selected since it represents one very important treatment modality for youth in crisis; long-term residential care. The Hillsides sample was also unique in that it afforded an opportunity to study the runaway phenomenon among the very young.

Diversion Programs

Diversion of youth from the juvenile justice system appears to be the popular trend in corrections. Certainly, the major federal initiative with regard to runaways and other status offenders is clearly toward deinstitutionalization. Many municipalities have developed comprehensive diversion networks designed to circumvent the juvenile courts and institutions. Both San Francisco and Los Angeles were late in the development of such a network. What existed at the time of the data collection phase of our research was quite loosely defined and emerging. By the time we were in the field, interviewing youth and agency staff, for one month the newly formed youth diversion program in San Francisco had failed to service a single runaway. Therefore, we sought cooperation from juvenile justice and diversion programs. The young women at Charila House were there in lieu of incarceration in juvenile hall or Youth Authority institutions.

The Way Home in Los Angeles was selected for study on much the same basis as Charila Foundation. The diversion network that existed in the Los Angeles area at the time of our research was also fragmented and ill-defined. The Way Home was an independent diversion program supported by county welfare and court referrals and funds.

Counterculture Programs

As with the selection of the private service agency in San Francisco, there was no difficulty in choosing the counterculture agency for study. Huckleberry House is perhaps the best known runaway center nationally. Huck's is by far the largest and most comprehensive program serving runaways and youth in crisis in the Bay Area.

By contrast to the wide variety of services available to runaways in the San Francisco area, we were able to locate only one runaway center in the greater Los Angeles area, 1736 House.

RECIPROCAL WORKING RELATIONSHIPS

A major area of concern to the agencies we studied, particularly the counterculture agencies, was expressed quite candidly by the director of Huckleberry House on our first meeting. He said, "We have been researched up to our ass. Every damn person concerned with youth comes here to find out how we work. They come; study our ways, and are gone. We never see or hear from them again. We don't need any more rip-off research." It has long been a policy of ISA that research is not a one-way flow of information. Reciprocal data sharing through the vehicle of formal and informal feedback sessions is an integral aspect of all ISA research. It was the promise of ongoing feedback as to what we learned from interviewing staff and clients as well as other youth and service providers that facilitated our gaining access and cooperation at Huck's. Upon completion of the preliminary draft of the final report, formal feedback sessions were scheduled. Additionally, we provided a vehicle by which these agencies representing a variety of treatment modalities for runaway youth could expound upon their perspectives on the runaway phenomenon.

LAW ENFORCEMENT PERSPECTIVE

The great majority of runaway youth get tangled in the juvenile justice web, from which extrication may be difficult. To learn more about the perspective and methods of law enforcement agencies, we interviewed all the juvenile division chiefs in the San Francisco and Los Angeles areas, a sample of juvenile court judges, and probation officers. It must be borne in mind that ours was not a study of the juvenile justice system and our efforts along this line were necessarily limited.

NATIONAL RUNAWAY SERVICE PROVIDERS CONFERENCE

Research staff attended the three regional conferences on runaway youth sponsored by the Office of Youth Development and the Social and Rehabilitation Service in 1974. At those meetings, a detailed questionnaire was distributed to all participants. We received an 80 percent response rate.

This questionnaire was supplemented by a follow-up questionnaire inquiring about the impact of the conferences on the participants' services and "pressure group" roles with regard to runaways.

APPENDIX II

Profiles of Eight Sample Agencies Serving Runaways

PUBLIC AGENCIES

Alameda County Welfare Department

The function of Children's Protective Services Division of the Alameda County Welfare Department is to serve children's needs for safety, protection, health and welfare.

This agency has progressed through many changes. In 1971, a major reorganization took place to group Welfare, Probation, and Human Relations Departments under one umbrella agency, the Human Resources Agency. This reorganization resulted in the transfer of Children's Investigation and Dependency units, formerly under Probation, to the Welfare Department. This has meant that many former probation officers, trained with probation philosophy and attitudes, perform the same function—but in a different system. Many tensions and adjustments ensued.

Headquarters are situated in two large buildings in downtown Oakland. Smaller service units are decentralized in local cities. Children needing residential services are placed at Senedigar Cottage, a residential treatment center, or occasionally in Juvenile Hall. Both are in San Leandro, 15 miles from Oakland.

This organizational analysis of the Welfare Department was limited to three major service units within the Children's Protective Services Division. These include one Foster Care Placement Unit, the Children's Investigation Unit, and the Children's Dependency Unit. These were chosen because of their familiarity with runaway youth.

In the Alameda Welfare agency, children who run away are seen primarily as abused, neglected, or abandoned. They are not likely to be counseled about the meaning of the runaway episode. Although staff agrees that such children and their families need intensive counseling, such therapeutic services are not readily available at these agencies. According to public welfare workers, demanding worker caseloads, court philosophy, and welfare structure prevent specific counseling for runaways. Many Alameda staff members regret the paucity of true family crisis counseling resources in the community apart from the Probation Department's Family Crisis Unit. Alameda Welfare staff frequently make referrals to available community counseling resources in an effort to keep youth out of the court system.

The route a youth follows in a public agency is predetermined, and all youth usually follow the same route. After referral a youth usually goes directly to the Investigations Unit. If the youth appears to need court protection, she/he is referred to the Supervision or Foster Care Placement Units for further services following the court disposition hearing. Until the time of the court hearing, and possibly afterwards, the youth may be placed in Senedigar Cottage, the county residential institution specifically for "dependent youth," as distinct from "juvenile offenders."

No young people are officially categorized as runaways within Children's Protective Services. Many more runaway youth are seen and categorized as runaway through the predelinquent "601 Category" within the Probation Department. If court dependent youth repeatedly run away or run for an extended period, they are referred to Probation's Family Crisis Unit.

Graphically this process looks like this:

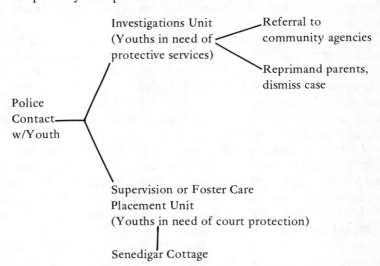

Many youth referred by community agencies or individuals never become court dependents because the Investigations Unit may decide the youth could be helped more quickly through other community resources. Or the Investigations Unit may decide the referred youth, by court standards, technically cannot be considered abused, abandoned, or neglected and thus not court dependent. In such cases, the youth and family are referred to other community resources for counseling, shelter or other needs. Additionally, the investigator may "reprimand" the parents but dismiss the case.

Of course there are standard guidelines that workers must follow before giving services. For example, youths and/or families must first prove eligibility for AFDC before receiving services from Foster Care Placement Unit. So a youth entering the public service terminal follows a process that leads to an agency assessment of his/her needs and services to be given.

COMMUNITY RELATIONS

The Alameda County Welfare Agency maintains contact with other agencies through agency conferences, reciprocal referrals, case consultations, and telephone contacts. These forms of community relationships are considered sufficient for basic exchanges of information, but insufficient for good rapport and image within the community.

For example, staff occaisionally has disagreements with individual police who see youth as troublemakers rather than as people with troubles. Conflicts exist with certain personalities within the school system who maintain rigid law and order attitudes. In relationships with the courts or juvenile delinquency facilities, difficulties sometimes occur because workers believe the child may run for good reason but is stamped "incorrigible" by the court, not listened to, and sent to Juvenile Hall. Problems also exist because of the distance between the central office and Senedigar and counterculture agencies predominantly because staff is unfamiliar with such services or is not encouraged to use them as sanctioned referrals.

Individual problematic relationships with all these agencies reflect both procedural and philosophical differences of orientation. Yet an additional factor is Welfare's controversial image in the community. To counteract this, the Children's Protective Services Division currently is involved in an educational campaign to present information on its services to local agencies.

STAFF

At Alameda Welfare Department all supervisors and workers are required through Alameda County civil service to have a bachelor's degree and some experience. Many of the staff also hold master's degrees in social work or a related field. The department did not have percentages available on staff's ethnic composition. Nearly all staff we interviewed commented that the fact that there are so few minority workers is a barrier in working with runaways from ethnic minorities, particularly Mexican-American and native American children.

FINANCES

Alameda County Welfare does not allot a specific amount of money for runaway services. Staff was unable to estimate the number of runaways seen per month. As previously stated, youth are not categorized as runaways within the Children's Protective Services Division. Unofficially, staff states that some youth are runaways from their homes, Senedigar Cottage, foster home placements, or institutional placements. The number of unofficial runaways is considered small in this legal "601 category" of dependent children. Many more runaway youth are seen and categorized as runaways through the Probation Department.

Because of the lack of records on runaways, it is impossible to do a cost analysis of the service program. In terms of the total Alameda Welfare program the funding sources are clear. Monies come from county, state, and federal governments. AFDC funds and county pay are direct funding sources for foster parents. Some parents of court dependent children contribute directly. The general populace contributes through taxes. An auxiliary group provides for specific needs, such as clothing, a nursery, and a camp with a contribution fund. No breakdown is available on the proportions of the various funding sources.

Also, it should be noted that Alameda Welfare has no easily accessible breakdown of categories of youth with other kinds of presenting problems.

Statistics exist on total numbers of children seen. About 1,700 children are seen monthly by the Foster Care Placement Units for ongoing supervision. During May 1975 a total of 1,780 youth were supervised overall. Of these 1,499 were court dependent, 253 were nondelinquent, and 28 were free for adoptions. Of these, perhaps 20 percent were also involved in a runaway incident of some type.

No official follow-up procedure exists except within the Supervision Unit where a youth and his/her parents may be informally supervised for six months. Additionally, AFDC workers and public health nurses may be asked to visit the referred family. Within Foster Care Placement, foster parents are sometimes called informally after termination of services. Workers of all three units write no formal follow-up reports at termination. Many will make informal phone calls to the referring agency.

DEMOGRAPHIC INFORMATION

No statistics are available on numbers of runaway youth. Records are not kept on the types of presenting problems.

Figures on age, ethnicity, or other descriptive factors were also unavailable.

EVALUATION PROCEDURES

No evaluation is done for services to runaways because there are no specific runaway services. For other agency services, evaluation is done through group meetings, case records, and agency statistics. Agency staff does ongoing evaluation of clientele served through similar means. Such information is used to gauge service effectiveness and as an indicator of new program needs.

BARRIERS TO SERVICE

Difficult or inadequate relationships exist sometimes with police, courts, or juvenile delinquency facilities, hotline services, free clinics, counterculture agencies, and private agencies or private counselors. Additionally, staff feels that crisis residential facilities for youth are grossly insufficient within the community, primarily for out-of-city and out-of-state youth. Poor relationships exist with welfare systems of other states having jurisdiction over clients served here.

The staff also specifically mentioned heavy caseloads and inadequate personnel as a barrier to service. It relates this problem to insufficient funds. It felt counseling services were inadequate and said it was often hampered by the legal restrictions on services to runaways.

Los Angeles Department Of Public Social Services

The Los Angeles Department of Public Social Services (DPSS) provides a variety of services to youth. This study focuses on the Children's Services Division of the Metro North DPSS office.

Metro North DPSS is situated northwest of downtown Los Angeles' business district. Social workers' desks were originally close together in a large room. There were small conference rooms for private sessions and larger rooms for group meetings. Recently, part of the Metro North Children's Services Division moved to a smaller building nearby. Social workers have more individual space in the new location.

The purpose of Children's Services is to serve families and children where there is some suspicion of neglect and/or abuse; to keep families together and help alleviate stress; to see that a child's placement is appropriate and effective; or to try to get a child back into the home under better conditions than when he or she left.

Changes that have occurred since the division's establishment have been due primarily to legislative or administrative policy changes. Recent changes have resulted in more short-term, crisis-oriented services. In addition, there has been a redefinition of goals, which stresses that placement is not considered a final solution, and protective services have been supplemented to meet client needs. Social workers also cite changes that have resulted in more accountability and standardization.

DPSS is well known in the community. Workers receive referrals from police and sheriff's departments, schools, private agencies, from the client's friends and relatives and self-referrals. Social workers keep in touch with community agencies referring clients to them.

RUNAWAY SERVICES

Alameda County Welfare and the Los Angeles Department of Social Services resemble each other and follow similar intake procedures. The Children's Services Division handles protective services, child placement, and court referrals. Here again the needs of the child and/or family are assessed according to standardization guidelines before services are given.

DPSS follows the typical public agency pattern in seeing runways as abused, neglected, or abandoned.

A runaway may initially become involved with DPSS through one of the crisis units, because of the runaway episode or because of ongoing problems. Runaways become clients of a crisis worker or supervision worker in the Children's Services Division. Service options for runaways include: return to parents, placement in foster homes, or a work and school continuation program.

The Los Angeles DPSS feels that the act of running away is a danger signal and usually a symptom of family problems. Its services are short-term: the counseling emphasis is crisis-oriented, and the need for long-term counseling of children and their families cannot be met by L.A. DPSS. Referrals to other social agencies are made when this is the case, according to L.A. DPSS workers' reports.

Termination occurs when a child is stabilized at home or when a family problem has been resolved. Termination could also occur if a client refuses services, if the client's whereabouts are un-known, or in the case of a child who becomes 18.

This diagram shows a youth's likely route through LA-DPSS:

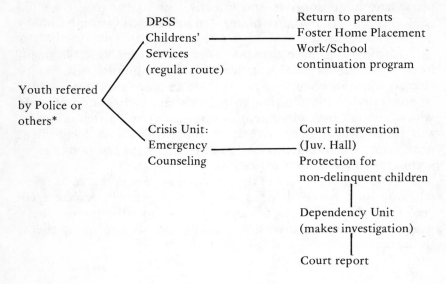

DPSS
Childrens'
Services
(regular route)

Return to parents
Foster Home Placement
Work/School
continuation program

Youth referred
by Police or
others*

Crisis Unit:
Emergency
Counseling

Court intervention
(Juv. Hall)
Protection for
non-delinquent children

Dependency Unit
(makes investigation)

Court report

*Others—schools, private agencies, friends, self-referrals.

COMMUNITY RELATIONS

Although DPSS is well known, staff feels that a better com-munity relationship could be established. This would result in greater understanding between agencies and more effective services. Staff is concerned that DPSS' image may not be adequate. It be-lieves that much of the bias against DPSS could be alleviated through personal contacts.

Social workers see a definite need for DPSS. Among reasons listed are that no other agency, excepting the police, is involved in placement and supervision of nondelinquent wards of the court. Social workers also point out that no other agency provides the same kinds of financial help for the poor.

STAFF

Los Angeles DPSS requires academic credentials of its staff. All DPSS social workers have college degrees, and promotions are based on training and experience with the department.

DPSS employs community workers to do outreach work. These workers have been receiving welfare benefits or are potential recipients. They are indigenous to the community they work in.

They are the only service staff personnel without an academic background. Although it can be assumed that many of these community workers are minority persons, no breakdown was available on ethnic composition.

Administrative staff works out of the central office in El Monte. At each district office, such as Metro North, a deputy director is in charge of a number of unit supervisors. Unit supervisors, and their supervision and intake workers offer direct services to children and families. Community workers assist social workers in providing transportation, translations for non-English speaking clients, and community contacts.

The following chart briefly describes the personnel positions for Children's Services, L.A. DPSS:

Chief of Children's Services   }   At the El Monte Office
Administrative Assistants

Deputy Director   }   At each of the District Offices
Unit Supervisors

Intake Workers   Supervision Workers (2+1 at Mariposa Annex Office)

FINANCES

The Children's Services Division of the DPSS Metro North office see about 10-12 runaways per month. This is a greater number than seen at the average DPSS office and is probably due to Metro North's location near Hollywood and the central Greyhound bus depot.

The L.A. DPSS receives county, state, and federal funds as well as some fees paid by clients. There is no fee for protective services counseling not involving placement. No breakdown of the yearly budget for the Metro North office is available and hence no estimate of the proportion spent on runaway services can be made.

DEMOGRAPHIC INFORMATION

Children's Services see 200 intake cases per month, involving both protective services and placement intakes. The office is concerned with about 500 additional ongoing cases. We do not have an ethnic breakdown.

EVALUATION PROCEDURES

Evaluation procedures take many forms. Auditing is done by the state and federal governments. A commission appointed by the Los Angeles County Board of Supervisors reviews different aspects of the program. Another form of evaluation measures whether money is being spent in accordance with regulations.

Treatment evaluation, which takes place during meetings between the deputy and the supervisor or the supervisor and the workers, is implemented through case reviews by the deputy and regional directors.

BARRIERS TO SERVICE

Barriers mentioned specifically by the L.A. DPSS staff include the agency's unsatisfactory relationship with its community (for details, see "Community Relations" above).

Additional barriers included: heavy caseloads and inadequate staff, related to insufficient funding; insufficient counseling services; and legal restrictions on services to runaways.

PRIVATE AGENCIES

Traveler's Aid Society of San Francisco

The Traveler's Aid Society of San Francisco was incorporated in 1914 as a private social service agency to help newly arrived persons become oriented and established in this area. It is affiliated with Traveler's Aid Association of America, a network of agencies in major cities designed to help transient people with information about housing, job leads, and travel arrangements, assist them in finding relatives, and offer casework counseling.

As migration patterns changed during this century, so did the kinds of people served. Formerly an agency that primarily focused on information and referral services, presently Traveler's Aid staff is composed of professionals who deliver services with a social casework orientation. During the past ten years, major changes have taken place within service components. This agency is more community-oriented and frequently speaks for client advocacy issues, such as nondiscriminatory tenant policy for families seeking rental housing in San Francisco. Traveler's Aid has become involved politically in the community and aggressive in establishing new programs and finding funding. As a resource agency having much experience with runaways, it assisted both Huckleberry House and Hospitality House in getting started. At many levels, Traveler's Aid encourages existing agencies in their programs and performs advocacy work for its own clientele.

Within the past few years the agency merged with the International Social Services of America for economic reasons. Services have broadened because of the merger. They now include intercountry work, such as assisting with family reunions and with family problems that cross international boundaries. During the hectic days of the Vietnamese orphan airlift, staff spent long, intense hours at the Presidio Gymnasium caring for the newly arrived children. Later staff assisted with travel arrangements to unite the children with their adoptive families, or helped locate temporary foster home placements.

Traveler's Aid Society is housed in an easily accessible office adjacent to Market Street. The atmosphere is comfortable and relaxed. Additionally, this agency maintains information booths manned by volunteers at the local Greyhound Bus Terminal and San Francisco International Airport. Presently office hours are Monday through Friday, 9 a.m. to 10 p.m., and 11 a.m. to 7 p.m. on Saturday and Sunday. The bus station and airport booths are open from 9 a.m. to 10 p.m. daily. No fee for service is required, with the exception that the agency may charge $7.50 for meeting young or disabled clients at the airport.

RUNAWAY SERVICES

Traveler's Aid is unique in providing services to transient persons. Some of its contacts with runaways are a result of Traveler's Aid's outreach activities at the San Francisco Airport and bus terminals. In addition it is used as a referral source by a wide range of community agencies. Traveler's Aid has referral reciprocity with the welfare department, private agencies, such as Aquarius House and the Salvation Army, and counterculture agencies such as free clinics or crash pads. Relationship with the police is a one-way referral process from police to Traveler's Aid. Clients also come on their own, or through friends, Traveler's Aid outreach workers, an effective hotline component, or recommendation by other agencies in the community. The agency's publicity is effective. Staff utilizes a vast number of community resources to help clients with needs: community-based counseling programs, Department of Social Services, Probation Department, or Juvenile Hall, an occasional church program, residential facilities, hotlines, shelter homes and crash pads, counterculture programs, free clinics, and legal aid services.

A client seeking services during day hours may be referred from the bus terminal or airport to the local office or may arrive as a "walk-in." After filling out a basic information form, the client is seen by a social worker. The interview defines the client's needs, and an approach is decided upon to meet these needs. Services may terminate at this point, with the client receiving the needed services, or the client may be referred to other community resources. Formal and written records are part of the intake procedure. Clients may be seen immediately or may wait several hours to be seen depending upon the activity level in the office.

The night outreach worker operates more informally as a street outreach worker after 5 p.m., visiting various restaurants where transients commonly congregate. The worker maintains communication with the volunteer staff at the bus terminal and airport.

No formal intake process, with face sheet or official interview, is required for clients seen at night. The worker may give brief counseling or referrals, provide scrip for food, temporary shelter or transportation. If needed, clients are referred to the office for continuing services the next day. Generally, no documentation is required for eligibility, the exception being the parental consent must be obtained to provide housing referrals or transportation assistance for youth under 18. Youth who refuse this parental contact are referred to crash pads or Huckleberry House.

Traveler's Aid limits housing and food assistance to two or three days, following which the client may seek other resources on referral. A discount of 25 percent on Greyhound bus tickets is given, if destination can be verified. Usually the client or his relatives must be able to pay the difference before a ticket can be issued to destination. Bus tokens are provided for local transportation. Decisions regarding the type of direct services needed are negotiated between client and worker at the time of the interview or following successive counseling sessions. On the average, clients are seen for three interviews while associated with the agency.

Many runaways are seen here, but no exact numbers are available. Traveler's Aid staff views runaways as having family problems, difficulties with school, police, and personal relationships. Seven percent of the clientele during 1973-1974 were under the age of 18, including runaways and the children of transient families. Many "outcast" youth, those asked to leave home by their parents, are seen here. Some young clients seek help returning home, others who wish to separate from their families are referred to shelter homes, crash pads or Huckleberry House. Some youth request further counseling to decide upon a direction.

There are many difficulties in arranging temporary housing for young people. Local hotels used are in shabby neighborhoods. Official shelter houses cannot accept youth under 18 without parental consent, and there are insufficient short-term housing resources in general. Huckleberry House, with specific runaway services, has limited bed space. Also, Huckleberry House's policy of refusing to divulge information on client progress has caused some problems for Traveler's Aid.

Some runaways are unable to profit from Traveler's Aid. These include youth who refuse to stop running away, those who resist allowing workers to contact parents regarding temporary housing, and those who are out of state residents with no family through which to make arrangements. Probably many runaways never seek help at Traveler's Aid because they mistrust establishment agencies or because of lack of knowledge of available services.

COMMUNITY RELATIONS

Traveler's Aid reports that difficult or inadequate relationships sometimes exist with police, courts or juvenile delinquency facilities, hotline services, free clinics, counterculture agencies, and private agencies and counselors. Poor relationships exist with welfare systems of other states having jurisdiction over clients served. The key point is that for Traveler's Aid such inadequate relationships do not occur as often as seems to be the case for public welfare departments.

In regard to improving the situation, Traveler's Aid maintains community contact through agency conferences, advisory committees, reports, referrals, and telephone contacts. Traveler's Aid is well known in San Francisco and is utilized as a resource by many agencies. Staff expresses the opinion, however, that more frequent formal contact and consultation is needed.

STAFF

Traveler's Aid is primarily staffed with credentialed social workers whose services are supplemented by graduate students and volunteers.

The primary responsibility for direct services is assumed by two social workers, one after hours outreach social worker, two graduate students, and about 100 volunteers. The full-time employed staff is all Anglo. There are no figures on ethnicity of volunteers.

Agency leadership regarding policy and philosophy is coordinated by a 25-member board of directors, composed of energetic, interested persons in the community as well as some staff members. Full-time, permanent, paid staff totals eight. Administrative personnel include the executive director, the social work supervisor, the volunteer director, and office manager. All administrative personnel, except the office manager, provide direct services to some extent.

FINANCES

Traveler's Aid has no special funds available for services to runaways. The major funding source (76 percent) is the Bay Area

United Way. Other sources include capital funds and investments (18 percent), contributions and one fund-raising event (5 percent), and fees for special transportation services (1 percent). Inadequate funding has been a constant dilemma as it forces undesirable limitations on staff size and diversity of services. Additional funds are expected from the government this year. Staff also plans to apply for a demonstration grant or proposal funds in the near future.

Many imaginative ideas for services have been proposed by staff, pending increased funding. These include an emergency housing facility and a half-way house administered directly by the agency, use of a mobile van for outreach work, more comprehensive financial and travel loan assistance, use of a storefront office for streetwork counseling, a more comprehensive outreach-night-work program, and improved feedback for clients through the use of video tape.

No breakdowns on ethnicity or on presenting problems were available.

EVALUATION PROCEDURES

No evaluation is done for services given to runaways because there are no specific runaway services. For general agency services, evaluation is incorporated through group meetings, case records, and agency statistics for presentation to the Social Work Supervisor, Executive Director, Board of Directors, and funding sources. Agency staff does ongoing evaluation of clientele served through similar means. This information is used as a reflection of service effectiveness as well as an indicator of new program component needs.

BARRIERS

Staff mentioned inadequate crisis residential facilities and a lack of appropriate referrals specifically as barriers to service.

Hillsides Episcopal Home

Hillsides Episcopal Home for Children in Pasadena is a private agency that provides services for children needing residential care, individual or group therapy, placement, and after-care foster homes. The program focuses on assisting the emotionally damaged child to regain a positive self-identity. Close attention is given to the family situation and the child's feelings regarding this problem area.

Hillsides began in 1913 as an institution for homeless children. It was the state's first cottage system of care and replaced large dormitories and large common facilities with a series of small residences. Today the facilities include small cottages, a dining area, administrative offices, recreational areas, and a special education classroom. Recreation and crafts are also part of the program.

RUNAWAY SERVICES

Hillsides receives referrals from the police, schools, and other public and private agencies, and individuals in the community. Although there is no special program for runaways, staff is familiar with this behavior both in children who run away from the Home and in children who come with such a history. About half of the 55 children in residence have engaged in a runaway episode.

Hillsides receives a majority of its referrals from county placement agencies, so its contact with public agencies is quite strong. The referral breakdown is as follows: 80 percent referred by DPSS, 15 percent referred by adoptions, and 5 percent referred by probation.

The intake procedure is formal. It involves a preplacement visit, getting the child's psychosocial and physical history, school reports when the child is a county agency referral, and sometimes a social worker visit to the child's home. Following the initial referral contact, a final decision regarding placement of the child is usually made within two weeks.

Hillsides' treatment program presupposes a client's stay of from nine months to one year. Upon termination a youth is placed in an appropriate "family" situation, which is usually either his natural family or a long-term foster home. There is no formal follow-up treatment procedure.

Hillsides' view of the causes of runaway behavior are not unlike those of other agencies. Staff sees running away as a symptom of other problems: family troubles, an angry response of a child whose needs aren't being met, and a way of reacting to a disturbing problem. In the case of children who run from Hillsides, the staff feels that the children don't believe the rejection at their homes and are running back home; feel a lack of trust in any adult and cannot believe that the new adults in their lives are going to meet their needs; are running away from the necessity of having to make changes in their new living situation; are running to one parent, if the parents are not together.

The staff hopes to develop in children the ability to face up to and deal with a crisis situation, instead of running away.

COMMUNITY RELATIONS

Hillsides Episcopal Home reports good community relationships, but feels it could be more visible.

Hillsides maintains relationships with the police, schools, public and private agencies, and individuals in the community on a formal as well as informal basis. Aside from the giving and receiving of referrals between agencies, the staff has excellent relationships with many individuals who are employed by other youth serving agencies. This encourages consultation and simultaneous efforts by individuals in the interest of Hillsides' residents. For instance, individual members of the Pasadena Police Department have come to the home to relate to youth on a "person-to-person" basis.

Staff hopes to increase the community's awareness of Hillsides' program. Past "open houses" have been successful in this regard, and similar efforts are planned.

Staff. The staff at Hillsides is composed of social workers and house parents. Although there are no academic requirements for houseparents, a background in childcare work is required. On the other hand master's degrees are required of all social workers. House parents serve as surrogate parents to children in each house. Each cottage has 24-hour coverage. There is also a secretarial staff and a home pediatrician. (See organizational chart).

HILLSIDES EPISCOPAL HOME FOR CHILDREN

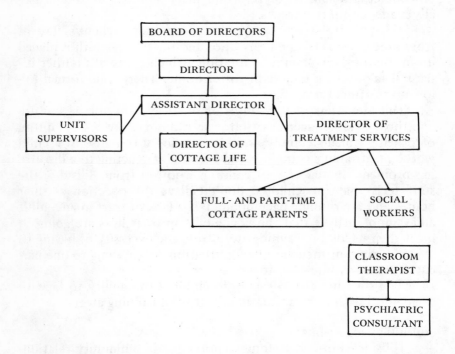

Finances. About 80 to 85 percent of Hillsides' budget needs are met by county funds, with the additional 15 to 20 percent being contributed by private donors. Since there is no treatment component aimed at working with runaways, no figures on monies spent directly on runaways can be given. It costs Hillsides $1,013 per child per month.

Demographic Information. Hillsides works with about 50 new children each year. Although the home is in Pasadena, children who live at Hillsides come from all over the Los Angeles area. Residents represent various ethnic backgrounds.

Evaluation Procedures. There is an annual county evaluation. Internal evaluation is done in staff meetings and in staff supervisory sessions.

In addition, Hillsides belongs to the California Association of Children's Residential Centers, which evaluates the program's standards of care, type of treatment, and quality of facilities.

Barriers to Service. Barriers which affect service to runaways at Hillsides involve funding and staffing. Staff feels that additional funds would enable expansion and provide a lower child-staff ratio. Lower staff turnover among cottage parents would provide more continuity and structure.

If the program were to be enhanced, staff has suggested peer group counseling, psychological counseling that focuses on running away, play therapy, and more time to spend individually with a runaway child.

THE DIVERSION AGENCIES

Charila Foundation

The Charila Foundation was founded in 1968 by two women therapists, a psychiatrist and a psychodramatist, as a private residential treatment center for adolescent girls considered dependent or delinquent wards of the court. No such facilities or foster homes were available at that time in San Francisco for girls 15 or older. Initially, four girls were referred to Charila by a probation officer. Two additional group homes were added in 1969 and 1971 to accommodate increasing referrals. Other changes have included a larger counseling staff, improved staff pay and working conditions, an informal aftercare program, and accreditation as a "therapeutic institution" by the Accreditation Council for Psychiatric Facilities.

The program operates 24 hours a day, seven days a week, although most of the girls are in school or vocational programs during weekdays. House counselors rotate day and overnight assignments to maintain 24-hour care. Administrative and therapy staff members are on call apart from their normal Monday through Friday day hours.

Charila is unique as a residential treatment center in the services it provides to girls aged 15 to 18. Other community agencies with similar structure and services include Mount St. Joseph's Home, Convent of the Good Shepherd, Homewood Terrace, and Sunny Hills Group Home. However, none of these agencies duplicates Charila exactly, and most serve a younger clientele.

Relationships with other agencies such as the Welfare and Probation departments, Huckleberry House, Sunny Hills, schools, and police do exist. Referrals are made to and from these agencies. Charila is known and used as a referral source mainly by agencies, not individuals.

Eighty percent of the young women who reside at Charila are referred by county probation departments. Fifteen percent are referred by county welfare departments. The agency is used as a diversion program. Community mental health programs and hospitals refer the remaining five percent. In rare cases, Charila accepts private referrals if parents are willing to pay.

Normally, a self-referred girl must first be involved through a county agency. While in residence at Charila, a girl may be referred by staff to other agencies for supplementary services. These agencies include Planned Parenthood, Neighborhood Legal Assistance, Pacific Medical Center for in-patient psychiatric treatment, welfare or juvenile hall for brief detention, and private doctors.

Upon termination of services, staff makes a recommendation to the referring agency regarding placement or disposition. At this point, a young woman may be referred to another agency, relatives or friends, a private counselor, foster placement, Huckleberry House, the juvenile detention facility, or a hospital psychiatric ward. Another option is independent living.

Charila, situated in a residential San Francisco neighborhood, is a nonprofit corporation governed by a board of directors of lay persons and a medical director. The three group homes are licensed by the California Department of Health and provide residences for nine girls per home. Since its inception in 1968, over 75 girls have become Charila graduates.

Runaway Services. The Charila Foundation is a long-term residential treatment center for older adolescent girls considered wards of the court because of a determined delinquent or dependent status. Girls remain in one of the three group homes for an average stay of one year.

Runaways who become Charila residents are most likely to be referred by a law enforcement or social contact agency. There is no separate treatment program for runaways, although most clients have run away at some point prior to referral or while in residence.

Charila's treatment process differs from that of the public agencies, and there is a heavy emphasis on counseling services. The public agencies (DPSS' Welfare) provide for the protection of children through a court process, and no other agency has the legal authority to remove a child from the home for reasons of neglect, abuse, or abandonment.

As a residential treatment center Charila provides the necessary life sustaining services (food, shelter, transportation). A great emphasis is placed on counseling: weekly individual therapy, weekly psychodrama groups, vocational counseling, and family counseling when appropriate. Additional services include group recreation, summer camp program, placement assistance, and an active referral service to other agency resources.

Treatment philosophy is based upon premises that girls receiving treatment need satisfaction of emotional and physical needs, love, direction, a sense of purpose, self-esteem, and a chance to find identity.

The Charila staff looks at runaway behavior as a symptom and sees its mission as giving disturbed, problem girls a beginning in their life perspective and relationships. The focus is on assisting the client in movement toward self-sufficiency and independence.

As previously mentioned, intake is dependent upon referral from county welfare or probation departments. Normally, these referring agencies send a fact sheet and some descriptive information on the girl to the intake social worker. If successfully screened, the girl is then interviewed jointly by the social worker and three house directors to determine her interest and ability to fit into the program. Additionally, she is given testing and an in-depth interview by the psychologist. Girls who are accepted may then begin Charila residence and treatment immediately if an opening exists or may have to wait for one month until space is available. Charila does not accept girls with a history of violence or prostitution, pregnant girls, habitual users of hard narcotics, those with I.Q.s under 84, or those that are not motivated to use services.

Termination of services is normally planned as a decision of the client, therapist, and house director. Following termination, staff must send an evaluation of the girl's school progress, health, personal relationships, and community relationships to the referring agency. An evaluation is also prepared monthly.

Although there are no formal follow-up programs, there are unofficial services. Girls may return for informal visits and for counseling with house staff. Ideas on handling finances or referrals may also be given.

Recently, the three house directors started a monthly women's group for Charila graduates. Future plans include an official aftercare program including assistance in finding housing, jobs, schooling, and help in developing an appropriate self-support system. Monthly group sessions will be held for aftercare women, and crisis intervention will be provided as needed. This future program does not include longterm psychotherapy. Those needing it will be referred.

Community Relations. Charila reports good community relations with occasional problems arising only with individual school personnel, probation officers, or neighbors. Intercommunity relationships are maintained through frequent telephone contacts, referrals, quarterly reports on each girl to the referring agency, and conferences with the California Children's Group Home Association.

Staff. At Charila, all staff who work with runaway youth hold academic credentials. The direct service staff includes one vocational counselor, a psychologist, three house directors, 13 counselors, and a psychodramatist. The executive director and the medical director provide some direct services. There are also six community volunteers.

Executive and administrative staff works from 9 a.m. to 5 p.m. Other staff members schedule flexible and rotating hours to meet the needs of a 24-hour care program.

Finances. Charila Foundation has no special treatment program for runaways, and consequently it is impossible to put a price tag on it. However, most girls living at Charila have run away at some point prior to referral or while in residence. Since the majority of residents are referred by probation departments, county welfare, mental health centers, and hospitals, most of the funds come from public sources.

Major funding sources (90 percent) incorporate state and county funds through the participating county welfare and probation departments. Parents may be billed through court pay orders according to ability to pay. Some federal funding (5 percent) may be given through Champois insurance in specific cases. The vocational counselor's salary is paid through the California State Department of Rehabilitation. Contributions and donations from businesses, individuals, and private foundations comprise other funding sources (5 percent). Finally, young women who reside at Charila contribute to funding through such activities as dinners, an annual fashion show, and organizing car washes.

Demographic Information. The area served includes all northern California counties, with Santa Cruz county as the southern boundary. No statistics are available on numbers of runaways, nor was a breakdown on age and race available. Statistics for 1973-1974 show Charila received 56 new referrals, with 31 accepted for treatment.

Average daily population was 94 percent capacity or 25 girls in residence.

Evaluation. Agency evaluation takes several forms. Clients regularly evaluate services. These are sent to each girl's probation officer. Other evaluations are done by staff through written reports, individual and group meetings. The Bay Area Placement Committee, which includes probation officers, does an annual evaluation of Charila.

Additional outside evaluations are made by United Bay Area Crusade and the Joint Accreditation Committee on Hospitals. No actual program effectiveness statistics have been compiled. Client evaluation is continuous, with testing, weekly evaluations, and follow-up reports to the referring agency.

The Way Home

The Way Home Foundation, a community clinic located in the San Fernando Valley, is a nontraditional counseling center that contains a diversion component. Its purposes are to improve adult-child communication, to help youth develop self-awareness, to improve decision-making ability, and to improve family relationships through therapy.

The Way Home offers therapy and consultation for individuals, couples, families, and groups. Special ongoing groups and programs have been designed for women, children, teenagers, single parents, and divorced persons. Areas served include drug and alcohol-related problems, school and learning difficulties, and diversion from correctional systems.

The foundation was begun over three years ago by six family therapists interested in starting a nontraditional counseling center in the San Fernando Valley. It developed without any major funding grants. The program has grown and now includes facilities in West Los Angeles, Santa Clarita Valley, and Canoga Park. The Way Home has also recently acquired land near the Sequoia National Forest. This site will be used for a residential center, ecological sanctuary, retreat and conference grounds, which it is planned, will be ready for use by summer 1977.

This report focuses on the San Fernando Valley facility, which serves Reseda, Woodland Hills, Canoga Park, the West Valley, Chatsworth, Sepulveda, and Van Nuys.

The Way Home maintains relationships with police, schools, and other public and private agencies. Relationships exist on a formal and informal level. The Way Home is also a member of the

San Fernando Valley Drug Abuse Coalition-West, San Fernando Valley Drug Abuse Coalition-East, and the Interagency (Task Force) on Drug Abuse and Related Problems. Staff feels that more effective public relations methods would increase visibility in the community.

The Way Home is licensed as a community clinic with the county and state. The San Fernando Valley center is at 15643 Sherman Way in Van Nuys.

RUNAWAY SERVICES

One component of The Way Home counseling center is a diversion program. Diversion programs provide youth with an alternative to involvement with the juvenile justice system. A juvenile who is in a diversion program usually has been charged with a first offense or nonserious crime. The youth is given the alternative of becoming involved with a community counseling program. Under this program, the youth's offense is not recorded. The Way Home's diversion program is comprised primarily of referrals from probation, police, and schools. Some also come from the sheriff's department.

The Way Home handles many diversion cases a month, of which one-fourth are listed as runaways. Runaways may receive services here as diversion cases or through referral from schools, friends, or private agencies. The Way Home sees its mission as providing counseling services: to assist youth in developing a deeper self-awareness and understanding of available alternatives, to improve family relationships, and to educate those involved with youth in effective adult-child communication.

The Way Home views running away as a symptom of an individual's family and emotional problems. In counseling, the focus is on assisting the client in developing feelings of self-esteem, autonomy, and understanding of self.

Staff members are assigned to coordinate the intake process. Minimal funds are available for administrative or secretarial staff. Most counselors arrange their own schedules. A switchboard operates at all times. Walk-in cases are discouraged, unless there is a crisis.

Therapy is usually short-term, and termination of services is decided on by all involved. There is no formal follow-up procedure except for funded programs.

Strengths of the program include: a diversity of counseling techniques, no waiting list, and a treatment philosophy that is responsive to the needs of youth.

STAFF

At The Way Home, only an executive director, administrator, intake worker, and a secretary are full-time employees. The direct service staff is composed of 30 part-time professional counselors, graduate students, and community volunteers. The professional staff does receive a percentage of fees paid by clients for services. Students receive professional supervision and credit for placement training.

FINANCES

The Way Home Foundation offers a contrast to public agencies in that it operates on a much smaller scale and is not primarily dependent on public funding. The foundation relies partly on the state to support its adult diversion program. These funds, SB 714 diversion money, account for about 12 percent of the program's funds.

In 1974, the San Fernando Valley program's budget was $41,000. The 1975 budget was almost double that amount. It costs the foundation about $40.85 for each client per month at an estimated $9.50 per session. Fees paid by counselors for training and client fees respectively contribute another 20 and 68 percent of the funds. Clients are charged for services on the basis of a sliding fee scale devised by the State Departmentof Health. GRS funds of $71,000 were received for 1975-76 for the youth drug program.

DEMOGRAPHIC INFORMATION

Aside from funded programs, The Way Home works with a total of 403 clients annually. A majority are residents of the largely white and middle-class San Fernando Valley.

EVALUATION

Evaluation of the counseling program takes place during staff supervisory and training sessions. Accountability reports are filed with the state in connection with SB 714 diversion funds and GRS funds. A program report is also given to the county.

BARRIERS TO SERVICE

Barriers to providing services to runaways center around legal restrictions as they apply to runaway situations, lack of adequate referrals, and inadequacy of funds. Staff feels the program could be improved in the following areas: more space, additional administrative staff, a staff outreach worker, and the ability to provide services for any juvenile regardless of circumstances.

THE WAY HOME

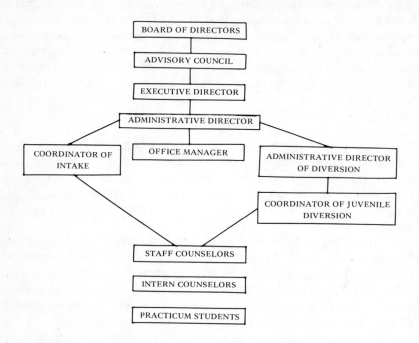

THE COUNTERCULTURE AGENCIES

Huckleberry House

Huckleberry House (Huck's), a counterculture agency in the San Francisco area, was born out of a need for temporary housing and crisis services for runaway youth.

Huckleberry's for Runaways opened in June 1967, with direct housing facilities for young women and housing resources for young men through local families. Many runaways were helped that first summer either with housing services, crisis counseling, and/or family counseling. Unstable and insufficient funding was a major problem until 1971, when funds for a runaway program were granted through the National Institute of Mental Health and a San Francisco city and county contract was awarded. By this time, Youth Advocates assumed administrative responsibility for Huck's.

Third-world persons now comprise half the staff. They have brought many new viewpoints to the program. From its early roots as a "counterculture" agency, Huck's is seen now as an established, alternative agency. Services have increased along with bureaucratic procedures, paperwork, and adjustment stresses as new staff has been hired.

Many young persons in crisis seek counseling here before considering a runaway episode. Thus, they differ from the original runaway clientele in that they seek help at the outset for serious problems. Finally, Huckleberry House staff recognizes improvements in its own development as a working group. In the early years, staff members banded together against the establishment and attempted to find themselves through a group identification. Presently, staff has developed much more expertise, individual strength and a tolerance for differing viewpoints. Services operate on a 24-hour basis, and no fees are charged for these services.

 Oganizationally, Huckleberry House is one component of the umbrella agency Youth Advocates, but it is the major component and receives about 90 percent of new cases served by the larger organization. Philosophically, Huck's staff has been in disagreement with Youth Advocates codirectors around economic and political issues.

RUNAWAY SERVICES

Youth more often seek services at Huck's because of their own motivation, rather than by direction of the juvenile justice system or welfare institutions. Relationships do exist between Huck's and the established public agencies.

Some youth come by referral from the police or sheriff's office, probation department, a court, schools, friends, outreach workers, a hotline component, mental health agencies, or private and public agencies. Because Huck's focuses on crisis services, staff utilizes referrals to every conceivable public, private, counterculture, and diversion program available in the community in order to assist youth with their unmet or continuing needs.

When Huck's opened, runaways were the primary client group, but it was origianlly intended as a crisis center. Now it serves about half as many runaways as it did originally, and offers preventive services to troubled youth as well. According to staff, there is a greater incidence of youth seeking help before considering a runaway episode. Referral percentages illustrate this point:

33 percent self-referred
20 percent by parents
13 percent by schools
8 percent by relatives
6 percent by other agencies
5 percent by police and courts
5 percent by welfare agencies
4 percent by community agencies
6 percent by "other" sources

These percentages are for all clients served, not just runaways. The "other" category includes referral by outreach workers and house hotline. All the referrals, and especially the self-referrals, attest to the publicity given the agency.

Huckleberry House provides comprehensive services for youth with any kind of problem. Self-determination for clients is strongly encouraged. Primary emphasis is on supporting the stated goals of the client rather than telling the client what his/her goals should be. Staff tries not to evaluate client behavior in an isolated, judgmental manner, but views behavior in the context of individual growth.

A crucial aspect of service delivery is helping clients be aware of their personal power. Clients are encouraged to focus on the process of their self-development rather than the outcome. Staff is committed to presenting clients with a number of alternative ideas for crisis resolution, based upon the belief that at a time of crisis a person is more able to accept alternative directions and to grow in self-mastery.

Services offered include a financial allowance, meals, crisis counseling, medical help, a hotline, and temporary residential facilities on a 24-hour basis. Long-term residential facilities are available through other components of Youth Advocates. Counseling is offered on a long-term and short-term basis and includes the options of individual, family and group counseling. Other services include 24-hour availability of legal counseling, some vocational counseling, comprehensive referral services, recreational outings, and placement counseling to assist youth with alternatives to living at home. Unofficial services are given in the form of talking with some youth over 18 and with former clients following termination of services about their progress and experience with other agencies. Many staff members provide unofficial services through overtime work and political activism in the community.

Intake procedures involve two steps. First, the client fills out a questionnaire for basic information. Then, two counselors have an in-depth interview with the client to assess the situation. A contract is made with the client, which may not include counseling. Counseling is optional for the client. The treatment contract is influenced by input from the youth and counselors, plus the family, if involved. The intake process is both formal and informal, requiring written records. Should the youth wish short-term residential help, she/he must call parents for consent. Sometimes there is a short waiting period before treatment begins.

Termination of services occurs primarily when clients leave the agency to return to their families, become self-sufficient, or choose an alternative placement.

Because this is a crisis center, clients generally do not reside at Huck's beyond two to three weeks. Referrals are made elsewhere for long-term residential placement if the client does not wish to return home. Many other clients who reside at home may continue in long-term counseling with staff.

Follow-up procedures are both formal and informal, including written reports to referring agencies and to parents. Frequently, terminated clients return or write to discuss their ongoing development with staff.

COMMUNITY RELATIONS

Huckleberry House staff is candid about its poor relationship with the police and the top hierarchy of the juvenile justice system, primarily with judges. Many philosophical differences exist with these groups. Recently the police asked Huck's to be part of a diversion program, necessitating an open records policy, which is antithetical to the treatment philosophy there. Police have threatened not to use Huck's for referral unless staff complies.

Sometimes staff reports experiencing conflicts with welfare departments over placement for certain youth. Relationships of variable quality exist with private agencies, private citizens, and schools. Difficulties occur more frequently with individuals than with entire agencies. It does not appear that staff maintains ongoing relationships with school personnel.

The least conflictual contacts exist with free clinics, hotlines, and counterculture agencies.

Huck's is well known and utilized by community agencies as well as the youth lay referral system. Agency image is variably positive or negative according to individual relationships. Some agencies express strong disapproval of Huck's confidentiality policy. Other agencies express strong faith in, and support for, Huck's staff, program components, and high credibility with youth.

Community relationships are maintained through occasional agency conference reports and newsletters, an active reciprocal relationship with public and private agencies, and through telephone contacts.

STAFF

Staff positions are separated by some role distinctions and differential financial remuneration. The two coordinators essentially act as administrators and assume clinical responsibility for the quality of services. Two counseling coordinators help execute all services rendered at Huck's, supervise the intake counselors, house managers and volunteers, and also direct counseling with youth.

Primary responsibility for intake screening and formation of contracts with clients is handled by two intake counselors.

Two house managers are responsible for physical house care, preparing meals, and counseling clients. Staff is hired mostly on the basis of sensitivity and experience with youth rather than formal education. Those primarily providing direct services are trained through individual supervisory sessions, staff sessions, and staff seminars with consultants. Additionally, every Huck's staff member is given an annual $600 stipend to use for personal therapy, or selected conferences.

Within the present staff structure, the group makes decisions by consensus and the coordinators take responsibility for decisions the group makes. A reorganization of this format in terms of decisionmaking, authority, and responsibility is expected to occur later this year. Essentially, the coordinators no longer wish to take responsibility for group decisions, but wish to encourage more individual responsiblity among staff members.

FINANCES

Like 1736 House, Huckleberry House does not have records of monies spent on runaway services, although almost two-thirds of the clients seen are runaways. Funding is provided through county, state, and federal grants. Some funding is given by the United Bay Crusade. No exact proportions are available per funding source. Most funding up to this point has come through drug abuse or juvenile delinquency prevention money. However, Huck's does receive funds through an Office of Youth Development Grant in the amount of $74,000 per year.

DEMOGRAPHIC INFORMATION

Youth from all over the nation are served at this agency, but generally close to 60 percent are Bay Area residents. Clients' ages ranged from 12 to 18. Two-thirds of them were 15 or 16 years old. Clients who defined themselves as runaways comprised 62 percent of those seen. Forty-six percent came from families living in San Francisco and 16 percent from families living within the greater Bay Area. Females comprised 57.9 percent of the client population. Ethnicity of clients was delineated as follows: 62.1 percent Caucasian, 18.4 percent black, 13.1 percent Latino-Chicano, and 6.1 percent other, mostly Asian.

Huckleberry House tends to see about 40 new clients per month and of these, about 12 participate with their families in explorative family sessions. Approximately 53 percent of the new clients are housed, with an average length of stay of 5.8 days. The house has accommodations for six young people at any one time, with an average capacity of 5.1 clients per night.

EVALUATION

Youth Advocates and all of its components, including Huckleberry House, are evaluated continuously by the Institute for the Study of Social Health Issues. This Berkeley organization is funded to evaluate Youth Advocates under a grant from the National Institute of Mental Health. An extensive report is published quarterly describing individual programs, staff trends, client statistical information, intracomponent relations, and intercomponent relations. Evaluators prepare their analysis through daily visits to component sites, attendance at staff meetings, and follow-up with clients who are willing to discuss their experiences with the agency. At Huckleberry House, an evaluator holds a conference with one of the coordinators on a monthly basis, gives evaluation questionnaires to all staff, and attends group meetings. Four evaluators interview clients on a daily basis and talk with some clients for follow-up information.

Other types of evaluation are performed by the Youth Advocates Board on an informal basis, by staff, by clients themselves, and by the community-at-large through open houses attended by neighbors, police, and so on. Clients are evaluated by staff twice daily and through termination and follow-up reports. Staff evaluates itself on a continuous basis during staff meetings and individual supervisory conferences. This ongoing process aids staff in defining new goals and changes in treatment procedures.

BARRIERS

Huck's staff reported that conflicts with its supervising agency, Youth Advocates, creates problems. This conflict evolved out of differences in orientation between Huck's staff and the leadership of Youth Advocates.

1736 House

1736 House, a large home next to the pier in Hermosa Beach, a Los Angeles seaside suburb, provides 24-hour crisis service. The program began three years ago as an outreach effort of a local church and involved street work and short-term housing for youth. The program grew primarily due to the efforts of two individuals, one of whom, a probation officer, became the first staff coordinator.

At present the service emphasis is on short-term, crisis counseling. The focus is to provide an atmosphere in which clients can use crisis situations for growth. Less than one-fifth of the clients are runaways.

RUNAWAY SERVICES

As an agency serving runaways, 1736 sees a need for good relationships with police. This has developed gradually through contact between staff and juvenile officers. The staff works with the system, without losing sight of its primary concern for runaway youth. House records show a total of 97 runaway cases handled between May 1974 and April 1975. This included 27 brief crisis services.

At intake, a runaway's first contact with staff is intense. An effort is made to build trust immediately so as not to frighten the youth away when the necessary steps are taken to work within legal confines. The intake procedure usually takes place informally during the initial discussion and contact with a client. Often, a first contact is by phone, and when necessary the youth comes to the house. There is no waiting period.

It is necessary to contact a runaway's parents. Staff makes an effort to buy time in order to work with youth. Police are always contacted when there is a runaway who may have a missing person's report filed. The house strives to uphold an image of a place where people stay to work on a problem. It is not a crash pad.

Services offered to runaways at the 1736 House are intended to meet the needs of the individual as perceived by staff members. Services available include short-term crisis counseling, during which a youth is helped to look at alternatives, to define what he is going through, and perhaps to decide upon some immediate directions in life. Whenever necessary and possible, the individual's family becomes involved in the short-term or crisis counseling sessions.

There is living room for 12 residents at the house. The designated residential time is three days and rarely does anyone stay longer than one week. Services are provided strictly on the level of crisis intervention, thus treatment is short-term, often intense, and may include a referral to a long-term counseling program. The process of terminating a case varies depending on the presenting problem. Sometimes a social worker refers a client who is about to be placed and has nowhere to stay for a night to the house as an alternative to a brief Juvenile Hall placement. In this case, the length of involvement is predetermined. In an average counseling situation, the termination process usually involves a decision made by the counselor at the house, the client, and whoever else has become involved. No formal follow-up procedures are implemented.

Credibility exists with the adult community. Parents or police sometimes bring a teenager to the house. The house also has credibility with youth who often learn of services through friends.

1736 House is of counterculture vintage. Referrals for clients serviced between May 1974 and April 1975 were as follows:

> 21 percent by friend
> 13 percent by hotline
> 12 percent by unknown
> 9 percent by police
> 7 percent by other agency
> 6 percent by church
> 6 percent by Harbor General Hospital
> 5 percent by schools
> 5 percent by citizens
> 4 percent by self-referral
> 4 percent by doctors
> 3 percent by DPSS
> 2 percent by relatives
> 2 percent by county mental hospital
> 1 percent by probation department

This table includes all clients served, not just runaways. Only 17 percent of 564 clients served were listed as runaways.

COMMUNITY RELATIONS

Staff constantly strives to be in contact with the community, particularly with individuals who are involved in youth work. Relationships are maintained through giving and receiving referrals, tellephone contacts, and meetings with many local agencies. Staff also consults at school and community meetings and participates in training seminars.

1736 House is well known in the South Bay area and has become an established referral source. Staff feels that its methods for maintaining community relationships are sufficient; however, it would like to have more time to devote to this. Many staff members feel there is a constant need to stay in touch with "the pulse beat of the community."

STAFF

An organizational chart includes the Beach Ministry Commission, executive board, staff coordinator, four full-time, paid staff and three part-time staff.

Staff training is informal and usually involves on-the-job training, often in the form of coleading a counseling session. All staff members have been involved with 1736 before being hired. An important staff qualification is commitment to the program.

Staff at 1736 House always attempts to involve the youth's family in counseling. In addition, other significant individuals may become involved—school personnel or social workers—in an attempt to treat youth within the context of their environment. Runaway behavior is always seen as symptomatic.

FINANCES

The program is dependent on contributions from the city, local church, church dioceses, private industry, small clubs, or individuals. Present operating costs are about $1,200 a month. This includes staff salaries, phone, gas, utility bills, and petty cash. The facility is rent free; like the food supply rent is donated by the church. There is no fee charged for services.

DEMOGRAPHIC INFORMATION

A majority of 1736 clients live in the surrounding neighborhood, a predominantly white, middle-class area.

EVALUATION

Evaluation takes three forms: an annual report to the church, an evaluation by the executive board, and an informal evaluation by staff. The ongoing evaluation utilizes feedback from clients and staff.

BARRIERS TO SERVICE

The greatest barriers affecting service to runaways are financial. Funding is insufficient and unstable, and this affects the service potential. Staff is often occupied with fund-raising activities.

If the house were to expand, additional services for runaways would include: parent groups, peer counseling, educational workshops, a half-way house, and a job development program for juveniles who want to be independent.

1736 HOUSE

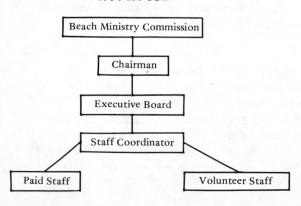

APPENDIX III

Runaway Resource Guide

YOUTH SERVICES IN CALIFORNIA'S SAN FRANCISCO BAY AND LOS ANGELES AREAS

INTRODUCTION

In 1974 the Institute for Scientific Analysis was awarded a grant by the Social and Rehabilitation Service of the U.S. Department of Health, Education and Welfare to study "Runaway Youth: How Are They To Be Served?" This study entailed a survey of services currently available to runaways in the San Francisco Bay and Los Angeles areas of California. A natural and useful byproduct of the survey was the compilation of a list of the agencies and facilities performing the relevant services.

Very few agencies are exclusively concerned with runaways. Our list, therefore, consists mostly of agencies that serve a more varied clientele, but are designed to meet needs that runaways are likely to have. As the list reveals, the fewest services are available for the most common needs, that is, free or low-cost shelter (without minimum age or parental approval requirements) and food. Counseling and medical services are more abundant.

We anticipate that the list will be used primarily by existing agencies to refer runaways to other facilities that can better meet some specific need. We also assume the agencies will make this directory available to runaways, so that they have an informational basis upon which to choose the resource that seems most appropriate to them. We have organized this directory by geographic locale and the principal category of service offered. The latter criterion posed problems, as some agencies offer several services, and do not themselves emphasize a principal service. Thus, for example, many agencies listed under "Youth Services" offer counseling, and yet we deemed it appropriate to have a separate listing for agencies that specialize in counseling. Generally, "Youth Services" is the designation that most resembles an umbrella, covering things that range from recreation and tutoring to food and shelter. Consequently, we have used this umbrella to also cover agencies that, strictly speaking, are not "Youth Services", for example, the Salvation Army and Travelers Aid. We hope we will be forgiven this transgression against categorical precision. At any rate, the reader is forewarned.

SAN FRANCISCO BAY AREA YOUTH SERVICES

There are two centers in the Bay Area with services designed specifically for runaways—Huckleberry House and Berkeley Youth Alternatives, which are listed and underlined below. However, because running away is frequently a sympton, as well as a problem, we have combined runaway centers, various youth services (including legal aid), and "juvenile delinquency prevention and control" programs here. These labels don't necessarily describe the nature or limits of the program, so don't let them stop you from finding out more. The many private residential youth homes in the Bay Area can be found in two of the directories listed in that section of the Resource Guide. Other good sources to explore for recreation, classes, and so on, are the parks and recreation departments of each city, and the YWCA and YMCA services offered in the area. We use asterisks to designate special types of programs as follows: *runaway center, **juvenile delinquency prevention and control program, ***legal aid.

Alameda County

Barrio Youth Service Center, 3334 E. 14th Street, Oakland, 94601 (415) 534-7002

Barrio is a bilingual program for Oakland residents, ages 12-17. Previously it served minor offenders who were referred by police, probation, and schools, but it has expanded to become a recreational program with a heavy emphasis on counseling for any youth needing its services. In addition to male and female youth clubs, it offers a variety of sports, field trips, tutoring, cultural information, and anything else it can do to improve a young person's situation.

Berkeley Workreation Council, Inc., 739 Allston Way, Berkeley, 94710, (415) 548-2281

A work program for Berkeley residents ages 14-18, who are in school. The jobs include clerical, park, and other city of Berkeley positions, and the salary is $2 an hour. Applications are made through the schools.

*Berkeley Youth Alternatives, 2141 Bonar Street, Berkeley, 94702, (415) 849-1402

Situated in a huge ex-warehouse, BYA offers a drop-in center, counseling services (individual, peer, group, family), legal services, streetworkers doing outreach in the community, as well as an in-school "pre-runaway" counseling service. A crisis housing facility in the building is being expanded. BYA runs a group home on 8th Street, Berkeley, with beds for six males, most of whom are court wards, and the organization has state health department approval to license and operate foster homes for its own placements. Through its volunteer training program, it provides alcholic counseling, and is developing several new components, including men's and women's awareness groups, drug counseling, health and sex education counseling, and vocational and occupational counseling.

Kairos Unlimited, 6001 Camden Street, Oakland, 94605, (415) 635-5787

A nonprofit crisis center dealing with adolescent and family problems. It houses up to six young women, ages 12-18, on a five to 15 day basis while counseling them and their families. It is chiefly a diversion program. All counselors live at the center, which is open 24 hours. Appointments can be made from 8 a.m.–11 p.m., seven days a week. The low sliding scale fee depends on the monthly income of family and number of children at home.

San Antonio Area Youth Project, P. O. Box 925, 1811 - 11th Avenue, Oakland, 94604, (415) 533-5800

SAAYP provides boys of different racial backgrounds, age 13 and up, with counseling, tutoring, recreation, employment referrals, medical/dental care, encouragement to remain in school, clothing, food, housing, and court services. The boys are referred to the project by the Juvenile Court of Alameda County or the CYA Board.

**Thresholds, 4801 East 14th Street, Oakland, 94601

Programs include job development, formation of United Youth Community Council, crisis intervention, a school counseling program, parental involvement, exposure to educational, cultural, and recreational activities, a library, clothes closet, and food locker for needy families. It is seen as a diversion from police custody as well as a walk-in program for East Oakland residents. The original concept was developed by ex-offenders.

**Youth Adult Project, 3051 Adeline Street, Berkeley, 94703, (415) 848-7342

Sponsored by Recreation and Parks and Community Services Departments of Berkeley, YAP has recreation, educational, and cultural activities for young adults between the ages of 15 and 25. It offers a variety of classes, excursions (free to participants), tutoring services, and individual, family, educational, and employment counseling. Berkeley's "only newsletter for young adults," the YAP *RAP* is published by it.

Xanthos House, 2528 Clement Street, Alameda, 94501, (415) 522-8363

Xanthos is an alternative youth service for people in the city of Alameda, ages 15-25. It has a drop-in center from 3:30 p.m. to 10 p.m. Monday through Friday, and an information and referral switchboard open 2 p.m. to 10 p.m. on those days. In addition to a diversion program oriented toward drug users and a variety of counseling services, it offers recreational classes and a Friday night coffeehouse.

Berkeley Emergency Food Project, University Lutheran Church, 2425 College (Haste St. Entrance), Berkeley, 94704, (415) 843-6230

Dinner served Monday through Saturday at 5 p.m., is 35 cents or free if you work in the Coffee Cellar, the project's evening recreation program at the First Baptist Church on Dana and Haste. The Coffee Cellar is open Monday, Tuesday, Thursday, and Friday, 6 p.m.–10 p.m., and offers movies, crafts, games, and occasional cooking projects as well as some personal and vocational counseling. Open to all ages, the program is free.

Berkeley Street Work Project, 2736 Bancroft Way, Berkeley, 94704, (415) 848-3378

A resource, referral, and advocacy center whose purpose is to work with low or nonincome people, especially in the South Campus Community. It hooks people up with the service that will meet their needs (food, shelter, medical, legal, counseling, and so on. It also has a panel of doctors, lawyers, and other professionals to help with special problems.

Emergency Shelter Program, 24679 Second Street, Hayward, 94541, (415) 537-0170

ESP is a home that accommodates from six to ten persons at one time, for up to seven days. It does not accept people under 18 without consent from parents or guardians, which can be arranged if necessary through the Family Crisis Intervention Unit (see separate listing for FCI information.) It has Human Service Assistants available on a 24 hours basis for counseling, referrals, securing aid from public agencies, or finding medical care. There is a homelike atmosphere in which three meals a day are provided.

Newman Hall, 2700 Dwight Way (corner/College), Berkeley, 94704, (415) 848-7812

Free showers are provided Tuesdays and Fridays, 1 p.m.–4:30 p.m., towel included (no soap). Open to all ages.

Salvation Army Service Center, Clay Street Center, 810 Clay Street, Oakland, 94607.

Lunch (11:30 a.m.) and dinner (4:30 p.m.) are served. Price is according to income: if you cannot pay, be there on time, since a limited number of free meals is available.

Spanish Speaking Information Center, (Centro de Informacion de Servicios), 1924 Fruitvale (before Foothill), Oakland, 94601, (415) 261-7839

This is a community center which offers survival assistance to both Spanish and English-speaking people. It provides general information and referrals, assistance with welfare, and help in finding jobs.

It will be offering a free clerical training class (typing, shorthand, office skills) with bilingual instruction, open to people of all ages. It also has Neighborhood Youth Corps slots for those who are eligible.

Marin County

C.C. Riders, (mobile unit), 890 Tamalpais Avenue, Novato, 94947, (415) 897-6155

C.C. Riders operate a GMC van which is in radio contact with the Novato house. They station themselves in various spots in the community to do counseling and make referrals. Call the Novato house to make an appointment for counseling if you wish to go directly there.

Rites of Passage, 1010 Grand, San Rafael, 94901.

A counseling program for young people (10-18) who have become in some sense dysfunctional through drug or alcohol use. Its hours are 10 a.m. to 6 p.m. Monday through Friday. In addition to family sessions, individual counseling and groups, it takes kids on wilderness trips. Individual minors are free, families on a sliding scale basis.

Sunny Hills Children's Services, 300 Sunny Hills Drive, San Anselmo, 94960, (415) 457-3200

Sunny Hills has three program components: (1) Residential psychiatric facility. A voluntary non-lock-up campus focusing on group work and passing through four "Phases" to graduation. Complete medical care is given, and the average stay is six to eight months. Referral sources are unrestricted although the 24-hour intensive program is an expensive one. There is an on-campus school. (2) Day treatment program. The young people attend 9 a.m. to 5 p.m., and there are parents' groups in the evenings. (3) Two group homes in the Richmond District of San Francisco. The emphasis here is keeping the kids in the community, training for jobs or in school.

Youth Advocates, Inc., 9 Grove Lane, San Anselmo, 94960

This facility has a 24-hour crisis line, crisis housing for six people (ages 12-18) for up to 30 days, individual and family counseling, video taping, and a placement service for foster and group homes. It takes referrals from DPSS, Juvenile Hall, local police, and the general public. Also, it has two attorneys on call for legal representation and counseling.

San Francisco

Big Brothers, Inc. of the Bay Area, 693 Mission Street, San Francisco, 94105, (415) 989-1250; San Rafael, 453-3022; Oakland 452-1219

Bay Area Big Sisters, 1356 Cole Street, San Francisco, 94117, (415) 982-4190; Alameda, 444-2596; Marin, 924-6282

These two organizations match on a one-to-one basis young people between the ages of 6 and 16 with adults for friendship. The Big Sister's or Brother's commitment is to see the youth twice a month for one year. Referrals may come from anywhere, including the youth her/himself.

**Chinatown-North Beach Youth Services, 250 Columbus Avenue, San Francisco, 94133, (415) 433-7163

Youth Services offers individual, family, and small peer group counseling to people ages 13-17. It encourages youth to plan their own fund-raising activities for trips, and so on. Translators are also available for parents who accompany youth to the Youth Guidance Center or the Youth Authority.

**Community Streetwork Center of the San Francisco Bay Area, 693 Mission Street, San Francisco, 94102, (415) 398-7737

Mainly for persons, ages 8-21, who are on probation or parole, to reduce their recidivism by working with people from their own communities. Activities, summer jobs program, recreation, and a 24-hour crisis intervention line are offered. There are general meetings Thursday at 5:30 p.m. at 697 Mission St.

Defensores de la Juventud, 259 Divisadero Street, San Francisco, 94117, (415) 863-2139

Three third-world staff members train people between the ages of 14 and 18 in skills that are valuable and necessary in working with community groups. The program is open all year and will teach media, community organizing, resource and counseling techniques to motivated youth.

Energy, 1287 - 11th Avenue, San Francisco, 94122, (415) 681-2500

Energy houses a drop-in, recreation program for young people who live in the Sunset district. Its counseling and referral services are extensive, and it welcomes agency and court referrals, as well as neighborhood people coming by to check it out. New peer groups are being formed around young men's and women's issues. If you have a need or idea for such a group and live in the area, drop by the program to discuss it.

Horizons Unlimited of San Francisco, In., 3001 - 22nd Street, San Francisco, 94110, (415) 285-2172

Situated in the Mission, this is a high school drop-out prevention program, for people ages 14-18, who meet poverty guidelines set by the government, and are in high school working towards a diploma. Participants are given part-time jobs in fields that they are interested in exploring. It also offers workshops in hiking, photography, silk screen, and so on. Counseling is available, and trips and programs are planned. The staff is bilingual, and the office is open 9 a.m. to 6:30 p.m. Monday through Friday.

*Huckleberry House, 3830 Judah Street, San Francisco, 94122, (415) 731-3921

Huck's has a full-time counseling staff and is licensed to house six young people, generally from a few days to three weeks, with individual, group, and family counseling provided (legal referrals included). Parental permission is necessary before a runaway can be housed, but other services are available to those who do not wish to contact home. It has its own foster home recruitment and placement service for those not returning home; it also provides assistance to those looking for independent living arrangements.

Mission Rebels, 674 S. Van Ness, San Francisco, 94110, (415) 431-2224

Programs for youth include recreation, occasional field trips, employment referrals, counseling, and nutritional services, all for free. This is a multiethnic, self-help organization housed in an old building that serves as a headquarters and community center.

***Potrero Hill Youth Legal Center, 991-A Wisconsin Street, San Francisco, 94701, (415) 826-5646; 826-7170

The Youth Legal Center is, in part, an alternative to the Youth Guidance Center, and it is working to do away with YGC altogether. Its primary activity is organizing youth in the Potrero Hill community to work for change, along with helping them through the YGC system, through education, employment counseling, and so on. Open seven days a week, 9 a.m. to 6 p.m.

RAP - Real Alternatives Program, 2901 - 23rd Street, San Francisco, 94110, (415) 826-6474

A free, blingual service for Mission District youth. As an alternative to the Youth Guidance Center, it provides community foster homes for temporary and/or permanent placement, education, recreation, ethnically matched counseling, crisis intervention, and a resource center for youth. Its hours are 9 a.m. to 6 p.m. Monday through Friday, and it has a 24-hour answering service.

Telegraph Hill Neighborhood Center, 660 Lombard, San Francisco, 94133, (415) 421-6464

A recreation, tutoring, and counseling program for Telegraph Hill youth. Open from 9 a.m. to 9 p.m. in the summer months; 3 p.m. to 10 p.m. during the school year.

***Youth Advocates, Inc., 3841 Judah Street, San Francisco, 94122, (415) 731-3921

Staff lawyers offer 24-hour assistance to teenagers. They represent them in court, give them information, and offer advice. For those eligible under California law, they offer assistance in achieving emancipated minor status.

**Youth for Service, 25 - 14th Street, San Francisco, 94103, (415) 621-5555

YFS has a community program for youth (16-25 years of age) who cannot or will not return to regular school, a Job Search Program designed to teach young adults how to find their own jobs, and a Multicultural Arts and Tutorial Program through the public schools. Services are free.

Youth Law Center, 693 Mission Street, 2nd Floor, San Francisco, 94105, (415) 495-6420

An OEO funded legal agency involved with law reform in juvenile cases. At no charge for its services, it will take cases that can be used to pursue larger reform issues, such as working to change procedures in juvenile court. It does referrals but does not take individual cases generally and is not a counseling or resource center as such.

Aquarius House, 1222 - 2nd Avenue, San Francisco, 94107, (415) 644-9888

Free housing for up to 30 days. Fourteen beds (eight men, four women, one couple). Ages 18-31, although sometimes people who are 17 are accepted with parental consent or emancipated minor status. Some vocational and employment counseling available.

Travelers Aid Society of San Francisco, 38 Mason Street, San Francisco, 94102, (415) 781-6738

Travelers Aid Society of Alameda County, 577 - 14th Street, 3rd Floor, Oakland, 94606, (415) 444-6834

The purpose of Travelers Aid is to provide services (counseling, a free meal, low cost housing, aid in transportation) to persons newly or recently arrived in San Francisco who are stranded for one reason or another and who need help in first identifying the alternatives available to them and second, in carrying out a plan of action.

MEDICAL/BIRTH CONTROL/ABORTION CLINICS

This is just a sampling of some of the health and sex-related clinics in the area, with an emphasis upon those that have special "teen" services. In addition, there are Planned Parenthood centers in each of the Bay Area counties, and these all have teen clinics and low or no fees. Look in your phone directory to find the one nearest you.

Alameda County

Berkeley Community Health Project, (Free Clinic), 2339 Durant Avenue, Berkeley, 94704, (415) 548-2570

The Free Clinic offers medical care as an all-purpose walk-in service for people of any age. It includes a medical clinic, psychiatric and psychological rap center, first aid station, dispensary, laboratory, dental clinic, crisis intervention and psych emergency, drug abuse educational programs, well-baby clinic, women's medical clinic and counseling, gay men's medical services, gay men's counseling, 24-hour switchboard, and the availability of on-the-street emergency medical services.

Berkeley Women's Health Collective, 2908 Ellsworth Street, Berkeley, 94705 (415) 843-6174

The Health Collective offers a gynecological clinic on Wednesdays and Thursdays, a general medical clinic and a pediatric clinic on Thursdays. It is necessary to make appointments on the day of the clinics, between 9:00-9:30 a.m. Other services include medical referrals, pregnancy testing, pregnancy/abortion counseling, crisis counseling, and self-help and rap groups for women. It asks a voluntary sliding scale fee for medical attention, and can accept Medi-Cal.

Feminist Women's Health Center, Women's Choice Clinic, 2930 McClure Street #201, Oakland, 94609, (415) 444-5676

During pregnancy, an under 18 year old woman is considered an emancipated minor, that is, does not need parental permission for decisions concerning her pregnancy. The Feminist Women's Health Center has a 24-Hour hotline, where sympathetic women counselors are always available to give as little or as much information as is desired. Pregnancy counseling appointments are scheduled for each woman to help her determine if she is pregnant, discuss alternatives, explain medical qualifications, and to talk about the abortion procedure. The abortion clinic is open Mondays, Tuesdays, and Fridays (call for appointment and times) and charges a sliding scale fee of $160-$235, but will make every attempt to arrange the procedure for those who cannot afford that. Self-help, pregnancy screening, and gyn clinics are also open at various times during the week.

People's Free Medical Clinic, 3236 Adeline Street, Berkeley, 94703, (415) 653-2534

Free medical services to everyone: free pharmacy, sickle cell testing and genetic counseling, pregnancy tests, VD diagnosis and treatment, family planning services (including minors without parental consent), lab work for hepatitis. General Clinic on Wednesday, 8:30 p.m. to 11 p.m., Pediatric Clinic Thursday, 2 p.m.--4p.m. Call for schedule of additional hours.

Teen Family Panning Program, Y.W.C.A., 1515 Webster Street, Room 107, Oakland, 94612, (415) 444-4326; 444-5364

The program's Birth Control Clinic is open Wednesdays 6 p.m.--9 p.m., and Saturdays noon--3 p.m. It has hours Tuesday--Saturday for pregnancy testing, as well as pap, venereal disease, sickle cell, and so on. It offers Teen Rap Sessions. Call to make arrangements. All services are free and confidential.

San Francisco

Haight-Ashbury Free Medical Clinic, Pediatric Clinic, 558 Clayton Street, San Francisco, 94117, (415) 431-1714; 431-1715

Offers free medical services. For times and appointment, call in advance. A dermatology clinic and podiatry clinic are offered once each week also.

Women's Need Center, 1698 Haight Street, San Francisco, 94117, (415) 621-1003

The center's free clinic is open Tuesdays and Thursdays, 9:30 a.m.--3 p.m., for gynecological problems. It is necessary to call Mondays to make an appointment. Pregnancy testing ($2) and abortion counseling are offered daily. Center personnel also teach how to do breast examinations, and they give birth control raps (they do not insert IUDs but do generally have diaphragms, birth control pills, and so on, available for free). No parental permission is needed for any of these services.

HOTLINES/SWITCHBOARDS

The telephone has been put to use in a variety of new ways in the past few years. It can be particularly useful to young people who need information/counseling, or other help without the risk of being identified. Two of these hotlines were created specifically for runaways nationally, and are underlined below. Included in this section are groups that see as their main function supplying information and referral service or crisis counseling over the telephone, although usually within that definition each has its own specialties. There are switchboards connected with some of the Youth Services listings, just as some of the switchboards listed have housing, food, and so on.

National

National Runaway Hotline, MetroHelp, 2210 N. Halsted, Chicago, Illinois 60614 (800) 621-4000

The National Runaway Hotline, operating a toll free number, attempts to help youngsters by giving them information and referrals in the area from which they call.

Operation Peace of Mind, Holiday Inn, Travis Room, 4640 South Main, Houston, Texas 77002 (800) 231-6946

Operation Peace of Mind operates a toll free number; its main service is getting in touch with parents for kids who either don't have the money to do so or who don't want their calls to be traced. It does not ask where you are if you don't want to volunteer the information. It relays your exact message, and you can call back to get any messages that your parents might have left. It also gives referral information concerning available services in the area from which the runaway is calling.

Alameda County

Berkeley Switchboard, 1901 - 8th Street, Berkeley, 94710, (415) 848-0800; 848-9583

Open daily, approximately 10 a.m. to midnight. Provides clothes, showers, referral service, and 15 beds for crashing (no couples, no pets), all for free. A phone call must be made first—do not go directly to the switchboard.

East Oakland Switchboard, 1909 - 73rd Avenue, Oakland, 94605, (415) 569-6369

Open Monday through Friday, 10 a.m. to 9 p.m., the switchboard gives information and referrals for people needing assistance about health, welfare, housing, and so on. It gives emergency food to people who need it without hassling about income or status.

Bay Area

Damien Switchboard, Daly City, (415) 992-5600

Extensively trained staffers of all ages, some of whom speak Spanish, Chinese, or French, offer confidential, free phone services 24 hours a day. They do crisis counseling, problem solving (runaway, drug, pregnancy), and offer information and referral.

San Francisco

Haight-Ashbury Switchboard, 1931 Hayes, San Francisco, 94117, (415) 387-7000

It has one of the most complete referral lists in the area. Call or drop in to its Hayes Street storefront to ask about cheap housing, rides, medical care, welfare and service groups, gay groups and services, legal aid, and so on. Free, although donations are gladly accepted.

Nite Ministry, c/o 942 Market, Suite 1464, San Francisco, 94102, (415) 986-1464

The ministry's switchboard is open from 10 p.m. to 6 a.m., and is unique in that a minister will make calls if necessary. It can provide free housing for one to three nights through the YMCA, and does counseling and referrals over the phone.

Sex Information of San Francisco
Volunteers staff the phones from 3 p.m. to 9 p.m., Monday through Friday. They provide sex information and help people understand options they have in sex-related problems. Many of their calls are from young people, so they are becoming experienced in relating to their questions and problems.

COUNSELING

The Bay Area offers one of the widest ranges of counseling techniques and services in the country. Listed below are a few of those that might be most appropriate for runaways and their parents, above and beyond the various Youth Services presented previously. Again, the emphasis is on free programs that are easily available by phone.

Alameda County

BAWAR, (Bay Area Women Against Rape), P. O. Box 240, Berkeley, (415) 845-7273

    BAWAR has a 24-hour hotline for women (of any age) who have experienced a traumatic crisis such as rape, or other forms of attack. After initial counseling or referral information is given over the phone, a meeting can be arranged in the office, at the home of the counselor, or in the caller's home if desired. Counselors will accompany the victim to the hospital or police station, arrange a supportive group in which to express feelings and reactions, and/or help put up street sheets with the rapist's description.

Berkeley Department of Public Health, Family Youth and Children's Center, 2515 Milvia Street, Berkeley, (415) 644-6617

    The center offers creative approaches to individual, family, and group therapy. Among its wide variety of treatment and counseling services are a Psychodrama for Families with Teenagers Group, an Evening for Couples who are also parents, and an adult-teenager Wednesday evening drop-in (all three for free).

Family Crisis Unit, (North Alameda County) 400 Broadway, Oakland, (415) 874-5731

(South Alameda County), 2200 Fairmont Drive, San Leandro, (415) 351-0420

    The FCU deals primarily with "incorrigibles" who are in need of crisis intervention with their families before the problem becomes a legal one. The first of five sessions lasts from two to five hours, and the emphasis is on as many family members being present as possible, in order to better understand the dynamics among them. The service is free and referrals can come from individuals or agencies.

Parental Stress Service, 154 Santa Clara Avenue, Oakland, 94610, (415) 655-3535 (crisis), 655-8988 (business)

Parental Stress provides a 24-hours-a-day, seven-days-a-week telephone hotline to aid in family-parent-child crises. It has professionally trained volunteers to intervene in a crisis or stressful situation on behalf of parent and child, referrals for counseling, a speaker's bureau, and parents groups. It is no-fee service.

Vocations for Social Change, East Bay Liberation Information Center, 5957 Canning Street, Oakland, (415) 653-6535

VSC has a library of materials dealing with various people's liberation groups and movements, including information on alternative education and schools, how to organize a high school newspaper, magazines for young people, resources concerning gay and women's groups, and so on.

Marin County

Marin Rape Crisis Center, P. O. Box 823, Kentfield, 94904, (415) 924-2100

Center personnel operate a 24-hour answering service. As "advocates" they will go with a woman to the police, hospital and court if necessary, and provide medical and legal information to rape victims.

San Francisco

T.A.L.K., Telephone Aid in Living with Kids, (800) 826-0800

A 24-hour telephone service that gives support to families in order to prevent abuse or neglect of children. The professionally trained volunteers are of varied ages and come from different living situations. They also provide a few groups for parents with professional leadership, and make referrals.

San Francisco Women Against Rape, (415) 647-RAPE

SFWAR provides support, information, and referrals for women who have been raped, all in confidence. Its personnel will accompany the woman if she wishes to go to the police, and will locate medical treatment, emergency childcare, and housing if necessary. Their answering service operates 24 hours a day, and group members are available through the service from 3 p.m. to 7 a.m.; in emergencies at all times.

EDUCATION

There are many fine alternative schools in the Bay Area, but in order to support themselves, it is necessary to charge tuition above most people's means. (There are scholarships available for most schools, however.) Among the directories, we have listed "A Guide to Alternative Education in the Bay Area," the most comprehensive catalogue available of such institutions. Those few we have included below are either publicly funded or comparatively inexpensive.

Alameda County

East Oakland Academy, 609 - 98th Avenue, Oakland, 94603, (415) 569-1190

Fruitvale Street Academy, 3137 E. 14th Street, Oakland, 94601, (415) 532-7556

Central Office, 1319 Fruitvale Avenue, Oakland, 94601, (415) 261-3673

This is a no-tuition alternative to the Oakland Public High School system for youths, ages 15-20 years, who have dropped out or are having difficulty learning in the public schools. There is individualized instruction and students make contracts to fulfill a certain quantity of work in social studies, mathematics, English, and science, for which they are rewarded. There are field trips to factories, and museums. A career counselor attempts to obtain part-time work for the students.

San Francisco

Morrisania West Postal Street Academy, 914 Divisadero Street, San Francisco, 94115, (415) 556-6343

An alternative educational school, servicing 16 to 24 year old dropouts, juvenile delinquents, or those simply turned off by the present educational system. Classes are geared toward preparation for taking the G.E.D. test. The most unique aspect is its ability to offer many supportive services to youngsters as well as educational and vocational training. Classes are from 9 a.m. to noon. Office hours are from 8 a.m. to 5 p.m.

Opportunity High School, 160 S. Van Ness, San Francisco, Ca. 94103, (415) 626-6207

A public high school offering alternative education. "A place where kids can come and participate actively in their own learning, on all levels, from hiring teachers to determining how money ought to be spent... Because everybody is a learner, traditional role disparities are non-operative." There is no charge, because this is a part of the public school system.

Symbas Experimental High School, 1380 Howard Street, San Francisco, 94103

An alternative high school that offers its students classes and apprenticeships with more than 50 teachers. Symbas is part of Project ONE, a six-story warehouse community of craftsmen, artists, technicians, workmen, and academicians. Students have access to workshops and studios in the building. They may also join the workers' co-operative and gain on-the-job training and in this way learn skills to survive economically. Symbas is for those who are ready to take responsibility for their own education as well as help run the school. Tuition is $60 a month; however, no one is turned away for lack of money.

LOS ANGELES AREA YOUTH SERVICES

The Big Sisters League, 701 South New Hampshire, Los Angeles, 90005, (213) 385-5104

The Big Sisters League provides 24-hour residential services for single pregnant girls between 16-18, as space permits. It is equipped to handle 30 women at a time, and if there is room non-pregnant teens are accepted. It provides prenatal and postpartum medical care, recreational, and educational programs. It has a bilingual staff (Spanish-English) and a helpline for pregnancy counseling. Hours: Monday-Friday, 9:00 a.m.--9:00 p.m.

1736 House, 1736 Monterey Blvd., Hermosa Beach, 90254, (213) 374-9334

1736 House offers 24-hour-a-day services, seven days a week. It provides counseling, (for individuals and families) and crisis intervention. If runaways wish to spend the night or longer, they must agree to permit counselors to seek parental consent. 1736 House will provide housing and meals under the condition that the runaway undergoes counseling and permits the staff to attempt a reconciliation with the family, or to secure an alternative placement. Counseling can be secured whether or not you live in the house.

Youth Crisis Housing Task Force, 6622 Van Nuys Blvd., Van Nuys, 91405, (213) 787-4920

This agency primarily aims at runaway prevention. For youth having trouble at home, it has set up a program through which they can be placed in foster homes for a seven day cooling off period. Parental consent is required as are joint parent-child counseling services. All services are free, but the agency tries to match the foster home location with the childs' own residence so that he or she can continue in school.

Boys Club of Venice, 2232 Lincoln Blvd., Venice, 90291, (213) 391-6301

The Boys Club provides counseling services and referrals to other resources for medical or dental help, food and clothing. Hours: Mon-Fri. 9:00 a.m.--9:00 p.m.

La Crescenta/Canada YMCA, 1930 Foothills, La Canada, 91011, (213) 790-0123

YMCA provides counseling, referrals for housing, recreational activities, and free food and gas for those in need.

Salvation Army, Family Services Department, 914 West 9th Street, Los Angeles, 90015, (213) 627-5571

Runaways needing living accommodations are invited to attend Thursday night open meetings and orientation from 3:00-4:00 p.m. If you are interested, you may spend a weekend at one of the Salvation Army homes. At the end of the weekend you and the staff will confer and decide if you can remain. Counseling and emergency relief are also provided. Payment is based on a sliding scale. Hours: 8:30-4:30.

MEDICAL SERVICES

Los Angeles Free Clinic, 8405 Beverly Blvd., Los Angeles, 90036, (213) 653-1990

The clinic accepts all patients on a free basis. Walk in or phone for an a appointment. The following services are provided: medical, psychological and related social services, pregnancy and abortion counseling, and employment assistance. Dental services are available with an appointment. Hours: Mon-Fri. 10:00 a.m.-11:00 p.m., Sat. 12:00 p.m.-5:00 p.m.

Rap House, 2032 Marengo Street, Los Angeles, 90033, (213) 226-5451

Rap House will treat males and females between the ages of 12 and 30 on a free basis. Walk-ins are accepted. Services include: minor medical treatment, counseling, sex education classes, and dental services. The staff is bilingual (Spanish-English). Hours: Mon, Wed, Thurs, Fri: 4:00 p.m.-8:00 p.m.

The Gay Community Service Center, 1213 North Highland Avenue, Hollywood, 90028, (213) 464-7485

Free medical services are provided during the above clinic hours. Counseling and referral services are avilable on request. Hours: Mon, Wed, Fri, 6 p.m. (Men), Saturday, 9 a.m. (Men), Thursday, 6 p.m. (Women), Tuesday, 6 p.m. (General Clinic).

Hollywood Sunset Free Clinic, 3324 Sunset Blvd., Los Angeles, 90026, (213) 660-2400

All ages are welcome and treated on a free basis. Services available include: general medical services, contraception information, and psychological counseling. Walk in or phone for an appointment. Hours: Mon.-Fri. 10:00 a.m.-9:30 p.m.

H.O.Y. (Help Our Youth) Free Clinic, 100 North First Avenue, Arcadia, 91006 (213) 446-2572

The clinic provides free services to individuals between the ages of 12 and 23. Services include individual, group, and family counseling, family planning, and venereal disease and pregnancy testing. Hours: 9:00 a.m.--9:00 p.m. daily.

Open Door Drug Clinic, 228 North Garfield, Monterey Park, 92754, (213) 280-0320

The center provides individual, family, and group drug counseling and a 24 hour hotline. It also helps with pregnancy counseling and referrals. Although it has no overnight accommodations, it may be able to put the runaway in touch with a place to crash.

Narcotics Prevention Project, Boyle Heights Center, 507 North Echandia Street, Los Angeles 90033, (213) 223-4017

Counseling services are available to all age drug abusers on a free basis by trained, bilingual (Spanish-English) staff. Call for an appointment or walk in. It may be able to help with job placement and training. Hours: Mon-Fri. 7:30 a.m.--5:00 p.m.

Central City Community Mental Health Agency, 4211 South Avalon Avenue, Los Angeles 90037, (213) 232-2441

This organization has a 24-hour emergency treatment center and a day treatment center. It prefers to limit its cases to residents of the geographic area, but may advise or help others. It has an ex-felon drug abuse center based on the ability to pay. Hours: Mon-Thurs., 8:30 a.m.-8:00 p.m., Friday 8:30 a.m.-5:00 p.m.

East Valley Free Clinic, 537 Vine Street, P. O. Box 385, West Covina, 91790, (213) 330-7428

East Valley Clinic offers several types of counseling, including legal advice. It provides crisis intervention and detoxification services for heroin users. Pregnancy tests are given on Tuesday, Wednesday, and Thursday at 7:00 p.m. and tests for venereal disease are given at this same time on Wednesday and Thursday. It refers runaways to other service agencies.

This is just a sampling of some of the medical and health-related clinics in the Los Angeles area that have special teen services provided free of charge or at a minimal cost. In addition, there are Planned Parenthood and Family Planning Centers in Los Angeles that will provide teen clinics, free or at a low cost. Check the telephone directory to find the one nearest you.

HOTLINES/SWITCHBOARDS

For two national hotlines offering toll-free service specifically for runaways, see section on "Hotlines/Switchboards" for the San Francisco Bay Area.

The Shepherd's Center, 23838 Kittridge, Canoga Park, 91307, (213) 340-LIFE, (5433)

The Shepherd's Center is primarily a hotline, with telephone referrals and counseling. It is also able to provide temporary housing in some cases.

Downey Hotline, (213) 869-4511, 620-0144

Downey Hotline can provide referrals to crash pads (private homes) and gives telephone counseling on a crisis basis.

Helpline Youth Counseling, 12727 Studebaker Road, Norwalk, 90650, (213) 860-5578

Helpline Youth Counseling has a 24-hour emergency hotline manned by trained volunteers, who are bilingual (Spanish-English). In addition to the hotline, the HYC office is open from 9 a.m. to 9 p.m. to provide counseling services to youth and their families, and crisis intervention. Walk ins are accepted and services are free.

Hollywood Lifeline, (213) 466-4331

Trained volunteers man the lifeline and provide counseling and referral.

Airport Marina, 8015 Sepulveda, Los Angeles, (213) 645-3333

This is another hotline that can provide counseling services over the telephone and give referrals.

Palos Verdes Switchboard, P. O. Box 907, Palos Verdes Estates, 90274, (213) 375-6215

Palos Verdes switchboard is open 24 hours a day for referrals and communication for lonely people. Counseling and educational opportunities are available for a fee.

COUNSELING SERVICES

Child, Youth, and Parent Counseling, 812 West 165th Place, Gardena, 90247, (213) 532-8253

This organization provides crisis counseling. Charges are based on a sliding scale. Hours: 12 p.m.–9 p.m. Monday; 8:30–5 p.m. Wed.-Fri.

Hollywood Youth Counseling Services, c/o Hollywood YMCA, 1553 North Hudson, Los Angeles, 90028, (213) 467-4161

The agency provides counseling to all individuals on a free basis. Phone calls are preferred to walk-ins. It provides referrals for problems it cannot handle.

La Casa Community Center, 203 East Mission Drive, San Gabriel, 91776, (213) 286-2144

La Casa is open 9 a.m. to 5 p.m. on weekdays and serves people of all ages. Runaways from the San Gabriel Valley are served directly; others are referred to agencies in the Los Angeles area. In addition to crisis intervention and referral services, La Casa has job counseling and an alternative school (see Education).

Reach Out Counseling, 315 South Ivy, Monrovia, (213) 359-1137

Counseling is open 8 a.m.-5 p.m. daily, serving individuals between 8 and 18 years old. It is a nonprofit community agency offering a wide variety of counseling services. It also operates a hotline and acts as a referral agency.

EDUCATION

La Casa Community Center, 203 East Mission Drive, San Gabriel, (213) 268-2144

La Casa will take anyone from San Gabriel, Alhambra, Rosemead, and Monterey Park into its High School Alternative Program. If you live outside this service area, it will try to refer you to another agency that can help you.

DIRECTORIES

We have found the following directories helpful in our research and believe that both runaways and service providers should be aware of them.

National Directory of Runaway Centers (January, 1974), National Youth Alternatives Project, 1830 Connecticut Avenue, N.W., Washington, D.C. 20009, (202) 234-6664, 387-5760

In addition to the Runaway Center listings, the directory contains an inclusive but concise description of the goals, policies, and variety of programs across the country that are concerned with runaways and youth advocacy.

A Directory of the Human Resources of Alameda County, published by Human Resources Agency, Jack McKay, Director

A very comprehensive list of a wide variety of traditional social services as well as a few alternative agencies.

People's Energy: An East Bay Community Resource Handbook, 5316 Telegraph Avenue, Oakland, 94609, (415) 654-7038

The *Handbook* provides information on alternative institutions and social change efforts in the East Bay Area. The People's Energy Collective, located on the second floor of a church, offers vocational counseling and educational programs geared toward helping the individual clarify goals and values concerning future plans for work, which could be very helpful to young people whose school guidance departments are lacking time and services, or who have dropped out of school. It will help you evaluate your skills on a realistic level, suggest possible alternative workstyles (collectives, communes) and connect you with suitable job openings the staff knows of. It has an extensive resource library. A donation of at least $1 is requested. Hours: Wed. 1-6 p.m. Thurs., Fri. 10-6 p.m.

Directory of Private Placement Resources, Edited by John Callahan, et al., Copyright 1973

A directory of private placement resources utilized by various placing agencies of the Bay Area Placement Commission, a subcommittee of the Bay Area Chief Probation Officers' Association. Lists name of agency and such criteria as age range, sex, and type of problem; also, gives information on school availability, boarding rates, capacity, professional staff, program, and so on.

People's Yellow Pages Number 4, Box 31219, San Francisco, 94131

Available in local bookstores or $3 if ordered by mail. An A through Z listing of service groups, stores, collectives, individuals, and any other conceivable configuration of people who make a similarly wide range of offerings with people, not profit, in mind.

A Guide to Alternative Education in the Bay Area, Editor and researcher:
Victoria M. Gonzalez, Orpheus Publications, Bay Area Center for Alternative
Education, 467 O'Farrel Street, San Francisco, 94102, (415) 474-3775

Includes a directory of alternative forms of education from preschool
to adults. Also an extensive list of related resources, including publications
and groups. Updated yearly.

Youth Alternatives, Publication of the National Youth Alternatives Project,
1830 Connecticut Avenue, N.W., Washington, D.C. 20009

It is the purpose of this newsletter to publicize events, issues, and activities affecting youth and youth workers, thereby stimulating the development of new models of social service and advocacy programs for youth and
uniting the workers and consumers of these programs around common issues
and concerns.

Youth Liberation, 2007 Washtenaw Avenue, Ann Arbor, Michigan 48104,
(313) 662-1867

A group which helps young people organize aroung their schools, families, and prisons. It publishes "FPF: A magazine of Young People's Liberation,"
which goes to high school organizers, teachers, youth services bureau staff,
and others. It also puts out a Youth Liberation Student Organizing Kit ($3)
which includes sample copies of "FPS," several pamphlets (including "Student and Youth Organizing"), and other materials. Send enough money to cover postage when asking for information.

FURTHER READINGS

We did not aim at a comprehensive bibliography of the literature on runaways.
Our primary emphasis was on selected publications that runaways may find
useful. Secondarily we listed a few publications that might be of special interest to service providers.

Beggs, The Reverend Larry. *Huckleberry's for Runaways.* New York: Ballan-
    tine Books, 1969.

A chronicle of the evolution of Huckleberry House and the clients
who have been served there.

Department of the Youth Authority of the State of California. *California
    Laws Relating to Youthful Offenders, Including the Youth Authority
    Act, the Juvenile Court Law, 1974 Legislative Changes,* 1974.

Social Advocates for Youth (Newsletter)
975 North Point
San Francisco, 94109   (415) 928-3222

S.A.Y.'s main office, from which it distributes its newsletter, is in San Francisco. It is published monthly and contains articles of interest to people working with youth, particularly in legal contexts.

Strouse, Jean. *Up Against the Law, the Legal Rights of People Under 21.* New York: New American Library, Inc., 1970.

A comprehensive survey and description of the laws regarding minors, covering issues such as what to do when a cop busts you, what states have what laws regarding minors, and so on.

Students Rights Handbook
c/o American Friends Service Committee
2160 Lake Street
San Francisco, 94121   (415) 752-7766

A handbook compiled by a high school woman to inform California public high school students of their legal rights. 50¢ to adults, 25¢ to students.

U.S. Congress. *Runaway Youths.* Hearings before the Subcommittee to Investigate Juvenile Delinquency, 92 Cong. 1st Sess., January 13, 14, 1972.

APPENDIX IV

Can Running Away Be Prevented?
A Research Note

INTRODUCTION

Can running away be prevented? What are the "early warning signals," and what can parents, teachers, or others do to prevent a young person from running away from home? In this study we examined data from 215 runaways which afford some clues for prevention strategies.

For the past several decades, increasing attention has been devoted to the runaway phenomenon. Most of the evidence to date suggests that the level of runaway activity is either remaining at the presently high rate or even increasing. To deal with the problem, government expenditures have similarly surged with many millions of dollars now earmarked for social services to runaway youth in fiscal year 1977. Clearly, a social problem of some scope is represented.

The main thrust of runaway policy has been to return youths home. For example, the language of the Runaway Youth Act of 1974 (P.L. 93-415) established an official mandate to "locate, detain, and return" runaway youth and thereby relieve the burden of protection from law enforcement agencies serving in loco parentis. However, the high incidence of repeat or chronic runaway activity among the nation's juvenile population suggests that this tactic is somewhat ineffective. Approximately 40 of the runaways in this study reported running away from home five or more times. Findings concerning the dangers of running away for youths also suggest the need for early detection and prevention strategies. Almost half of the runaway sample reported being "ripped off"; 35 percent reported "bad" experiences while hitchhiking, and approximately one-fourth reported they depended primarily on delinquent acts to support themselves. Prevention efforts, rather than deterrence in the form of increasing penalties, seem consistent with current efforts to decriminalize runaways and to offer social services geared to diverting these youth from the criminal justice system.

This study dealt with a series of questions aimed at shedding some light on runaway prevention possibilities and the necessary precondition for a successful prevention program. Basically, as Simon (1972) suggests, prevention rests in part on the *foreseeability* of the act to be prevented and the actor's *willingness* to be prevented from engaging in the act. The following questions are addressed in our study.

1. Could some of the runaway incidents have been prevented?
2. If so, how many? Could a significant proportion have been prevented?
3. How could prevention efforts be effected?
4. How could potential runaways be isolated, identified, or predicted?
5. What kinds of prevention programs might be helpful?

To answer some of these questions, data gathered from recent interviews with runaways and nonrunaways were analyzed and served as the primary source of evidence for this study. A total of 215 runaways was interviewed in San Francisco and Los Angeles during 1974-1975, and 436 students from a local school system were interviewed for comparison purposes.

FINDINGS

The first evidence we have as to the potential utility of runaway prevention efforts is based on runaway responses to the interview question, *"Was there anything that could have changed your mind about leaving?"*, referring to the most recent episode, and if so, *"What do you think could have happened to change your mind?"* The runaway's own perception of the prevention possibilities is an important ingredient in any prevention program as Simon (1972) indicates. Certainly if the runaway himself sees the possibility of change, the chances for success in preventing the runaway act seem much greater. Of course, if parents or guardians also agree, chances would seem to be even greater.

In any case, one-third of the sample of runaways responded to the first question above in the affirmative. This high an incidence would seem to speak well for instituting prevention efforts and their potential impact on the runaway problem today. Responses to the second question by the one-third, who indicated their last runaway episode could have been prevented, are analyzed in the following table.

**TABLE A.1: RUNAWAY YOUTHS' RESPONSES TO THE QUESTION:
"WHAT COULD HAVE CHANGED YOUR MIND ABOUT LEAVING?"**
(For those who indicated such change was possible)

	N	%
If could work out longstanding problems	28	46
If could work out immediate problems	13	21
If could have found alternative placement	7	11
If legal problems could have been worked out	1	2
If someone tried to stop me	3	5
If school problems could have been worked out	1	2
If some social agent helped us	4	6
If friends or relatives could have helped out	1	2
Other	3	5
Total	61	100%

Table A.1 presents the data on what could have happened to change their minds. It is apparent that in the majority of cases the working out of "longstanding problems" was seen as necessary, rather than any simple request to stay. Also significant is that 12 percent (who were already in foster care) requested that alternative placement be arranged. Typically, the longstanding problems cited involved too much parental strictness, or child abuse or neglect. For example, some typical comments were "If my father had changed," or "If my parents were less strict," or "If my parents showed they cared." More will be said on these specific points later.

RUNAWAY PLANNING

The second piece of evidence from the data which suggested the feasibility of prevention efforts concerned the presence of prerunaway planning and discussion of plans with others, siblings, friends, or others. In Table A.2, we can see that one half of the runaways discussed their plans for running with somebody.

**TABLE A.2: RUNAWAYS' REPORTS ON WHETHER THEY DISCUSSED
RUNAWAY PLANS WITH OTHER (N = 215)**

	N	%
Discussed	110	51
Not discussed	105	49
Total	215	100%

This means that advance information on running away does exist and might be tapped with some success prior to the actual incident. The chances for discovering a potential runaway act seem greater when several people are aware of it, so in some sense this makes the runaway act more foreseeable or predictable.

In addition, one-third of the runaway sample reported leaving with others, rather than alone. Having traveling companions would also increase the chance of uncovering runaway episodes in advance.

RUNAWAY CHARACTERISTICS

A profile that encompassed typical or common runaway characteristics was compiled and seems also to suggest that many runaways could be identified as the first step in a counseling or other type of runaway prevention program.

Typically, the average runaway lives in a broken home or in an institution, is in trouble at school or with the law, or both, and/or is experiencing some degree of abuse or neglect in the home, and/or is affected by drinking problems in the home and/or has a history of friends and siblings who have left home.

TABLE A.3: RUNAWAY CHARACTERISTICS PROFILE
(N=215)

	N	%
Parents separated or divorced	Yes = 126	59
Suspended or expelled from school	150	70
Dissatisfied at school	122	57
Trouble with law	135	63
Child abuse	84	39
Child neglect	124	58
Parental drinking problem	89	41
Friends school drop-outs	164	76
Friends ran away	187	87
Brother ran away	74	34
Sister ran away	72	33

Runaways often come from multiproblem families, as described in Table A.3, and between efforts of school counselors, welfare workers, and medical services, should be relatively easy to identify and isolate to determine if running away is being planned. This pattern of characteristics should thus also act to make the leaving of home more foreseeable at least in the case of the chronic runaway.

RUNAWAY TYPES AND PREVENTION

In the larger study, a typology of runaways was developed, based on the runaways' own vocabulary of motives. That is, the reasons for running away from home given by each runaway were content-analyzed and coded into one of six runaway "types."

These six types reflect the natural world of the runaway as he perceives and reports it. Two major groups of runaways were distinguished by the degree to which they perceived their running away as a response to problems with their parents. Those who saw it mainly in this fashion were called "parent-locus" runaway types, while those who saw it in other or mixed terms were classed as "child-locus" types. Each of these were subdivided into three subtypes and were defined as follows:

Parent Locus

I. *Victims* are those runaways who report fleeing from physical abuse and assault by parents or guardians. These youth feel their parents are enemies and to return home is to endanger their lives. Thirty-eight percent stated their running away could have been prevented.

II. Those runaways who define their leaving home in terms of parental rejection were called *exiles.* Such runaways report leaving home because they were not wanted: in effect they are outcasts, kicked or thrown out. Even so, 42 percent felt their exclusion could have been prevented.

III. The third runaway types was the *rebel.* As the name implies, these youth are involved in serious and continual conflict with their parents, and running away from home is just another stage in this conflict, which they hope to win and thus remain at home on their terms. Only 31 percent of these youth indicated their runaway episode could have been prevented.

Child Locus

IV. The *fugitive* child is running from the consequences of his behavior in order to escape arrest and punishment for something he did. They are often in trouble with the law or the authority structure and with their families as well. Thirty percent indicated some prevention might have been possible.

V. *Refugees* are runaways without a family who are usually running from institutions or foster care homes. Like the *fugitives,* they are fleeing a social-control structure, but do not see themselves at fault necessarily. Thirty-eight percent felt they might have been prevented from running away.

VI. The *immigrants,* the final type, are basically, independent runaways who have taken matters into their own hands and are attempting to become autonomous or "free" to establish themselves and their own life-style. In a sense they have declared themselves grown or adult, and act on this premise. Only approximately one-fourth (27 percent) indicated their running away could have been prevented.

Several of these runaway types have significance when considering the questions of deterrence or decreasing the numbers who run away. The following will discuss some of the more obvious implications.

For example, the *fugitives,* runaways in trouble with the law primarily, could substantially be reduced as a group through a broadening of current *diversion* or other *decriminalization* programs.

Another group, the *refugees,* included many institutionalized subjects fleeing foster-home or child-care placements. Theoretically an improvement in these placements or programs could substantially reduce this kind of runaway. *Refugees* and *fugitives* as types were the most likely to mention immediate problems as the reason for their running away.

Still another type of runaway is typically the lower-class youth, literally pushed out of the home by various pressures, some of them economic, who was called the *exile.* The *exiles* as a group were the most likely to report a possible change of plans—some 42 percent of them did so. Some involvement with the law was also common for this group. This type of runaway would also profit from diversion or protective service programs noted earlier and also from some improvement in welfare policies and programs.

The greatest potential for counseling programs and crisis intervention or outreach programs was seen in the case of the *rebel* and *immigrant* types of runaways. Both groups are in some conflict with parents, but still retain some relationship to the home. Intensive counseling with these families located early enough could conceivably reduce the incidence of runaways from these situations. *Immigrants* as a group reported the *least* likelihood of averting the runaway as compared with the *rebels,* some 75 percent of whom reported they might have changed their minds.

The final runaway type, the *victim,* is, as the name suggests, the target of substantial amounts of violence and/or neglect in the home. Consequently, the prognosis for these cases is guarded, but perhaps psychiatric help or counseling under a protective service program could salvage these families. Often, though, alternative placements might be sought here as the treatment of alcoholics and addiction is often difficult. Indeed some 31 percent of the *victims* reported desiring such placements. Early detection and intervention also might be the key here.

Some clues about the possible content or goal of counseling or prevention programs are seen in the reasons for running away cited by runaways, especially those reporting they might be prevented from running. As Table A.4 indicates, often *strictness* by parents or guardians is cited by these runaways. *Disapproval of friends, use of drugs, dating,* and *dressing* were also frequently cited as areas of contention by those runaways reporting they might have been deterred from leaving home.

In summary, a review of these findings suggests strongly that at least two of the basic conditions necessary for effective runaway prevention programs are present, that is, foreseeability and motivation for prevention. Based on the evidence introduced, a substantial proportion, perhaps as much as one-third or so, according to their own statements, could be prevented from leaving home. Basic changes would have to be made in longstanding problem areas.

TABLE A.4: PROBLEM AREAS—

(Percent Who Report Parent Strictness*)	Could Have Changed Mind (N = 72)	Would Not Change Mind (N = 143)
Parents:		
Disapproval of friends	63%	55%
Too strict about drugs	49%	37%
Too strict about dating	34%	22%
Too strict about fashions	31%	17%
Too strict overall	83%	78%

Potential areas of change seem to consist largely of problems in the home or living situation, particularly with respect to friends, dating, clothing, and drug use, plus the control of perceived physical abuse in some cases.

With respect to the foreseeability of the runaway act, early identification possibilities seem present with a rather clear profile of multiproblem families, and trouble at school or with the law. The fact that many runaways discuss their plans with others and frequently run away with others also would seem to increase the likelihood of earlier detection.

The presence of school problems in many cases, that is, disciplinary actions, drop-outs, expulsions, and so forth, suggests that the school behavior of the youth is an early warning sign of impending running away and other problems. In this case, we would suggest that school teachers, counselors, and other school staff be alerted to serve as an early warning system. Similarly, medical personnel could be alerted in connection with evidence of child abuse and neglect. Advance notice and earlier detection of problem cases could assist in preventing future trouble.

The implications of prevention in general were discussed for each type of runaway, and a substantial reduction of *fugitives,* for example, seemed possible through increased juvenile *diversion* and *decriminalization* projects.

Certainly, further research is needed to replicate these findings and perhaps demonstrate or test the advisability and feasibility of various prevention programs or formats. Research into the situations of the many would-be runaways who indicate thinking about leaving home, but never do, would seem to be one fruitful approach. For example, data concerning the Berkeley School sample indicated that 20 percent have thought of leaving home, but haven't as yet done it. Other specific programs aimed at preventing runaways, such as diversion projects or counseling projects, could also be evaluated as to their relative effectiveness in reducing or stopping runaway incidents. A two-pronged approach, consisting of both prevention efforts and the customary detain and return programs, would seem to offer the best solution for a large and possibly growing social problem of youth in flight.

BIBLIOGRAPHY

Ambrosino, Lillian. *Runaways*. Boston: Beacon, 1971.

Antebi, R. "Some Charactersitics of Mental Hospital Absconders." *British Journal of Psychiatry* 133 (1967):1087-1100.

Armstrong, C.P. *600 Runaway Boys*. Boston: Boston 1932.

——. "A Psychoneurotic Reaction of Delinquent Boys and Girls," *Journal of Abnormal Social Psychology* 32 (1937):329-42.

Ball, Geoffrey H. *Classification Analysis*. Prepared for Head, Information Systems Branch, Mathematical Sciences, Office of Naval Research, 1970.

Bartollas, Clemens L. *Runaways at the Training Institution*. Ph.D. dissertation, Ohio State University.

Baumohl, J., and Miller, H. *Down and Out in Berkeley*. Berkeley: University of California Community Affairs Committee, 1974.

Beaser, Herbert W. *The Legal Status of Runaway Children*. Washington, D.C.: Educational Systems Corp., 1975.

Beggs, Larry. *Huckleberry's for Runaways*. New York: Balantine Books,1969.

Belkin, Alice. "Why Boys Run Away From Home," *Smith College Studies in Social Work* 11 (1940):438-41. *(Psych. Abs.* (1955):585.)

Berger, I., and Schmidt, R.M. "Results of Child Psychiatric and Psychological Investigations of Spontaneous and Reactive Runaways," *Prax. Kinderpsychol. Kinderpsychiat.* 7 (1958):206-10.

Bergeron, M. "Juvenile Running Away and Vagrancy," *Bulletin Graduate Etud. Psychol.* 6, University of Paris (1952):309-10. *(Psych. Abs.* (1954):1279.

Bettelheim, B. *Love is Not Enough*. Glencoe, IL.: Free Press, 1950.

Beyer, Margaret. *Psychosocial Problems of Adolescent Runaways*. Ph.D. dissertation, Yale University, 1974.

Blood, Linda, and D'Angelo, Rocco. "A Progress Research Report on Value Issues in Conflict Between Runaways and Their Parents," *Journal of Family and Marriage,* (August, 1974):486-91.

Bock, Richard D., and English, Abigail. *Got Me on the Run: A Study of Runaways*. Boston: Beacon Press, 1973.

Brennan, Tim. "A Social-Psychological Study of Runaway Youth," Paper presented to the American Psychological Association Conference in Salt Lake City, 1975.

Brennan, Tim, Brewington, Sue, and Walker, Lynn. *A Study of Issues Relating to Runaway Behavior*. Mimeographed report submitted to the Office of Youth Development, Behavioral Research and Evaluation Corporation, 1974.

Brennan Tim, Blanchard, F., Huizinga, D., and Elliott, D., "The Incidence and Nature of Runaway Behavior—Final Report," Behavioral Research and Evaluation Corporation, 1975.

Chamberlin, Cecil R., "Running Away During Psychotherapy," *Bulletin of the Meninger Clinic* 24 (1960).

Cloward, Richard, and Ohlin, Lloyd E. *Delinquency and Opportunity: A Theory of Delinquent Gangs.* Glencoe, IL.: The Free Press, 1960.

Cochran, William G. *Sampling Techniques.* New York: Wiley, 1963.

Cohen, Albert K. *Deviance and Control.* Englewood Cliffs, N.J.: Prentice Hall, 1966.

Coleman, James S. *The Adolescent Society.* Glencoe, IL.: Free Press, 1961.

Coleman, James S., Campbell, Ernest Q., Hobson, Carol J., McPartland, James, Mood, Alexander M., Weinfeld, Frederic D., and York, Robert L., *Equality of Educational Opportunity.* Washington, D.C.: U.S. Government Printing Office, 1966.

D'Angelo, R. *Families of Sand: A Report Concerning the Flight of Adolescents from their Families.* School of Social Work, Ohio State University, 1974.

Durkheim, E. *Suicide: A Study in Sociology.* Glencoe, IL.: The Free Press, 1951.

Dymally, Mervyn. *The Runaway Child.* State of California Senate Select Committee on Children and Youth Hearing, 1973.

Elliott, Delbert S. "Delinquency and Perceived Opportunity." *Sociological Inquiry* 32, 1962.

——,"The Dynamics of Delinquent Behavior: A National Survey. "Proposal submitted to Department of Health, Education and Welfare, 1975.

Elliott, Delbert S., and Voss, Harwin L. *Delinquency and Dropout.* Lexington, Ma.: D.C. Heath, 1974.

English, Clifford John. "Leaving Home: A Typology of Runaways (Transportation and People)," *Society* 10, 5 (July-August 1973):22-24.

Farber, Bernard, and Jenne, William C. "Family Organization and Parent-Child Communication: Parents and Siblings of a Retarded Child," *Society for Research in Child Development* 28, no. 7.

Farrington, Donald S., Shelton, William, and MacKay, James R. "Observations on Runaway Children from a Residential Setting," *Child Welfare* 42 (1963):286-91.

Foster, R.M. "Intrapsychic and Environmental Factors in Running Away from Home," *American Journal of Orthopsychiatry* 32, no. 3 (1962).

Goldberg, M. "Runaway American," *Mental Hygiene* (November 1972):9-12.

Greene, Nancy B., and Esselstyn, T.C. "The Beyond Control Girl," *Juvenile Justice* 2343 (1972):13-19.

Gunasekara, M.G.S. "The Problem of Absconding in Boys Approved Schools in England and Wales," *The British Journal of Criminology* 4, no. 2 (1963):145-51.

Hansen, M.H., Hurwitz, W.M. and Madow, W.G. *Sample Survey Methods and Theory.* New York: Wiley 1953.

Haskell, Martin R., and Yablonsky, L. *Crime and Delinquency.* Chicago: Rand McNally, 1970.

Haupt, Donald, and Offord, David R. "Runaways from a Residential Treatment Center: A Preliminary Report," *Corrective Psychiatry and Journal of Social Therapy* 18, no. 3 (1972):14-21.

Hildebrand, J.A. "Why Runaways Leave Home." *Journal of Criminal Law, Criminology and Police Science* 54, 1963.

Hirschi, Travis. *Causes of Delinquency.* Berkeley: University of California Press, 1969.

Homer, Louise, "Community-Based Resource for Runaway Girls," *Social Casework* 54, no. 8, 1973.

Howell, M.C., Emmons, E.B., and Frank, D.A. "Reminiscences of Runaway Adolescents," *American Journal of Orthospsychiatry* 43, no. 5 (October 1973).

Jenkins, R.L. "Classification of Behavior Problems of Children," *American Journal of Psychiatry 125, no. 8 (1969):1032-39.*

———,"The Runaway Reaction," *American Journal of Psychiatry* 128, no. 2 (August 1971):168-73.

Jenkins, Richard L., and Boyer, Andrew. "Types of Delinquent Behavior and Background Factors," *International Journal of Social Psychiatry* 14 (Winter 1967-68):65-78.

———. "The Effects of Inadequate Mothering and Inadequate Fathering on Children." *International Journal of Social Psychiatry* 16, London, 2 (1970):72-78.

Jenkins, Richard L., and Stahle, Galen. "The Runaway Reaction: A Case Study." *Journal of the Americn Academy of Child Psychiatry* 11, 2 (1972):294-313.

Jessor, Shirley L., and Jessor, Richard. "Maternal Ideology and Adolescent Problem Behavior." *Developmental Psychology,* 10 (1974):246-54.

Joos, J., Debuyst, C., and Sepulchre-Cassiers, M. "Boys Who Run Away from Home: A Belgian Study." *International Journal of Offender Therapy* 14, 2 (1970):98-104.

Kanner, L. *Child Psychiatry.* Springfield, Il.: C. C. Thomas, 1950.

Kaufman, Joshua, Allen, James R., and West, Louis Jolyon. "Runaways, Hippies, and Marijuana." *American Journal of Psychiatry* 126, 5 (1969): 17-20.

Kaufman, I., Peck, A.L., and Taguiri, C.K. "The Family Constellation and Overt Incestuous Relationships between Father and Daughter." *American Journal of Orthopsychiatry* 24, 2 (1954):266-79.

Kish, Leslie. *Survey Sampling.* New York: 1967.

Kitano, H., and Miranda, Manuel. *Ethnic Runaways.* Social Rehabilitation

Lerman, Paul. "Beyond *Guilt:* Injustice and the Child." In Paul Lerman (ed.), *Delinquency and Social Policy.* New York: Prager, 1970, pp. 236-50.

———. "Child Convicts." *Transaction* (1970).

Leventhal, Theodore. "Control Problems in Runaway Children." *Archives of General Psychiatry* 9 (1963):122-26.

Levinson, Boris M., and Mezei, Harry. "Self-Concepts and Ideal Self-Concepts of Runaway Youths: Counseling Implications." *Psychological Reports* 26,3 (1970):871-74.

Levy, Edwin Z. (Meninger Foundation, Children's Division, Topeka, Kansas). "Some Thoughts About Patients Who Run Away from Residential Treatment and the Staff They Leave Behind." *Psychiatric Quarterly* 46, 1 (1972):1-21.

Lowrey, Lawson G. "Runaways and Nomads." *American Journal of Orthopsychiatry* 11, 4 (1941):775-82.

McClosky, H., and Schaar, J.H. "Anomie in Psychological Dimensions of Anomie." *American Sociological Review* (1963):14-40.

McRae, D.J. "Multivariate Cluster Analysis." Presented at 55th Annual Meeting of American Education Research Association, New York, 1971.

MacLeod, C. "The Street People: The New Migrants." *The Nation* (October 1973):395-97.

Merton, Robert K. *Social Theory and Social Structure.* Glencoe, Il: The Free Press, 1957.

Mizruchi, E.H. *Success and Opportunity.* Glencoe, Il: The Free Press, 1964.

Nettler, Gwynne. *Explaining Crime.* New York: McGraw Hill, 1974.

Nowicki, S., and Strickland, B.R. "A Locus of Control Scale for Children." *Journal of Consulting and Clinical Psychology* 40 (1973):148-54.

Nye, F.I., and Short, J.F. "Scaling Delinquent Behavior." *American Sociological Review* 22, 3 (1957):326-31.

Outland, G.E. "The Home Situation as a Direct Cause of Boy Transiency." *Journal of Juvenile Research* 22 (1938):33-43.

Paykel, E.S., Myers, J.K., Dienelt, M.N., Klerman, G.L., Lindenthal, J.J., and Petter, M.P. "Life Events and Depression: A Controlled Study." *Archives of General Psychiatry* 21 (1969):753-60.

Piliavin, Irving, and Briar, Scott. "Police Encounters with Juveniles." *American Journal of Sociology* 10 (1964):206-14.

Ralston, William. "Intake: Informal Disposition or Adversary Proceeding." *Crime and Delinquency* (April 1971):160-67.

Reckless, W.C. *The Crime Problem,* 4th ed. New York: Appleton-Century-Crofts, 1967.

Reinholz, Mary. "The Throwaway Children." *New York News Magazine,* 1973.

Riback, Linda. "Juvenile Delinquency Laws: Juvenile Women and the Double Standard of Morality." *UCLA Law Review* 19, 2 (December 1971): 313-42.

Riemer, M. "Runaway Children." *American Journal of Orthopsyhiatry* 10, 3 (1940):322-26.

Robey, A., and Rosewald, R.E. "The Runaway Girl: A Reaction to Family Stress." *American Journal of Orthopsyhiatry* 34, 4 (1964).

Robins, Lee N. "Mental Illness and the Runaway: A 30 Year Followup Study." *Human Organization* 16 (1956):11-15.

Robins, Lee N., and O'Neal, Patricia. "The Adult Prognosis for Runaway Children." *American Journal of Orthopsychiatry* 29 (1959):752-61.

Rosenberg, Morris. *Society and the Adolescent Self-Image.* Princeton: Princeton University Press, 1965.

Rosenwald, R.J., and Mayer, J. "Runaway Girls from Suburbia." *American Journal of Orthopsychiatry* 37, 2 (1967):402-3.

Rotter, J.B. "Generalized Expectancies for Internal Versus External Control of Reinforcement." *Psychological Monographs* 80, no. 609 (1966).

Rousseau, Jean Jacques. *Les Confessions.* Geneva, 1782.

Schulz, David A., and Wilson, Robert A. "Some Traditional Family Variables and Their Correlations with Drug Use Among High School Students." *Journal of Marriage and Family* 35, 4 (November 1973):628-31.

Scientific Analysis Corporation. "The Sick, the Bad and the Free: A Review of the Runaway Literature." Study for Department of Health, Education and Welfare, 1975.

———. "Runaway Youth: How Are They to be Served?" A proposal submitted to Department of Health, Education and Welfare, 1974.

Shellow, Robert, Schamp, Juliana R., Liebow, Elliot and Unger, Elizabeth. "Suburban Runaways of the 1960's." *Monograph of the Soc. for Res. in Child Development* 32 (1967):1-51.

Shinohara, M., and Jenkins, R.L. "MMPI Study of Three Types of Delinquents." *Journal of Clinical Psychology* 23 (1967):156-63.

Short, James F., Jr. "Gang Delinquency and Anomie." In Marshall B. Clinard (ed.), *Anomie and Deviant Behavior.* Glencoe, Il.: Free Press, 1964, pp. 98-127.

Siegelman, Marvin. "Evaluation of Bronfenbrenner's Questionnaire for Children Concerning Parental Behavior." *Child Development* 36 (1965): 163-74.

Simon, W.B. "Some Issues in the Logic of Prevention." *Social Science and Medicine* 6 (1972):95-107.

Skinner, Mary and Alice S. Nutt, "Adolescents Away from Home," *Annals of the American Academy of Political and Social Science,* Vol. 236, 1944, pp. 51-59.

Spergel, Irving. "Deviant Patterns of Opportunities of Pre-Adolescent Negro Boys in Three Chicago Neighborhoods." In Malcolm W. Klein (ed.), *Juvenile Gangs in Context.* Englewood Cliffs, NJ: 1967, pp. 38-54.

Steirlin, Helm. "A Family Perspective on Adolescent Runaways." *Archives of General Psychiatry* 29 (July), 1973.

Stengel, Edwin. "Studies on the Psychopathology of Compulsive Wandering." *British Journal of Medical Psychology* 18 (1939):250-54.

Suddick, David E. "Runaways: A Review of the Literature." *Juvenile Justice.* (August 1973):46-54.

Sumner, Helen. "Locking Them Up." *Crime and Delinquency,* 1971, pp. 168-79.

Sutherland, E.H., and Cressey, D.R. *Principles of Criminology.* New York: Lippincott, 1960.

Time. "Runaways: A National Problem." August 27, 1973, p. 57.

Toby, Jackson. "The Differential Impact of Family Disorganization." In Daniel Glaser (ed.) *Handbook of Criminology.* Chicago: Rand McNally, 1974.

Tsunts, M. "Dropouts on the Run." *Atlas* (1971):158-60.

Walker, Deborah R. "Runaway Youth: An Annotated Bibliography and Brief Literature Overview." Department of Health, Education and Welfare, 1974.

Ward, Joe H., Jr. "Hierarchical Grouping to Optimize an Objective Function." *Journal of American Statistical Association* 58, 301 (March 1963): 236-44.

Wishart D. "Some Problems in the Theory and Application of the Methods of Numerical Taxonomy." Ph.D. Thesis, University of St. Andrews, Scotland.

Wylier, D.C., and Weinreb, J. "The Treatment of a Runaway Adolescent Girl Through Treatment of the Mother." *American Journal of Orthopsychiatry* 23, 9 (1950):188-95.

———. "Runaway Children—A Problem for More and More Cities." *U.S. News and World Report,* April, 1972.

———. "Casualties of Recession—More Kids on the Road," *U.S. News and World Report,* May, 1975.

Index